**GEORGIA GARDNER GRAY
PLAYS AND WORKS 2014–2019**

**KUNSTHALLE LINGEN
MOUSSE PUBLISHING**

„FAHRSCHEIN, BITTE"
Steven Warwick

Beim Betreten der Kunsthalle könnte man meinen, sich in einem Wartesaal zu befinden. Der Raum wurde zu einem öffentlichen Verkehrsmittel umgestaltet, mit Klappsitzen und skulpturalen Plexiglaselementen, durch die man hindurchgehen kann. Das Berliner U-Bahn-System ist von protestantischen Vorstellungen von Schuld und Vertrauen geprägt. Schwarzfahren ist möglich, doch wird in der U-Bahn-Station und in den Wagen vor dem Fahren ohne gültigen Fahrschein gewarnt. Das Thema verwandelt sich von einem ökonomischen in ein moralisches. Kontrolleure in Zivil mischen sich unter die Reisenden, nur um sich dann zu erkennen zu geben und die Fahrgäste zu überprüfen. *Controller* (2018) schildert dieses Szenario in leuchtenden Farben: Die Amtsgewalt macht sich gegenüber den Reisenden bemerkbar; im trubeligen Berufsverkehr sind angekettetes Gepäck und ein Hund mit Maulkorb zu erkennen.

In die Szenerie integrierte Skulpturen machen die Situation jenseits der Leinwand noch sinnfälliger. Drei U-Bahn-Klappsitze säumen den Raum mit Gegenständen, die absichtlich oder zufällig auf ihnen zurückgelassen wurden. Auf einem Sitz befindet sich eine gegossene Nachbildung eines saftigen Schinkenbratens in einer roten Plastiktüte; unter einem anderen liegt eine Sammlung von Einkaufstaschen, deren Inhalt seltsamerweise komplett weiß gefärbt ist.

Am unheimlichsten von allen ist *Pigeon Feather Stick* (2018), eine figürliche Skulptur aus einem Einkaufstrolley, geschmückt mit raubkopierten Accessoires von Luxuslabels, die mit Taubenabwehrspitzen versehen sind. Die bedrohliche menschenähnliche Gestalt hat eine unheimliche Präsenz, sie lauert im Raum und ist schon viel länger als vorgesehen da. Man grübelt, ob es sich bei ihr um eine Art Straßen-Proll, eine exzentrische Obdachlose oder einen harmlosen Straßenhändler handelt, der versucht, gefälschte Prada- und Gucci-Taschen an die Frau zu bringen.

Die Skulpturen verbindet die Frage, wie die Öffentlichkeit das U-Bahn-System zu den verschiedenen Zeiten zwischen Rush Hour und den trostlosen Nachtstunden besetzt, und vor allem, welche Teile der Öffentlichkeit vorüberziehen, welche verweilen und es besetzen.

Grays Arbeiten handeln oft von den sozialen und öffentlichen Räumen der allgemeinen Bevölkerung oder den Habermas'schen *loci publici*: den Bereich von Privatpersonen, die als Öffentlichkeit zusammenkommen.[1] *Feierabend* (2017) zeigt einen erschöpften Arbeiter, der zusammengesunken vor dem Fernseher zu Abend isst. An den Rand der Gesellschaft gedrängte Figuren kontrastieren mit denjenigen, die es sich auf sozialer Ebene bequem gemacht haben. Auf *Bad Habits* (2017) sieht man Nonnen mit weihevollem Gesicht, während *Ladies in the Toilet* (2017) die illegale Einnahme eines weißen Pulvers auf einem Smartphone zeigt. Das Wortspiel und die Wiederholung eines visuellen Wortspiels schildern vermeintlich akzeptable und inakzeptable Verhaltensweisen, im Besonderen da die Figuren auf beiden Bildern weiblich sind. *Monoculture* (2017) verweist auf den Zustand der kulturellen Diversität Europas, insbesondere Merkels berüchtigte Aussage aus dem Jahr 2010, der Multikulturalismus sei gescheitert.[2] Zwei weiße Frauen mit knallrot gefärbten Haaren sitzen leicht gelangweilt in der U-Bahn und essen Fastfood-Nudeln.

In der Ausstellung *Concorde* (UKS Oslo, 2017) war ein großes Foto von Roosevelt Island in New York zu sehen, wo Gray aufwuchs. Die relativ hässliche brutalistische Fabrikarchitektur erinnert an das Pseudo-Geschäftsleben am Potsdamer Platz, der angesichts der architektonischen Gesichtslosigkeit seines vermeintlich internationalen Stils vielerlei Orte oder paradoxerweise gar kein Ort sein könnte. Dieses für eine bestimmte demografische Gruppe erstrebenswerte Wunschbild könnte auch aus Immobilienanzeigen oder Bordmagazinen stammen. Eine ähnlich mimetische Semiotik der Concorde wird aufgrund ihres bewussten Retro-Charmes aufgerufen (hier eher als wissende satirische Anspielung).

Seit 2015 arbeitet die Künstlerin vor allem mit dem und durch das Medium Malerei. Grays Ansatz steht jedoch den konzeptuellen Strategien John Millers näher als dem Diskurs der Malerei per se. Miller lehnte die abstrakt expressionistischen Tendenzen seiner Lehrer ab, nur um später zu erkennen, dass deren Einfluss in seinen immer stärkeren Mixed-Media-Arbeiten wiederkehren sollte, wenn auch durch den Filter seiner eigenen Demontage. Ähnlich verwirft Gray die konzeptuellen und entmaterialisierten Strategien, die sie an der Cooper Union lernte, nur um sie dann im Medium Malerei wiederaufleben zu lassen. Sie verweist offen auf ihre Bezüge und zitiert Motive der alten Meister der europäischen Malerei wie Cranach oder Ensor, die sie mit semiotischem oder mimetischem Wert und nicht der einfachen ästhetischen oder allegorischen Entscheidung aus dem Diskurs der Malerei auflädt. Nachdem Gray zuvor im Medium Skulptur arbeitete und dann Performances und Theaterstücke schrieb, aktiviert sie nun temporär einen Raum mit figürlichen Gestalten in den unterschiedlichsten Medien auf und jenseits der Leinwand. Obwohl die Künstlerin vehement bestreiten würde, dass ihre Arbeiten von etwas „handeln", spielt sie mit den Bildern weiblicher Figuren sowie mit Dandy-haftigkeit in Bezug auf typische geschlechtsspezifische Vorstellungen (weiblicher) Performativität. Gray ist in erster Linie Malerin und möchte sich nicht durch ihr Geschlecht definieren lassen, so wie Frank Ripploh sagte, sein Film *Taxi zum Klo* sei kein Schwulenfilm, sondern spiele zufällig in einem schwulen Milieu.[3] In beiden Fällen steht die angesprochene Subjektivität im Vordergrund, eine Person in einen ideologischen Rahmen zu stellen, um diese Subjektivität dann zu zerlegen und sie frei entlang des Bahnsteigs laufen zu lassen.

1 Habermas, Jürgen, *Strukturwandel der Öffentlichkeit. Untersuchungen zu einer Kategorie der bürgerlichen Gesellschaft*. Frankfurt am Main: Suhrkamp, 1962.
2 http://www.spiegel.de/politik/deutschland/integration-merkel-erklaert-multikulti-fuer-gescheitert-a-723532.html.
3 „Back to the Toilet. An Interview with Frank Ripploh", übers. Christopher Duncan. *Little Joe Magazine* #2, 2011.

"FAHRSCHEIN, BITTE"
Steven Warwick

Entering the Kunsthalle, one could be forgiven for thinking they have entered a waiting room. The space has been designed to resemble a public transport carriage replete with flip-down seats, and Perspex sculptural vessels through which to pass. Protestant notions of guilt and trust pervade the Berlin subway system with the possibility of *Schwarzfahren* or riding without a (valid) ticket. Warnings against this practice are posted inside the station and on the carriages. The issue morphs from an economic to a moral one. Plain-clothes inspectors blend in with the public only to blow their cover and police the passengers. *Controller* (2018) depicts this scenario in vivid hues, as authority makes its presence known to the travelling public; it shows chained-up luggage and a muzzled dog during a dizzying rush hour.

Sculptures incorporated into the scene further concretize the situation off canvas. Three flip-down subway seats line the space, scattered with items deliberately or accidentally left behind. A cast replica of a juicy joint of ham in a red plastic bag rests on one seat; a collection of shopping bags sits beneath another. Curiously, the contents of the bags are exclusively colored white.

Eeriest of all is *Pigeon Feather Stick* (2018), a figurative sculpture made of a trolley adorned with bootleg luxury fashion accessories punctured with anti-pigeon spikes. The menacing human-like figure has an uncanny presence in the space, lurking, overstaying its welcome. One is left to ponder if the character is some kind of street oik, eccentric bag lady or harmless street trader trying to sell knock-off Prada and Gucci bags. These sculptures are united by the question of how the public occupies the subway system over the various periods between rush hour and the desolate hours of the night, and more importantly, which elements of the public pass through and which linger and occupy it.

Gray's work often inhabits the social and public spaces of the general population or the Habermasian *loci publici*: the sphere of private people coming together as a public.[1] *Feierabend* (2017) depicts an exhausted worker, collapsed in front of his television in the evening, eating dinner. Characters generally pushed to the margins contrast with the more socially comfortable. *Bad Habits* features some solemn-faced nuns, whilst *Ladies in the Toilet* (both works 2017) depicts an illicit act of ingesting white powder from a smartphone. The wordplay and repetition of a visual pun depict modes of socially acceptable and unacceptable behaviour, especially considering that the subjects in both paintings are female. *Monoculture* (2017) points to the state of European diversity, in particular Merkel's infamous statement from 2010 that "multiculturalism has failed."[2] In it, two white women with uniformly bright dyed red hair sit on the subway, looking somewhat bored, eating some cheap fast food noodles.

Concorde, 2017 at UKS Oslo, featured a large photo taken from Gray's neighborhood of Roosevelt Island in New York City where she grew up. Its somewhat ugly brutalist factory architecture brings to mind the corporate veneer of Potsdamer Platz which could be many places and paradoxically none at all, due to the architectural facelessness of its supposedly international style. This aspirational image, desirable to a certain demographic, could be found in real estate advertisements, or in-flight magazines. A similarly mimetic semiotic of the Concorde is mined for its consciously retro value (here more with a knowing satirical nod).

Since 2015 the artist has primarily worked with and through the medium of painting. However, Gray's approach is closer to the conceptual strategies of John Miller than the discourse of painting per se. Miller would reject the abstract expressionist tendencies of his teachers only to later realize the influence had resurfaced in his increasingly mixed media practice, albeit through a filter of his own dismantling. Gray would reject the conceptual and dematerialised strategies she was taught at Cooper Union only to have them return through the medium of painting. She openly lifts references and quotes motifs from the Old Masters of European painting such as Cranach or Ensor, charged with their semiotic or mimetic value rather than the simple aesthetic or allegorical choice that we find in the discourse of painting. Previously working in sculpture and going on to write performances and plays, the use of figurative characters, be it on or off canvas, activates a space for a determined amount of time, across media. Whilst Gray would resolutely state her works aren't "about" anything, she plays with tropes of feminine figures and dandiness in relation to gendered preconceptions of (feminine) performativity. Gray is foremost a painter and prefers not to be defined by her gender, just as Frank Ripploh stated that his film *Taxi zum Klo* isn't a gay film, but rather happens to be set in a gay milieu.[3] In both cases, the interpellated subjectivity of placing an individual in an ideological framework is highlighted in order to break it down and allow it to move freely along the platform.

1   Habermas, Jürgen, *The Structural Transformation of the Public Sphere: An Enquiry into a Category of Bourgeois Society*. Cambridge: The MIT Press, 1991.
2   http://www.spiegel.de/politik/deutschland/integration-merkel-erklaert-multikulti-fuer-gescheitert-a-723532.html.
3   "Back to the Toilet. An Interview with Frank Ripploh," transl. Christopher Duncan. *Little Joe*, Nº 2, 2011.

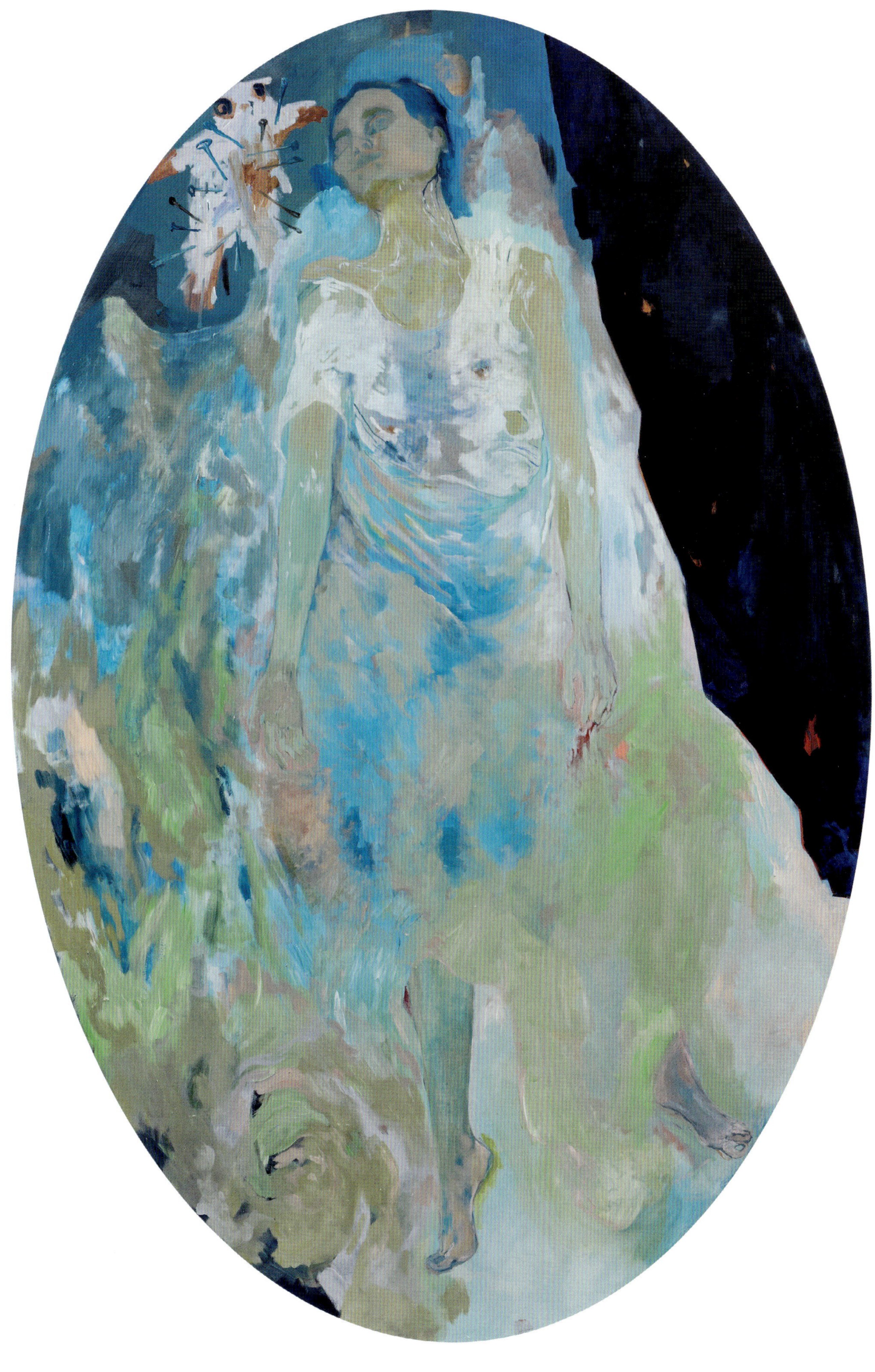

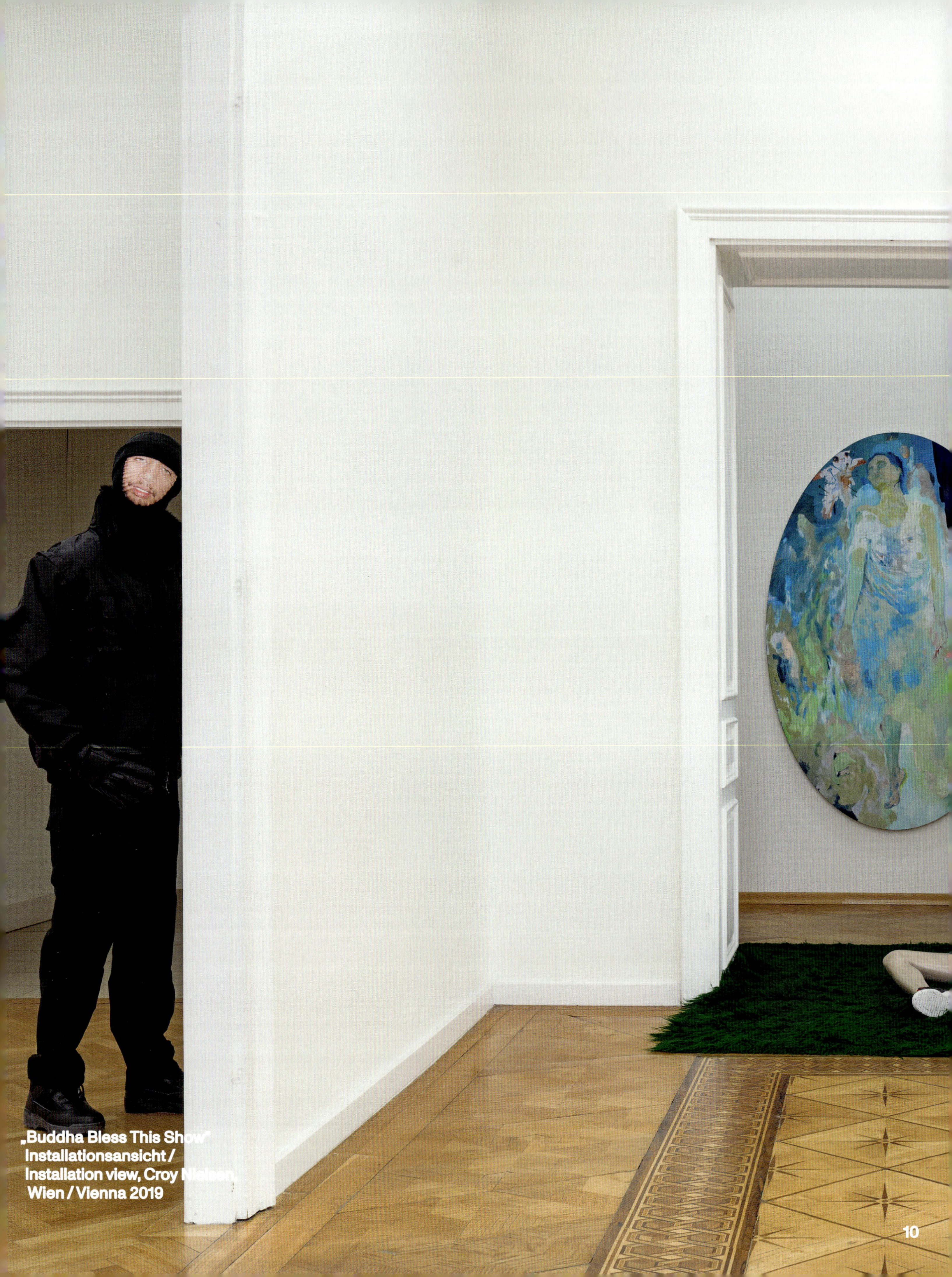

„Buddha Bless This Show"
Installationsansicht /
Installation view, Croy Nielsen,
Wien / Vienna 2019

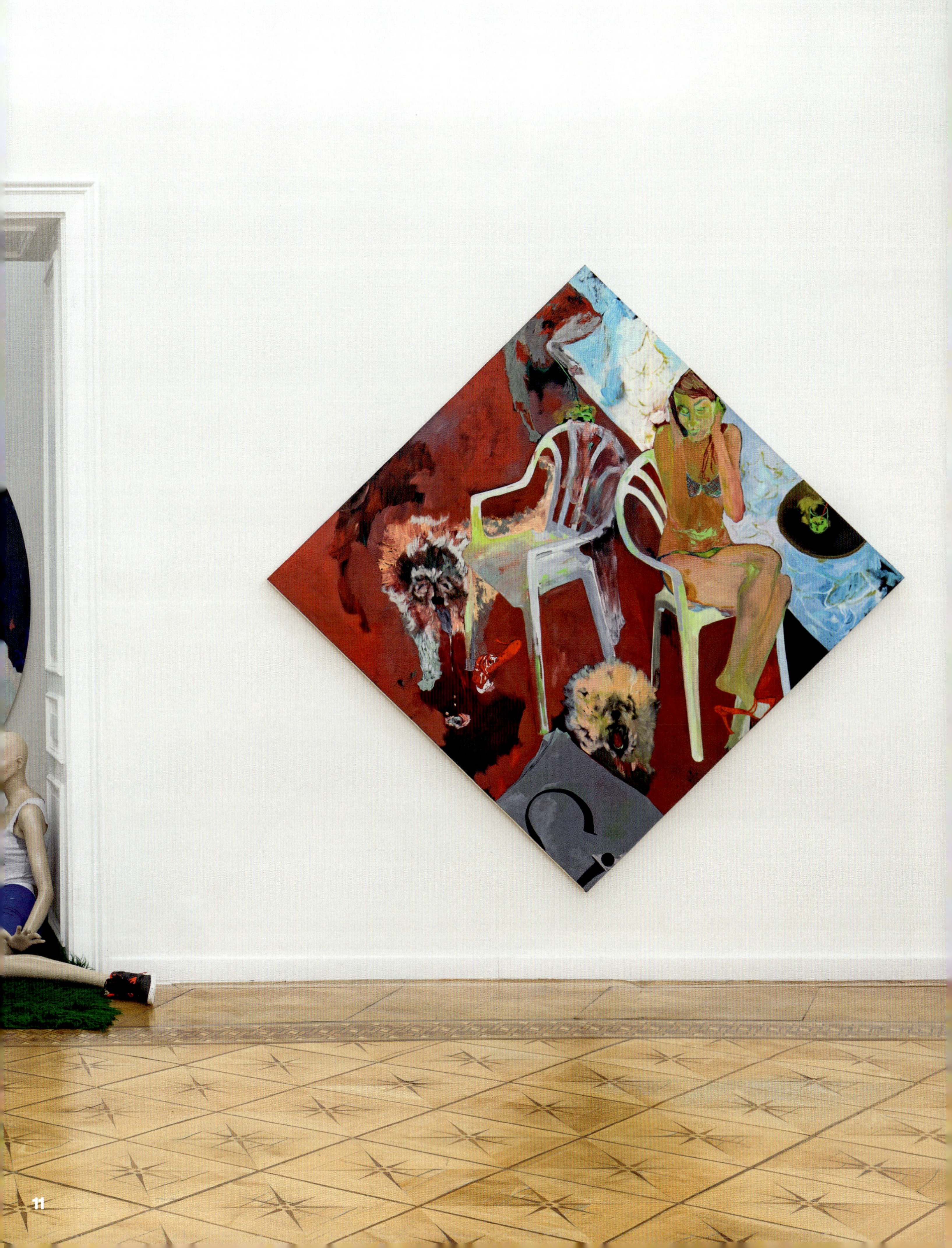

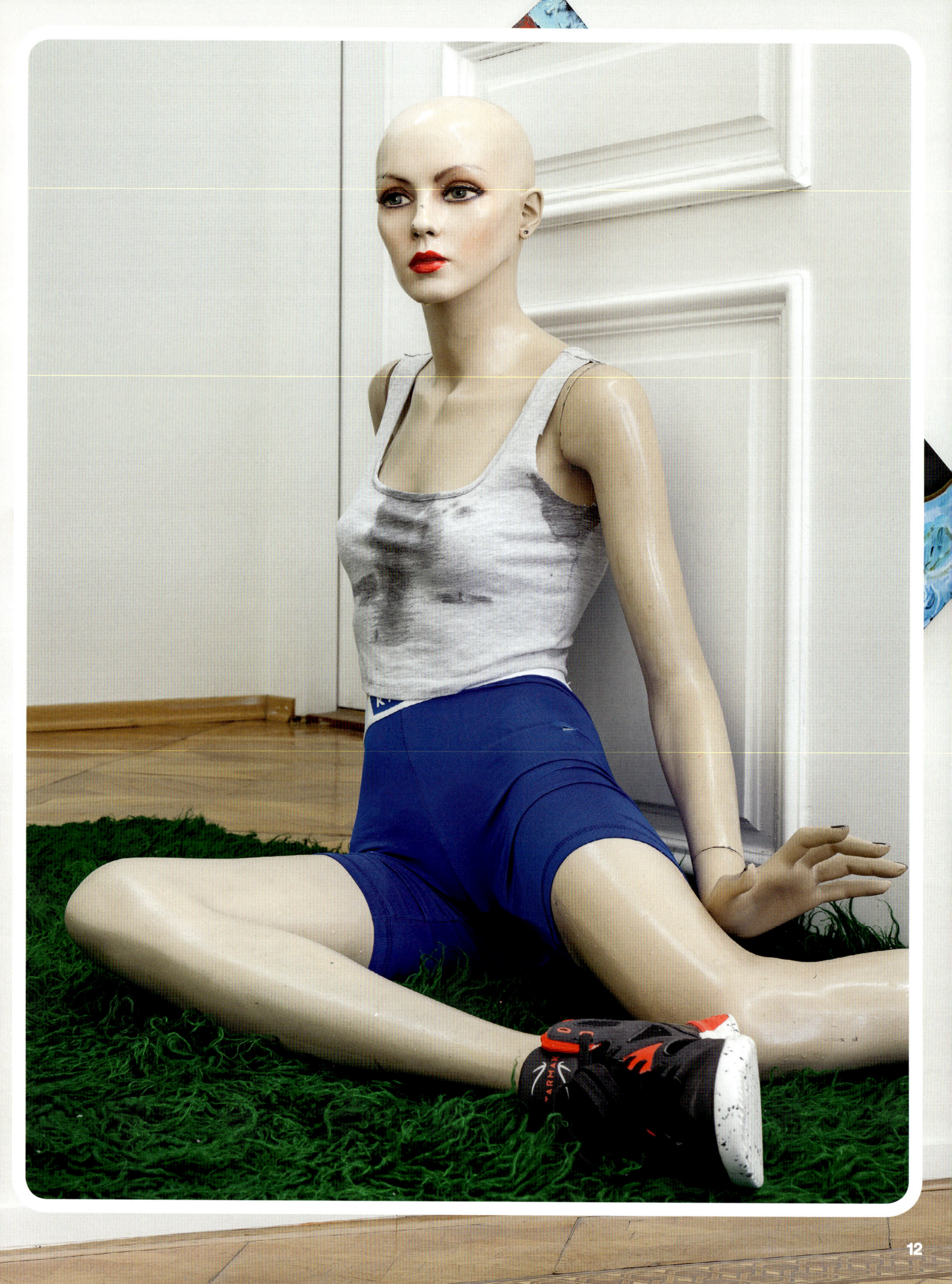

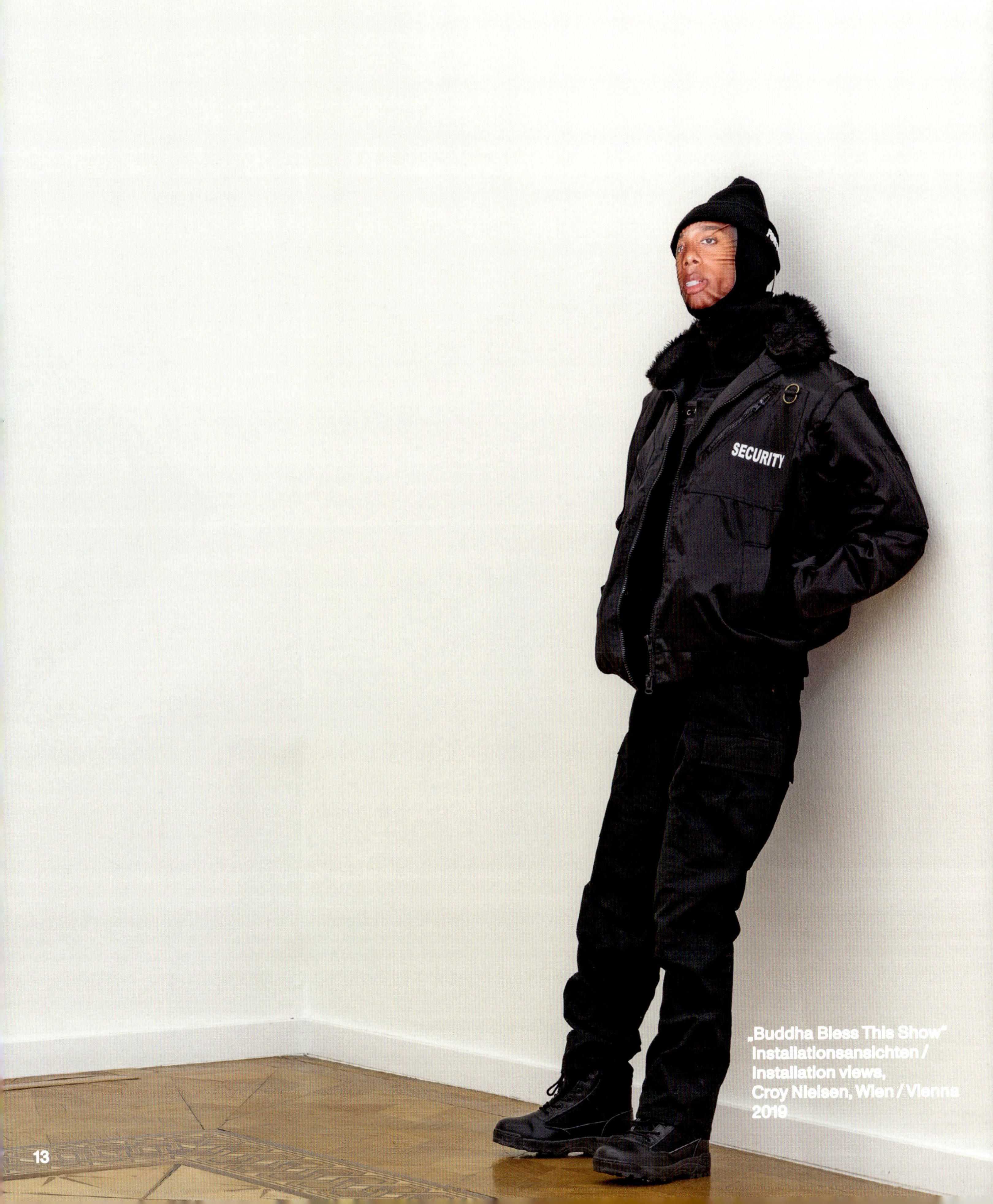

„Buddha Bless This Show"
Installationsansichten /
Installation views,
Croy Nielsen, Wien / Vienna
2019

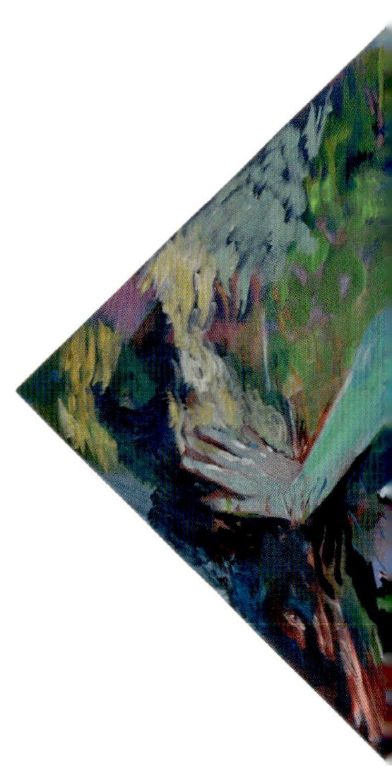

Age of Asexual Reproduction,
2019

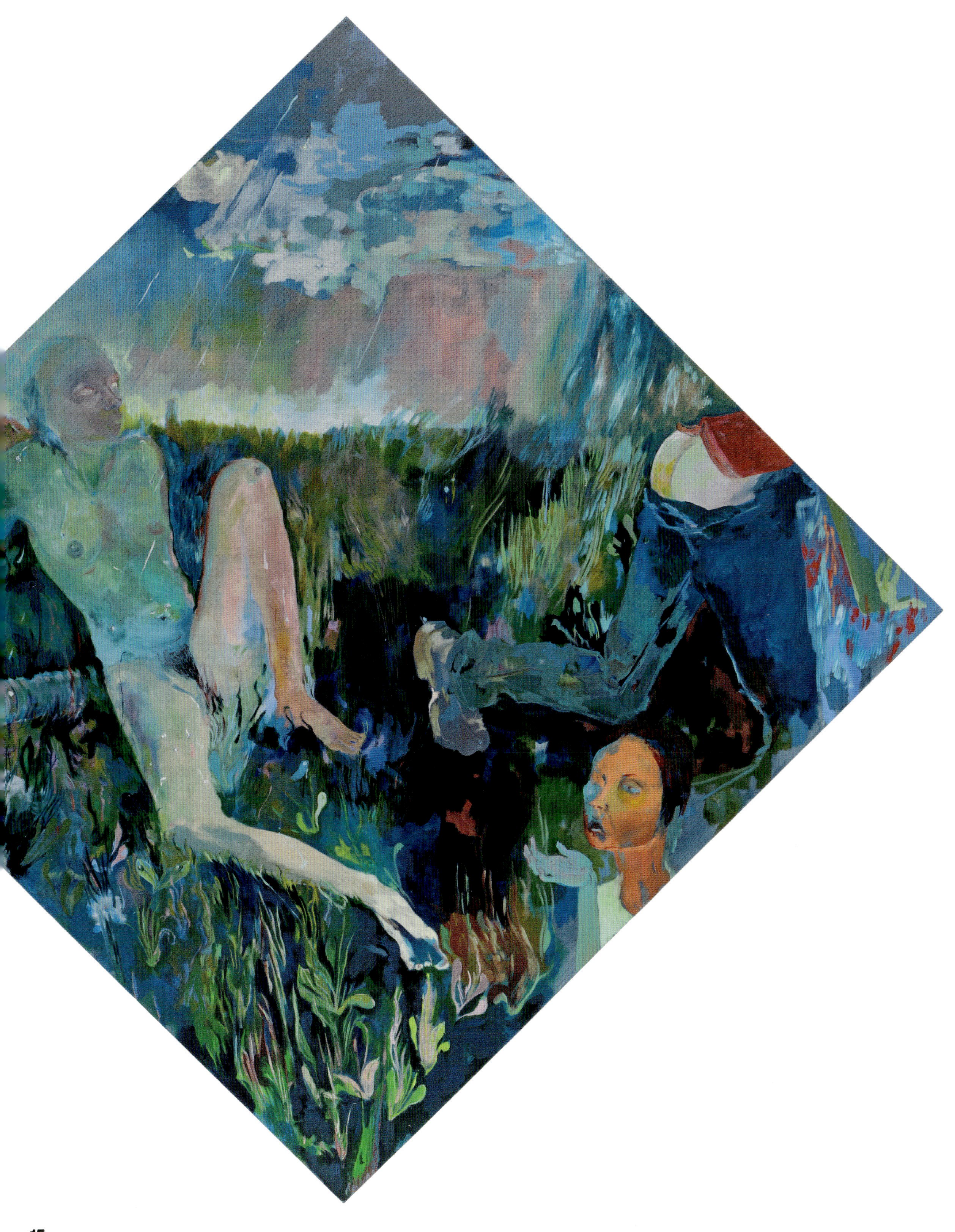

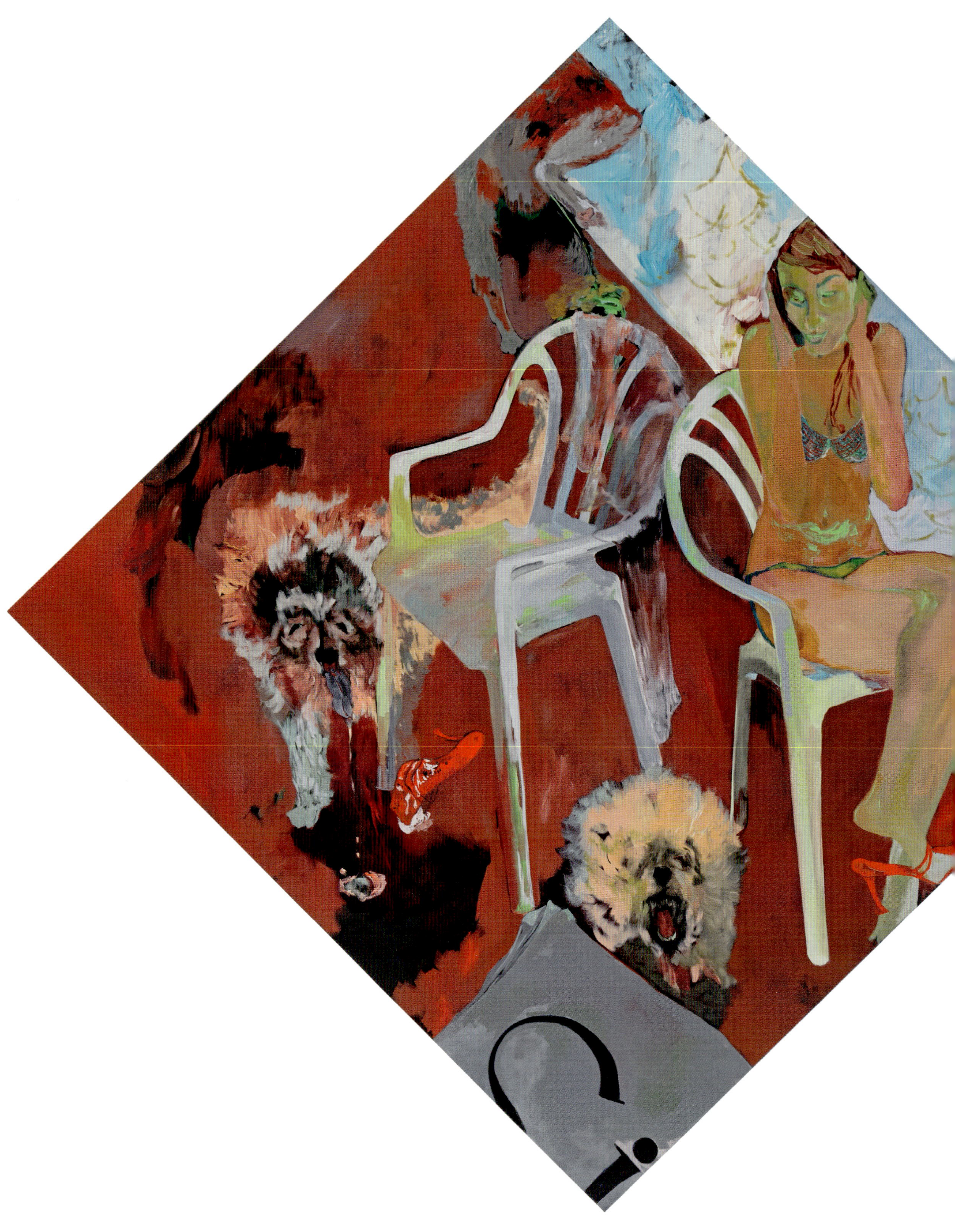

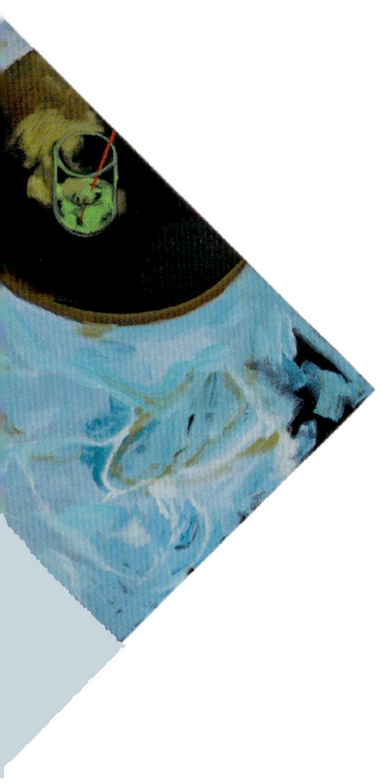

Snowflake (Buddha Bless
This Property), 2019

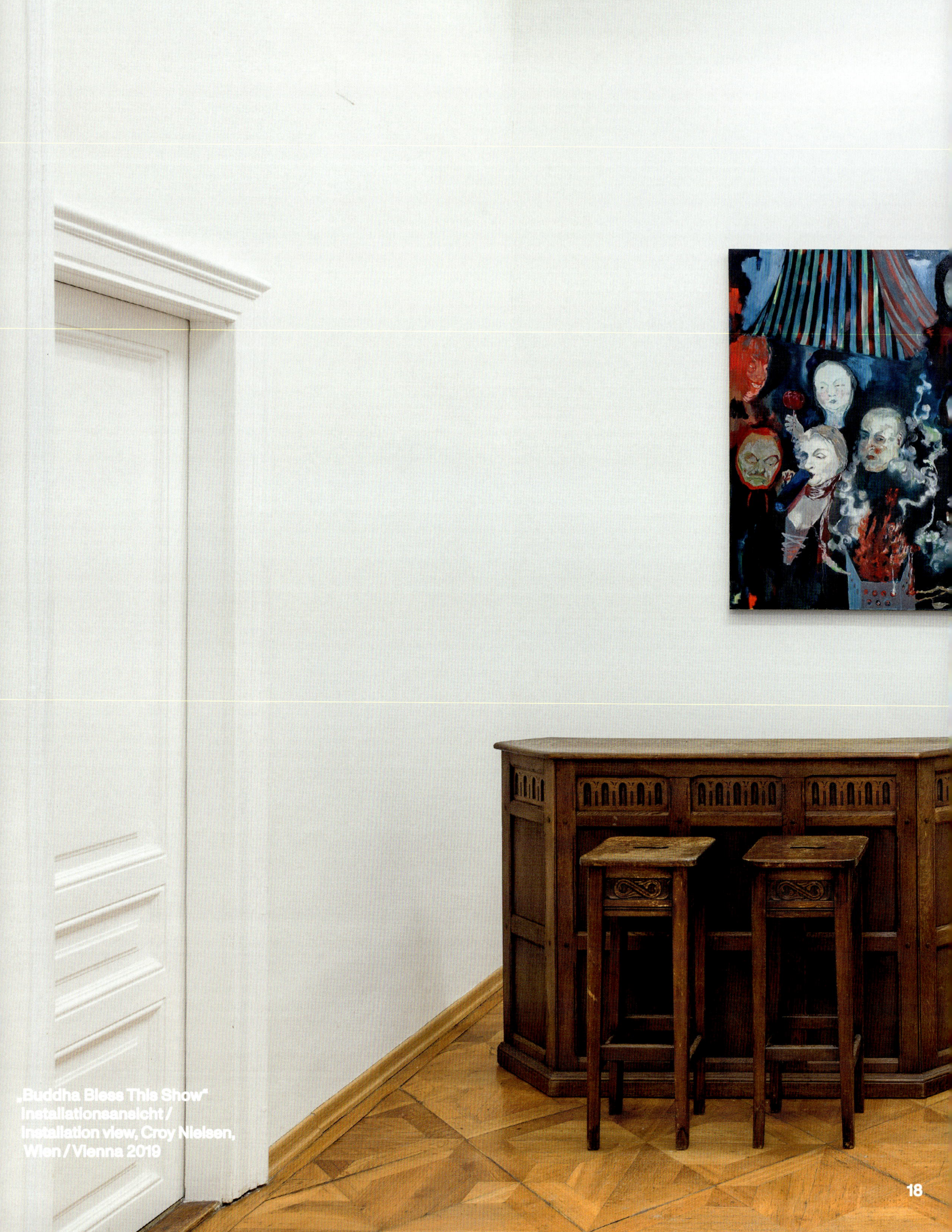

„Buddha Bless This Show"
Installationsansicht /
Installation view, Croy Nielsen,
Wien / Vienna 2019

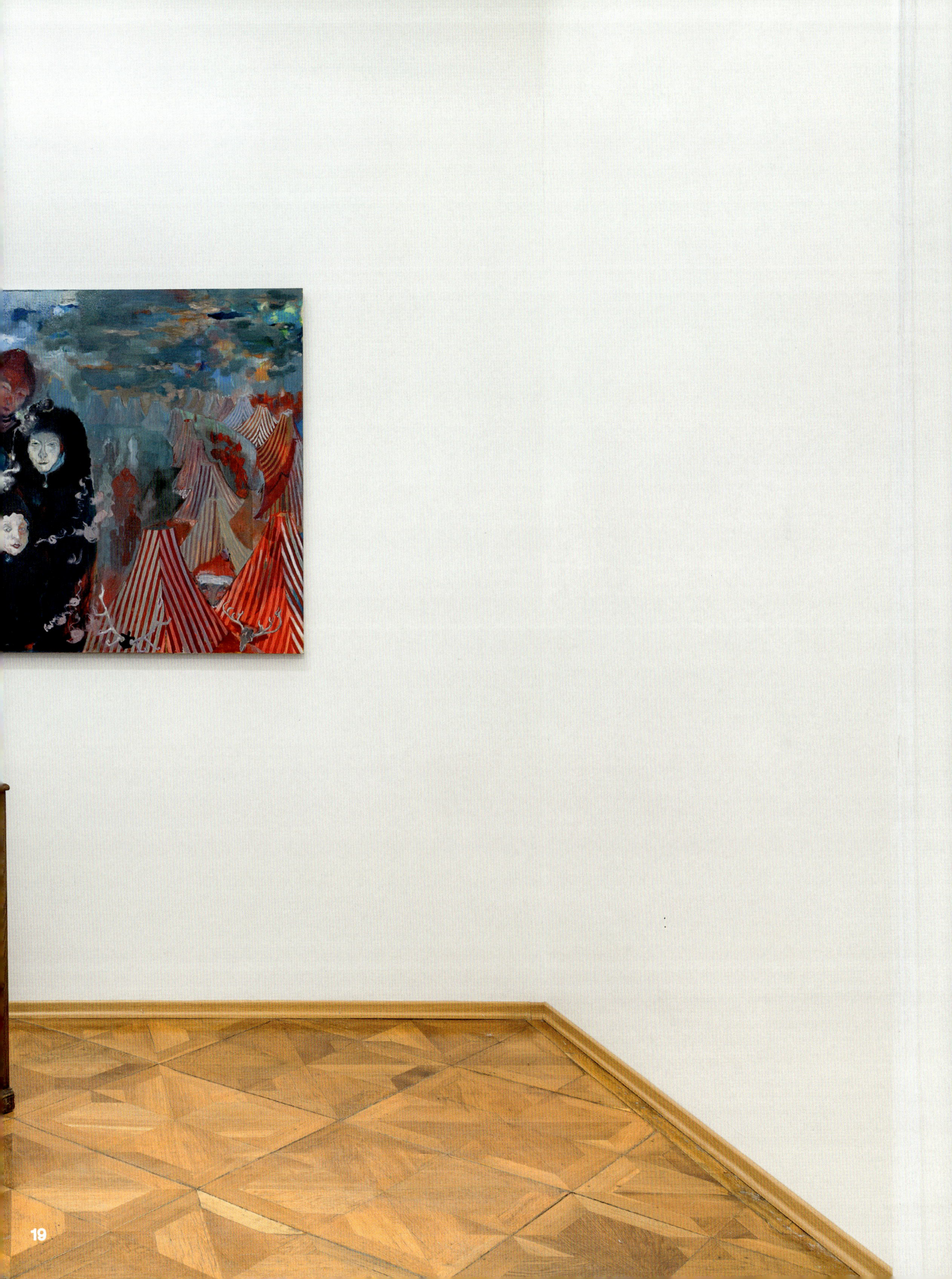

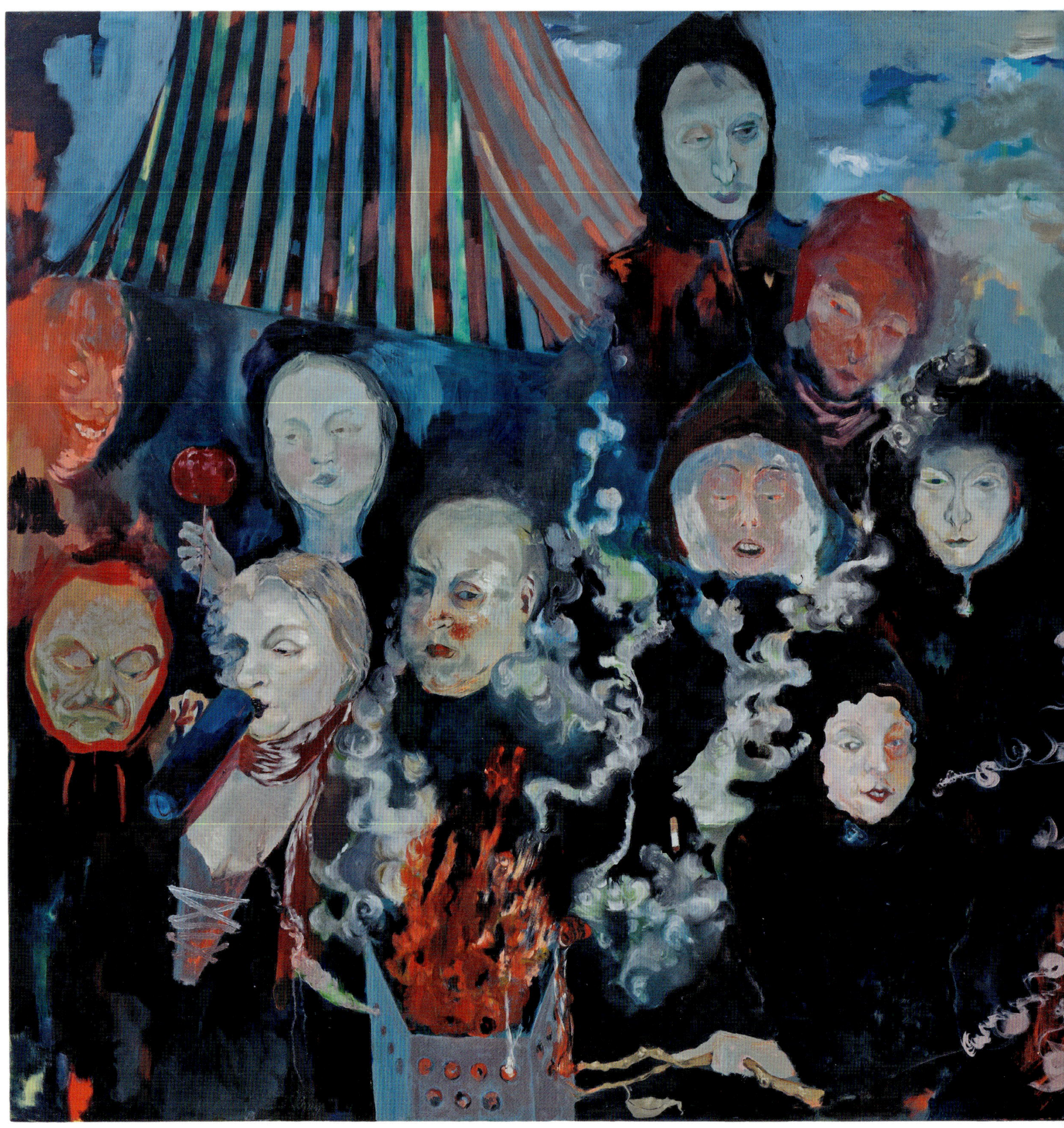

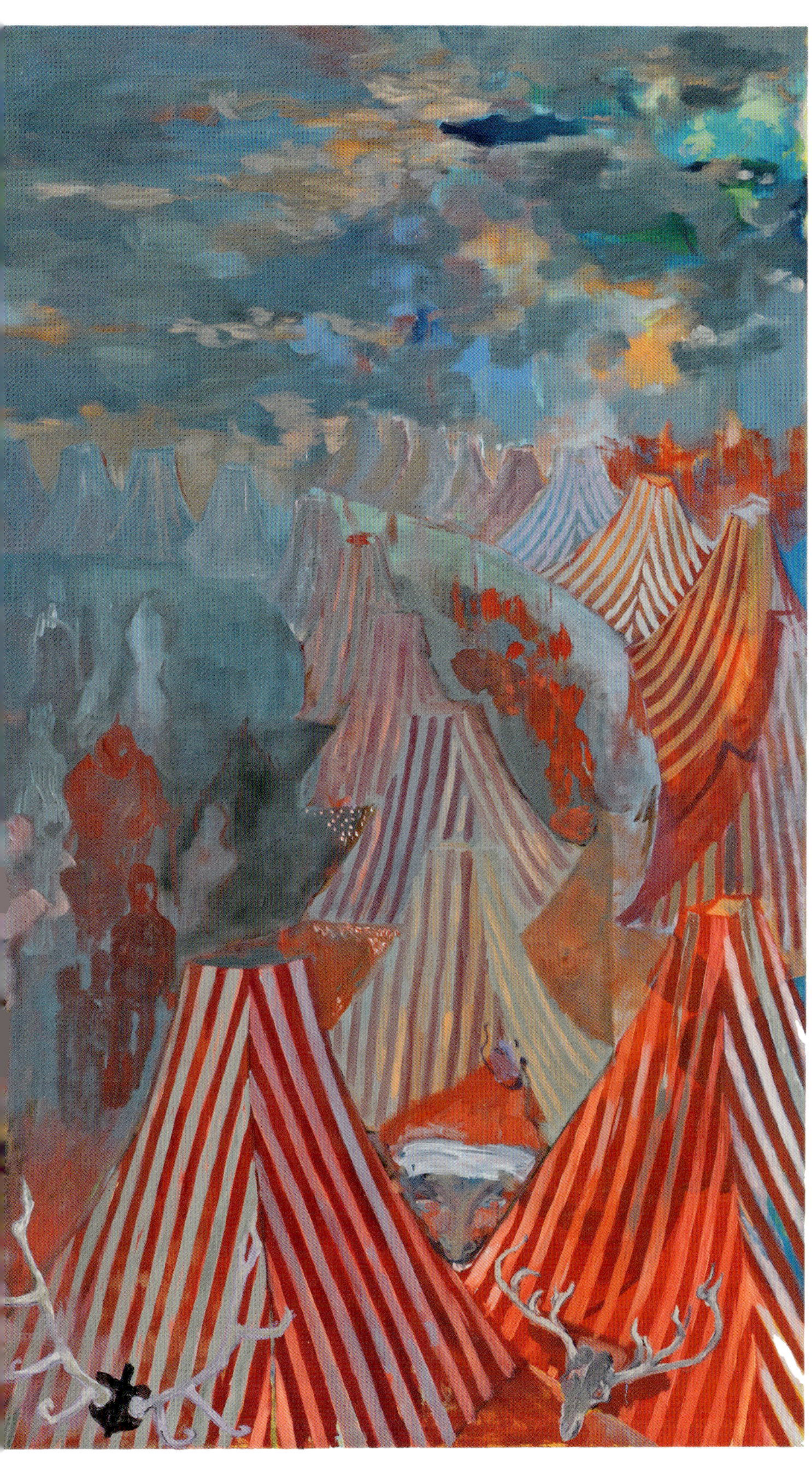

Christmas Market, 2019

Rhino and Dead Bird, 2019

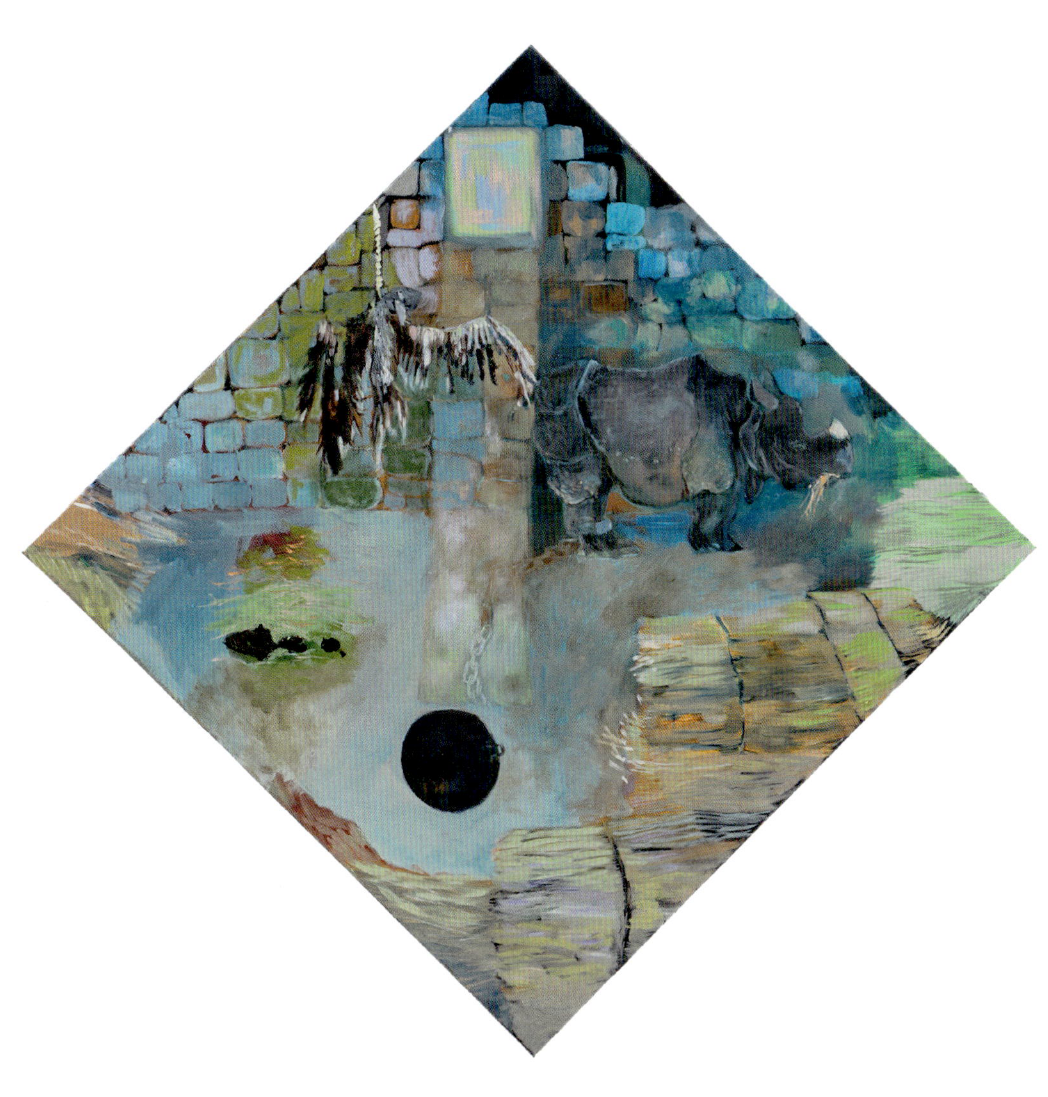

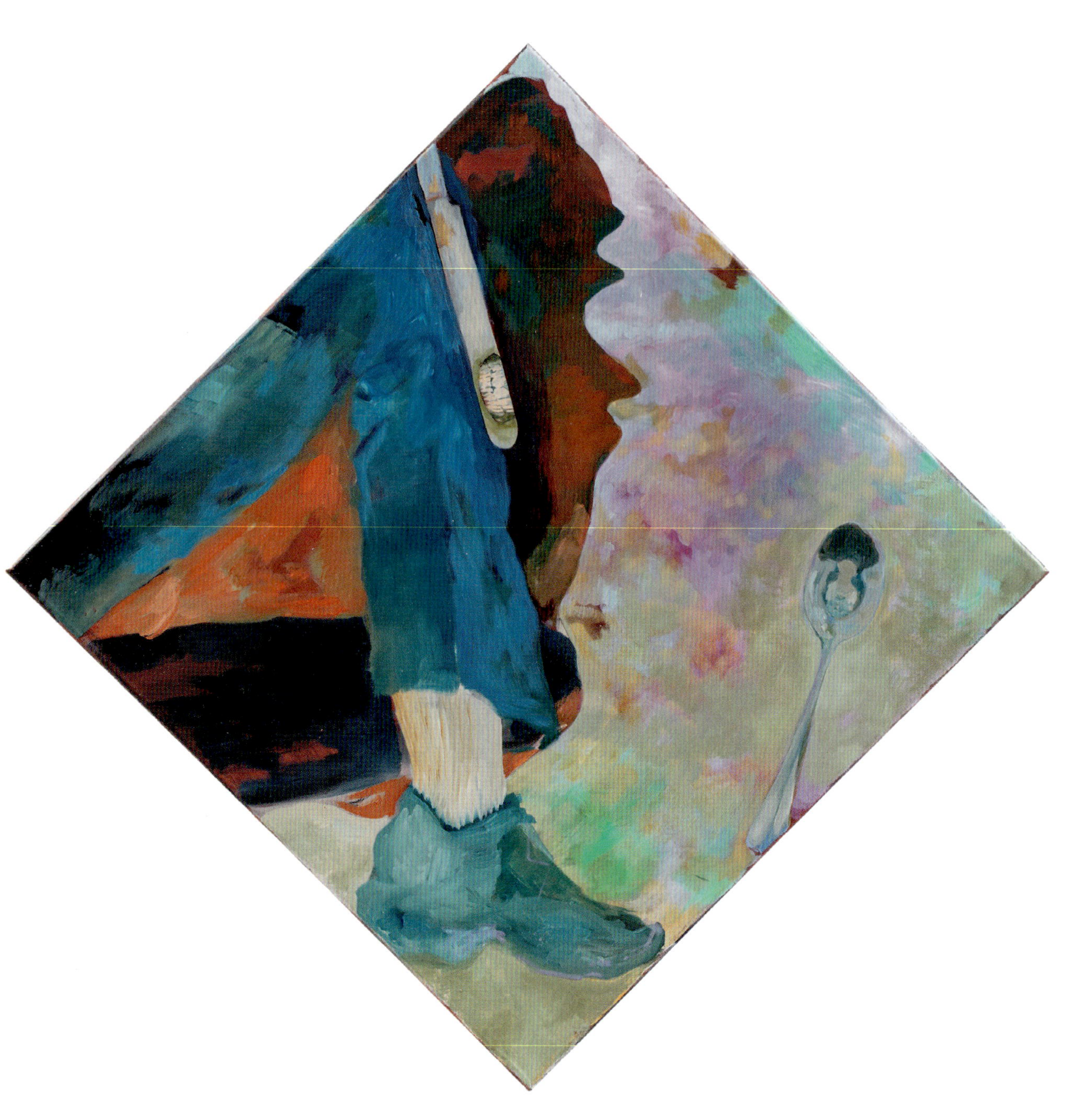

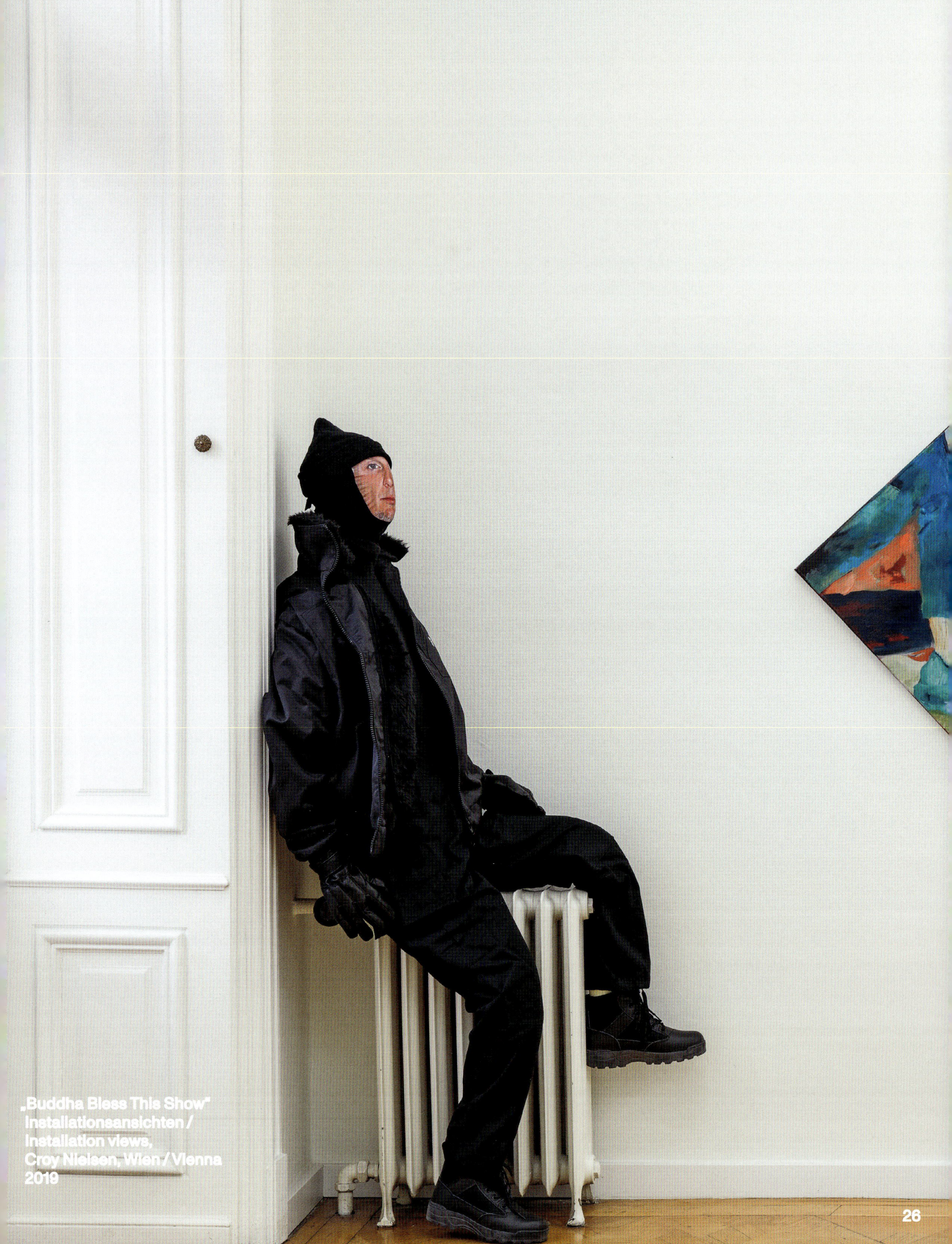

„Buddha Bless This Show"
Installationsansichten /
Installation views,
Croy Nielsen, Wien / Vienna
2019

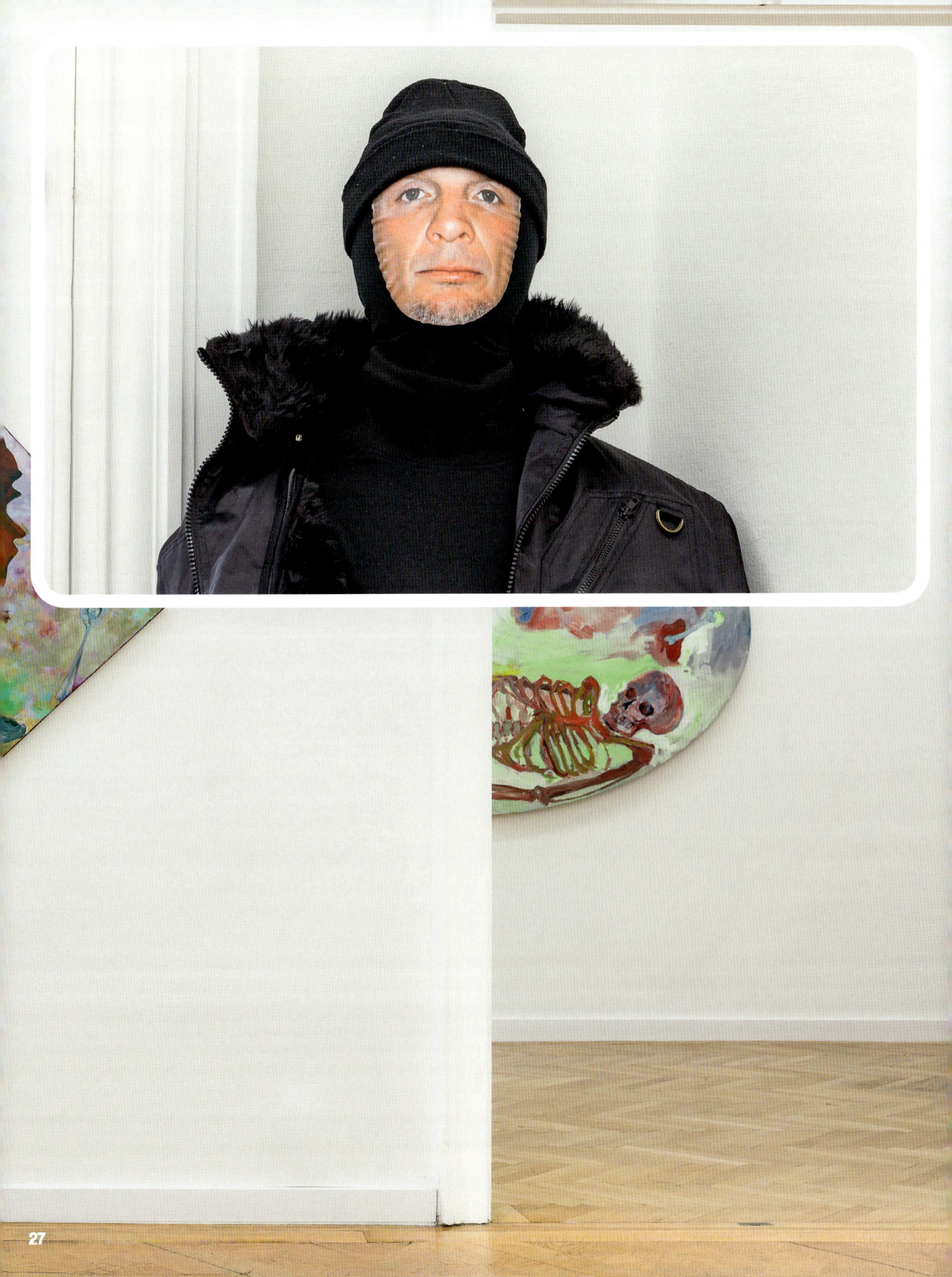

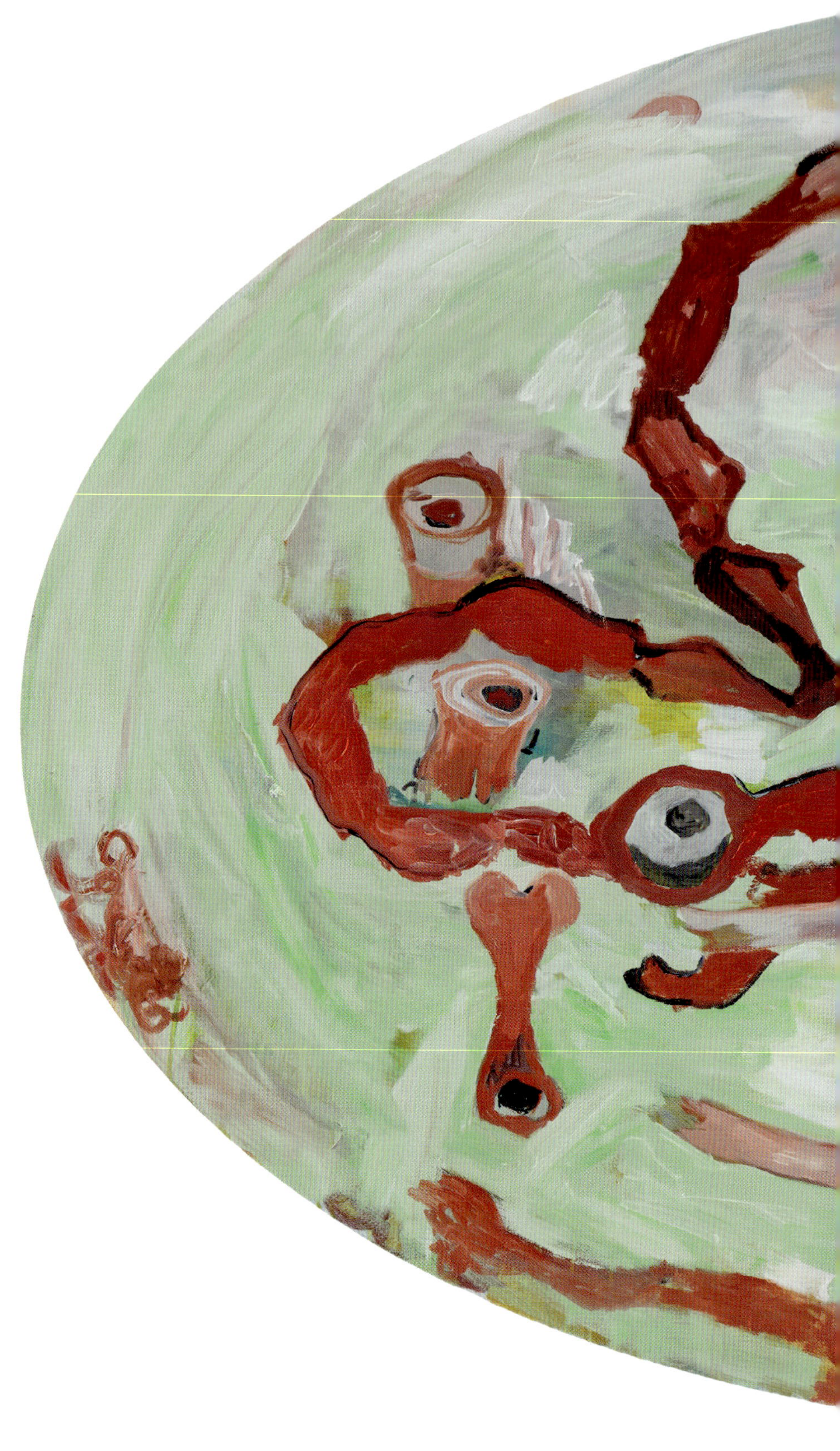

Obvious Death, 2019

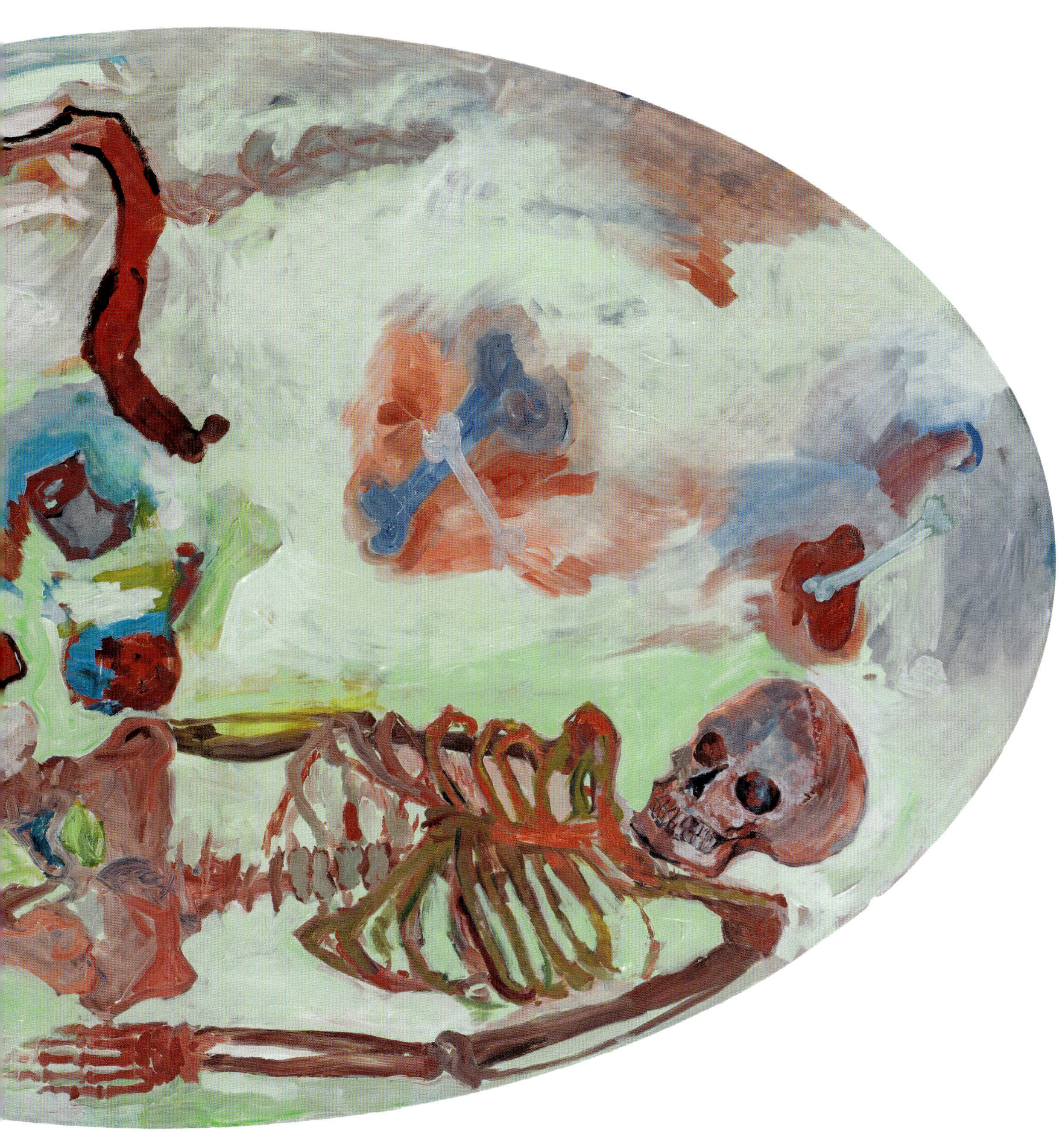

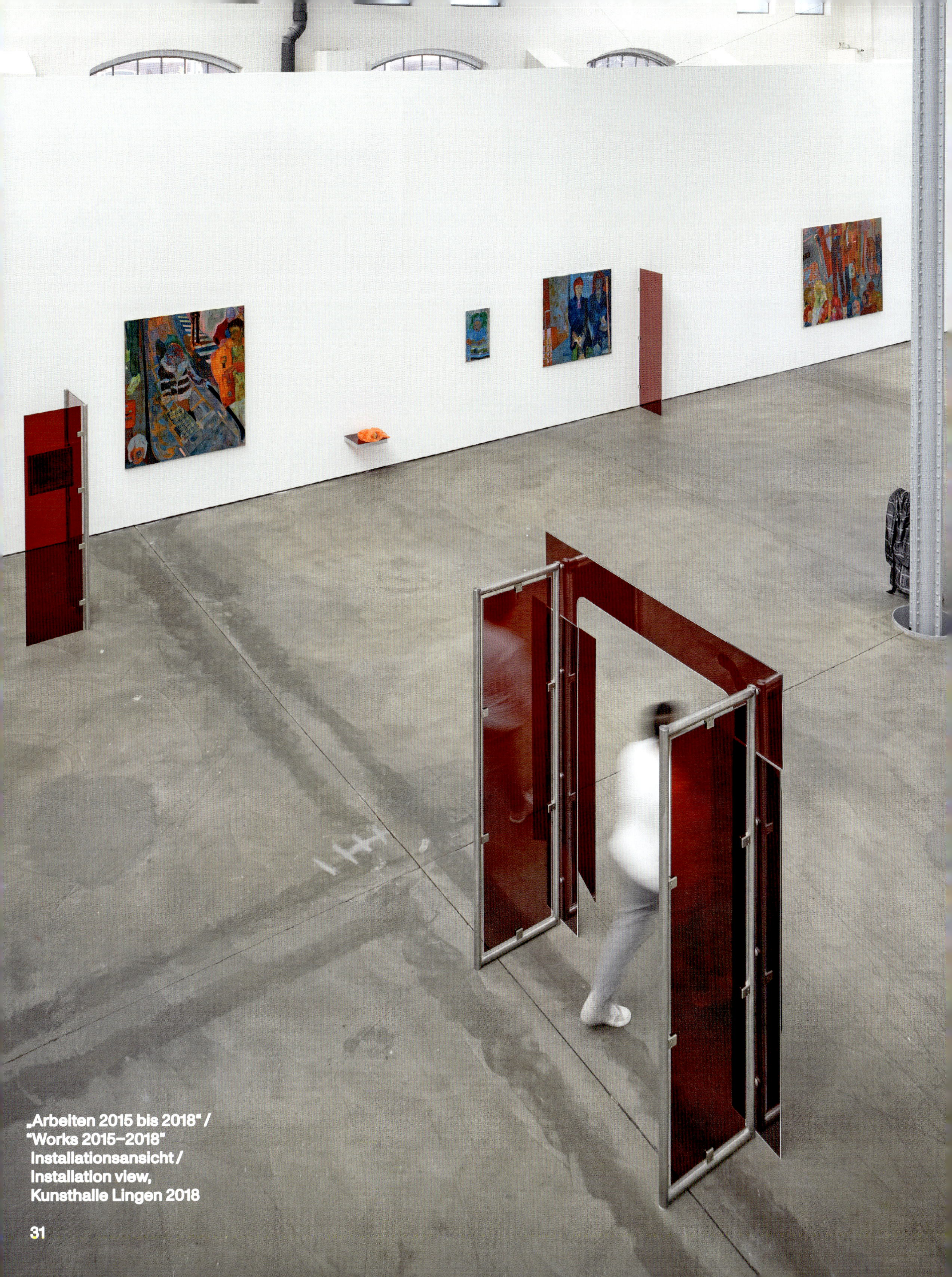

„Arbeiten 2015 bis 2018" /
"Works 2015–2018"
Installationsansicht /
Installation view,
Kunsthalle Lingen 2018

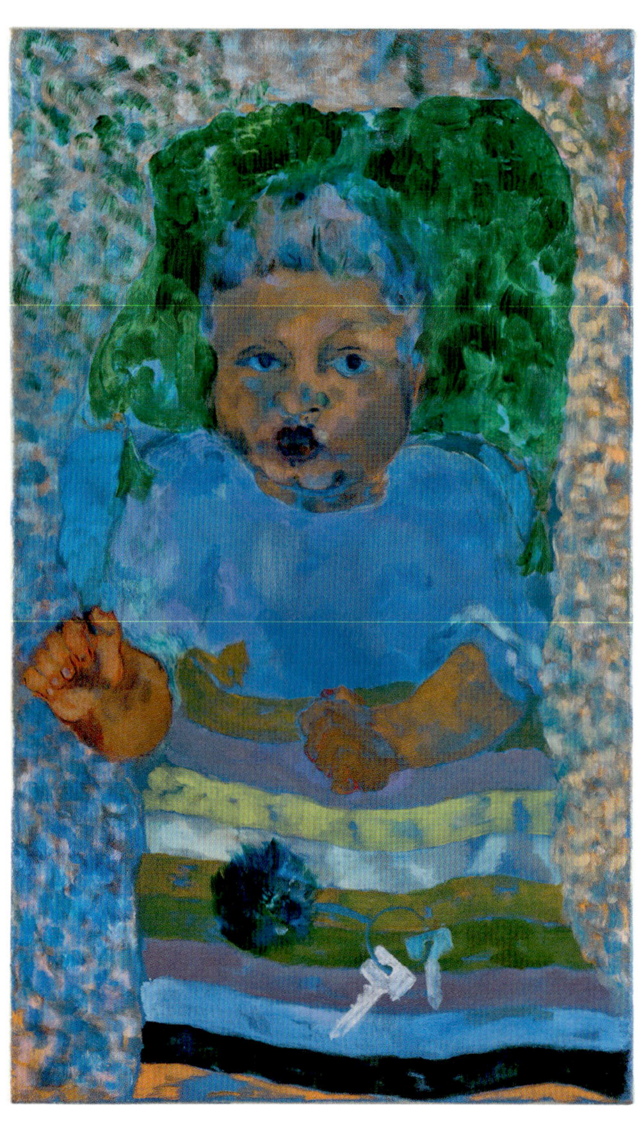

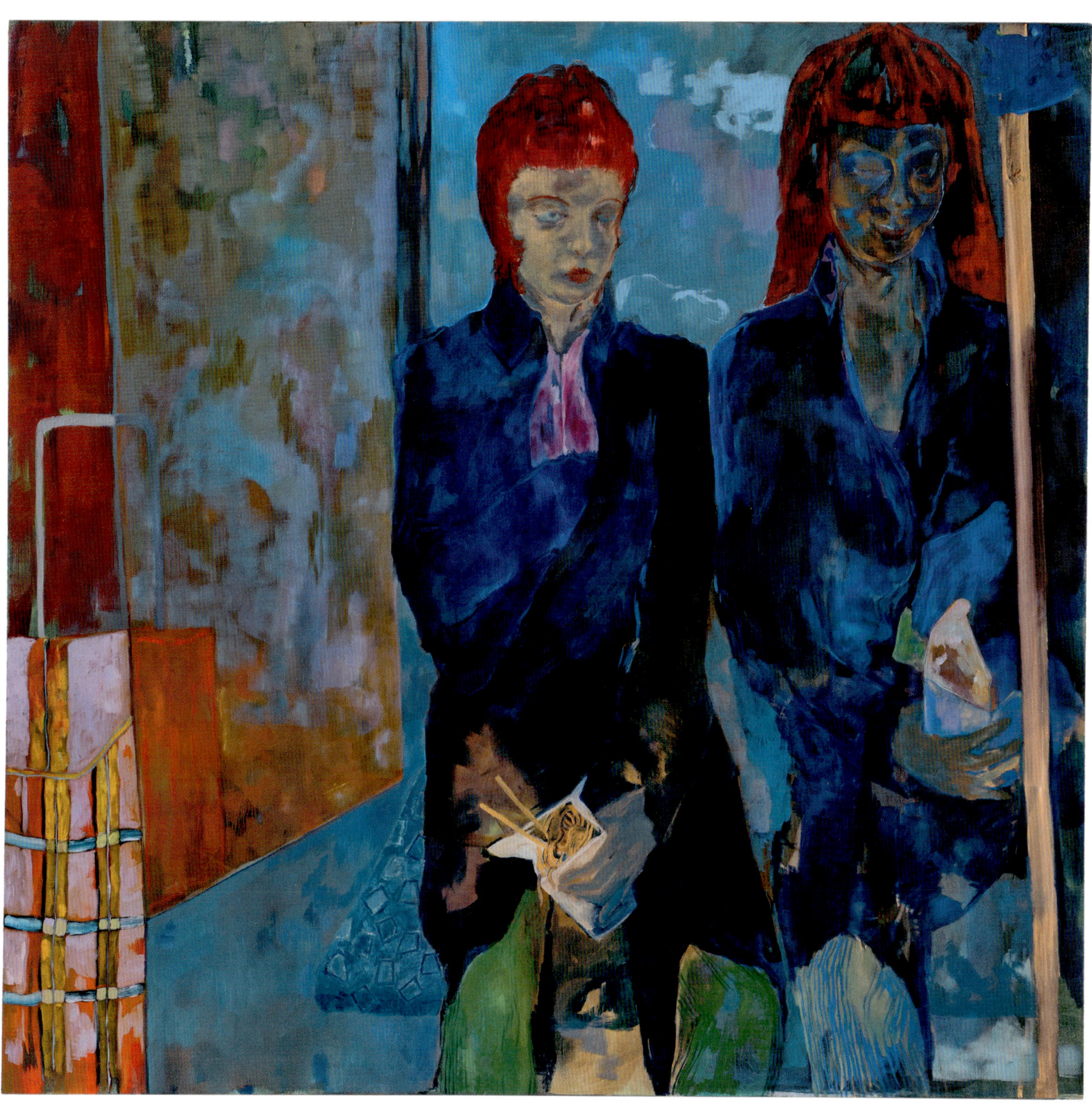

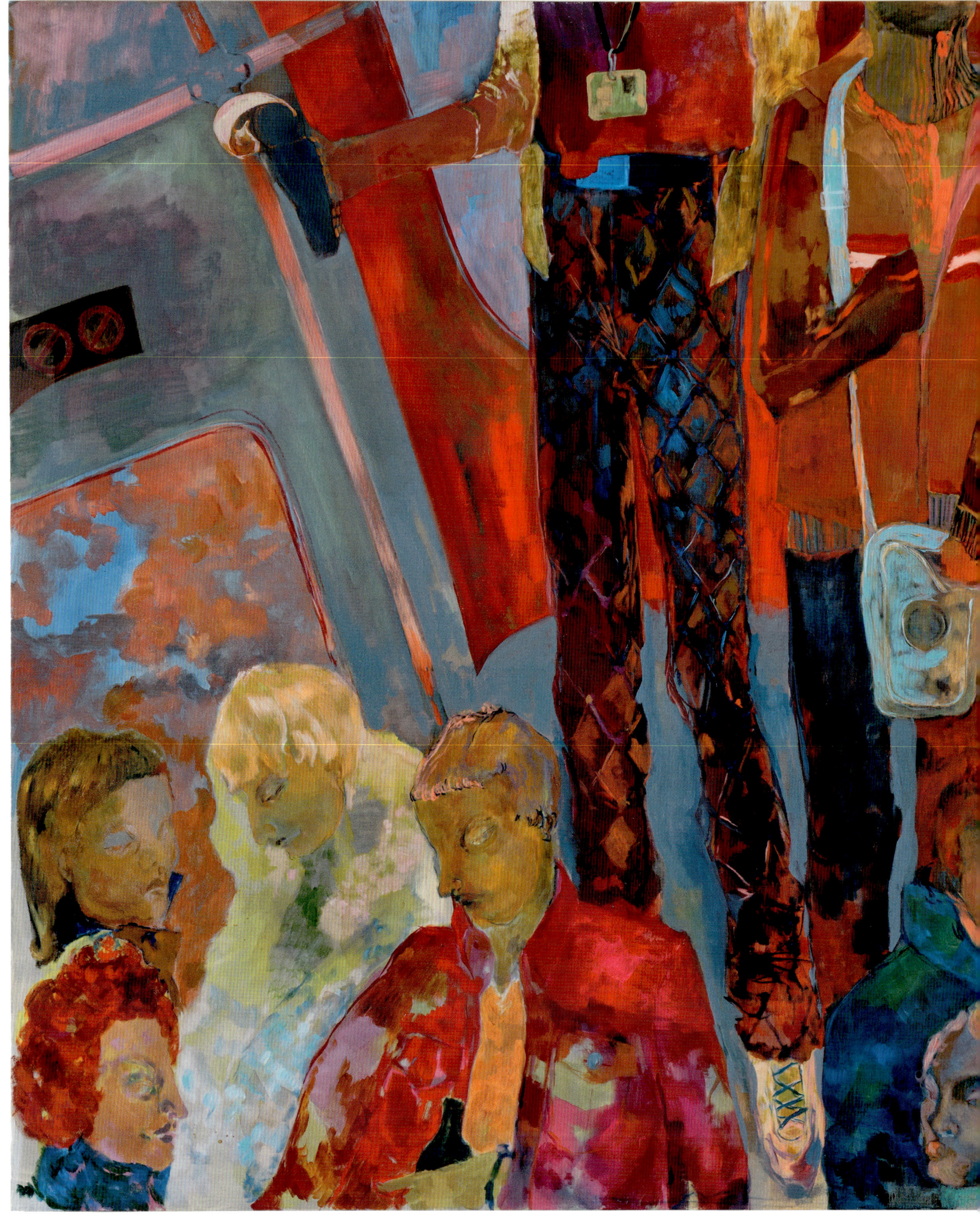

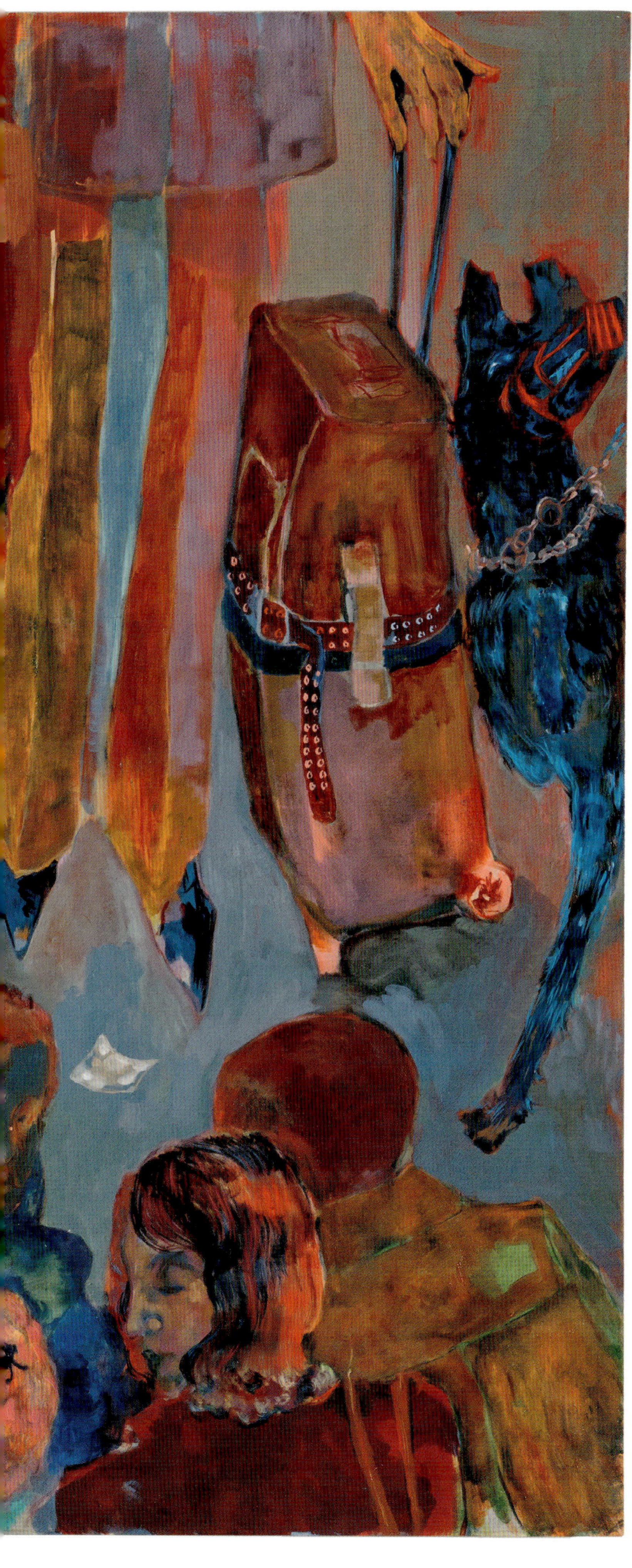

Controller, 2018

„Arbeiten 2015 bis 2018" /
"Works 2015–2018"
Installationsansicht /
Installation view,
Kunsthalle Lingen 2018

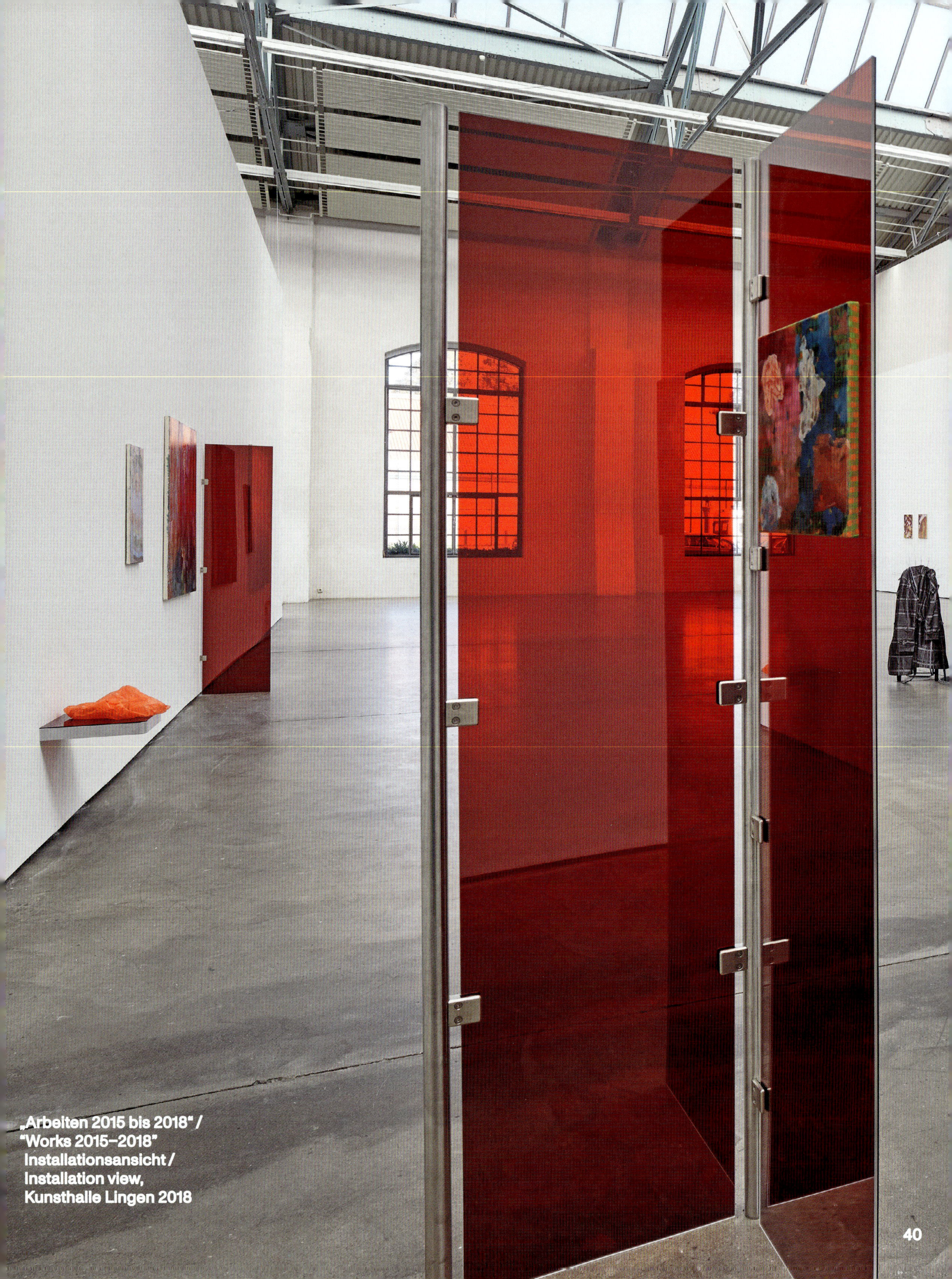

„Arbeiten 2015 bis 2018" /
"Works 2015–2018"
Installationsansicht /
Installation view,
Kunsthalle Lingen 2018

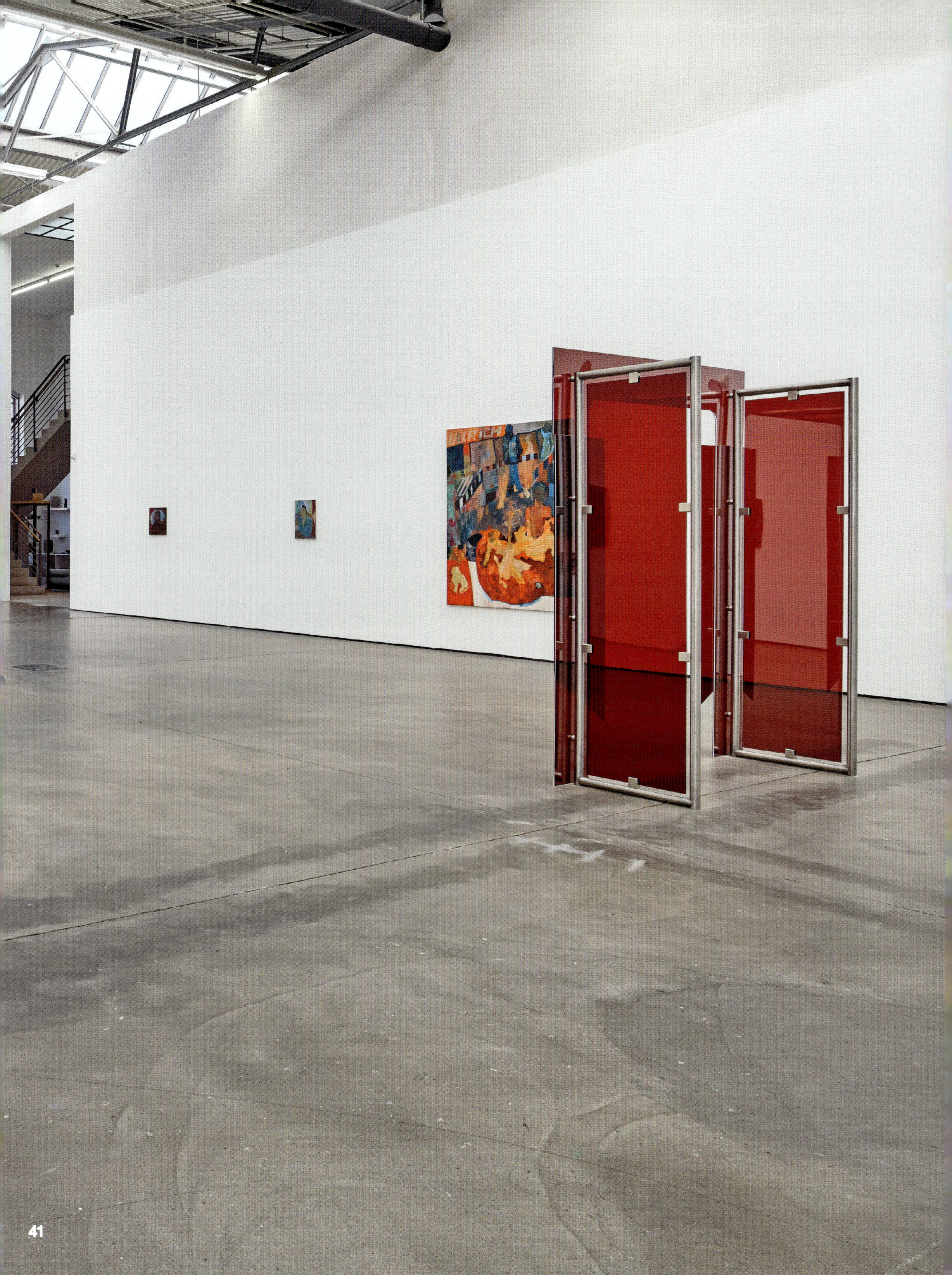

Mood, 2018

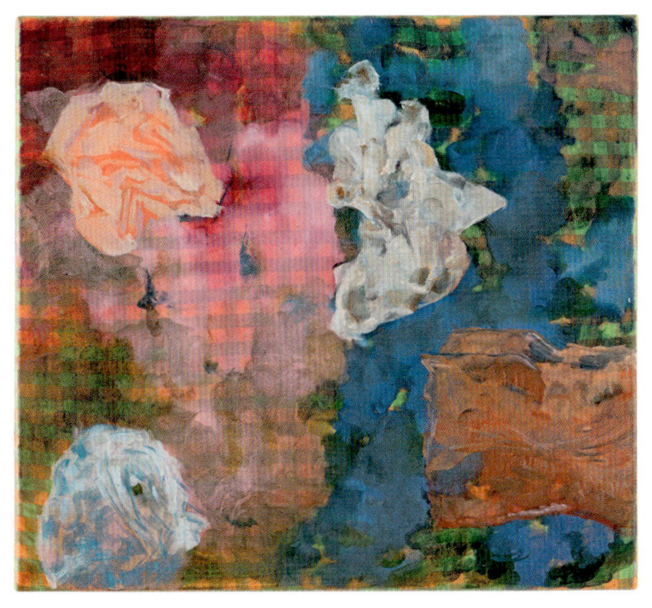

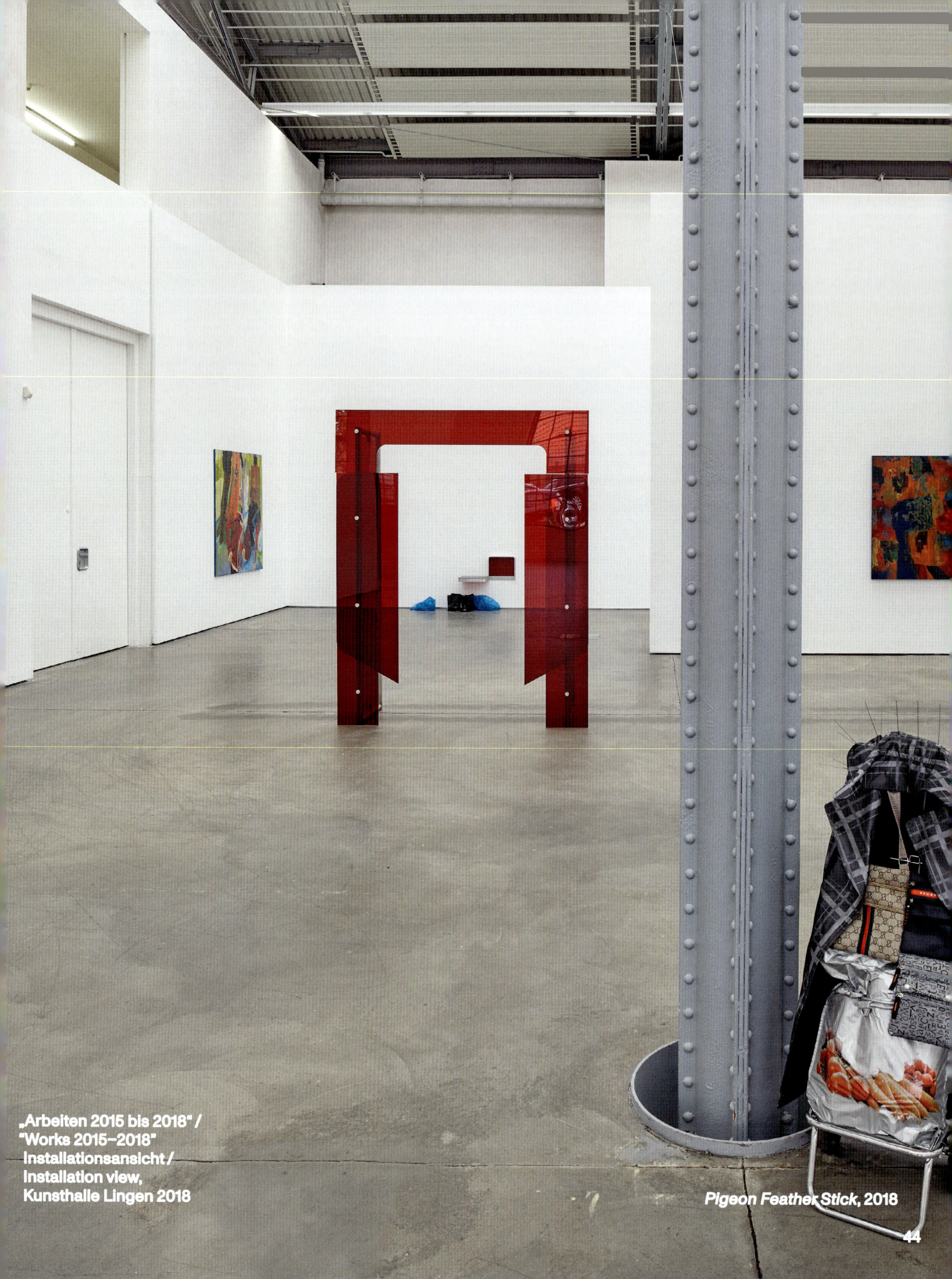

Pigeon Feather Stick, 2018

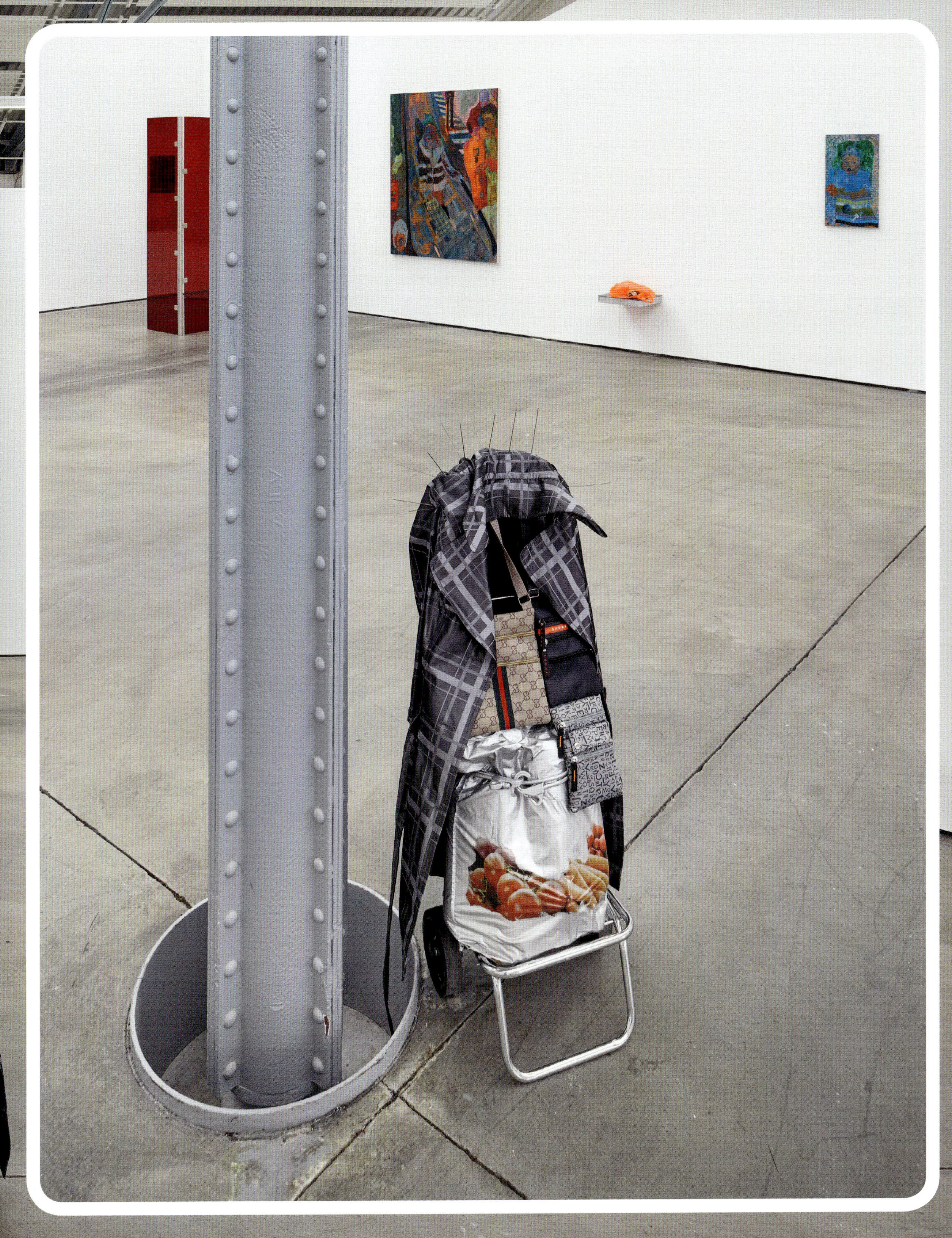

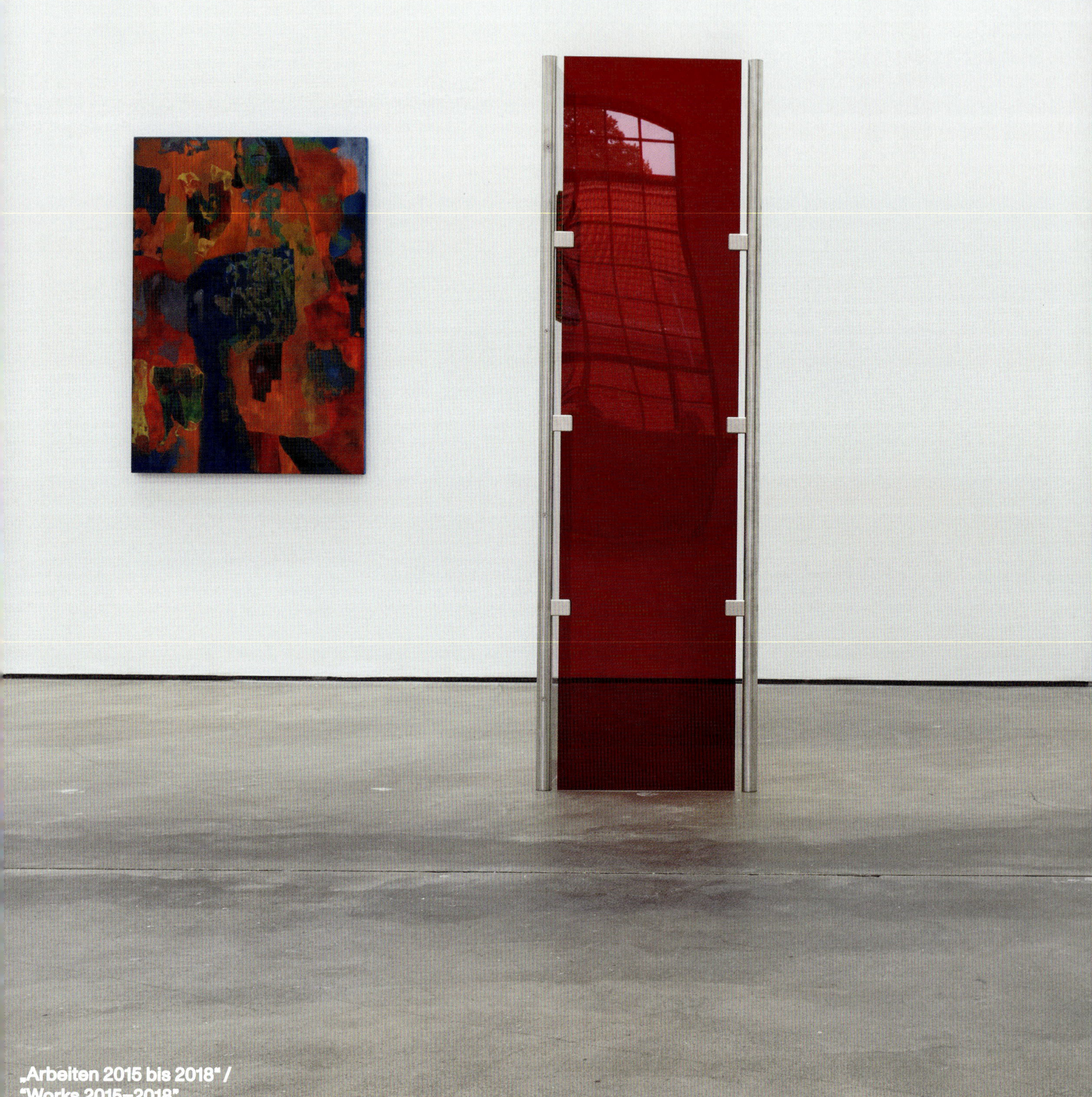

„Arbeiten 2015 bis 2018" /
"Works 2015–2018"
Installationsansichten /
Installation views,
Kunsthalle Lingen 2018

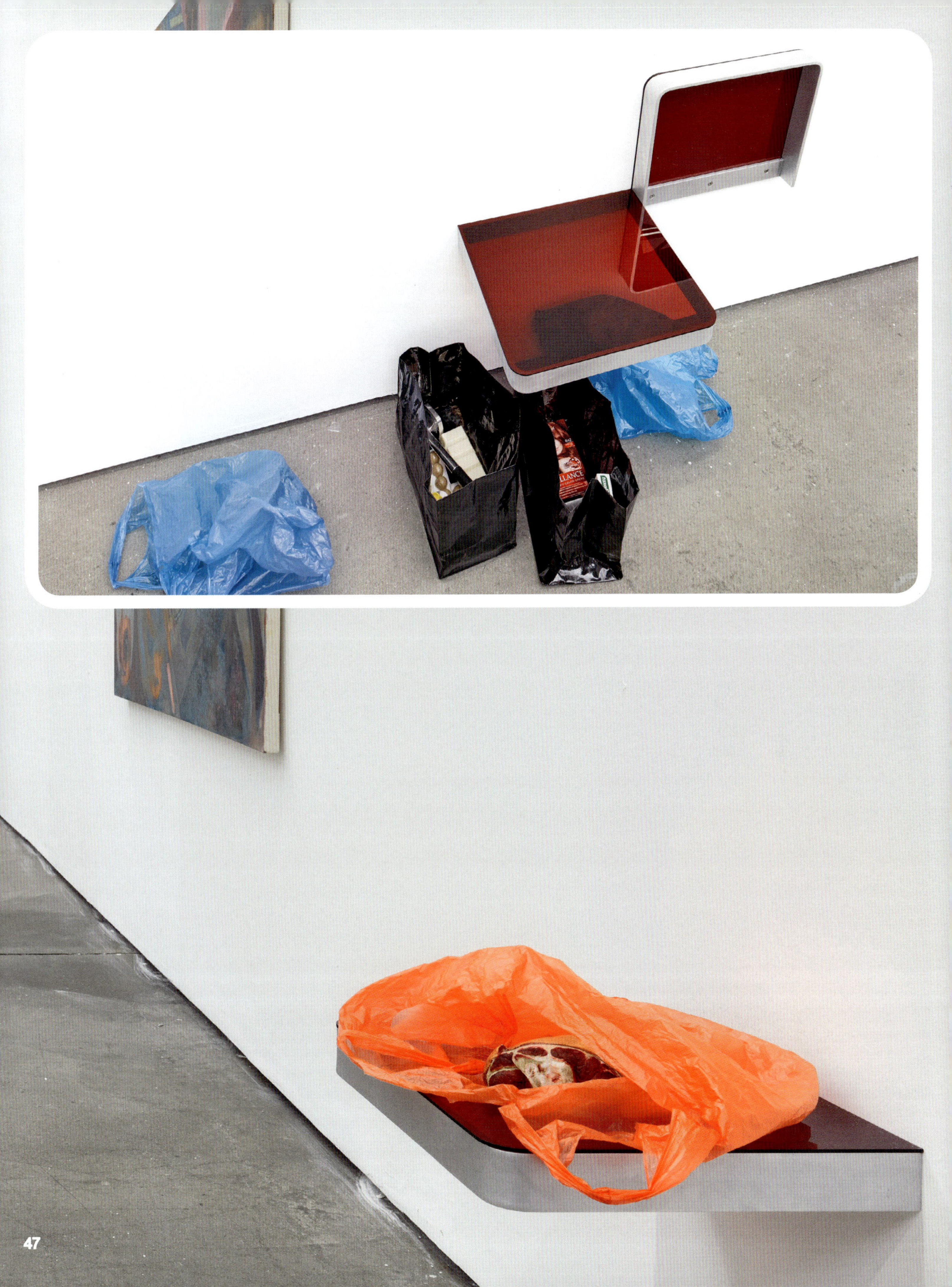

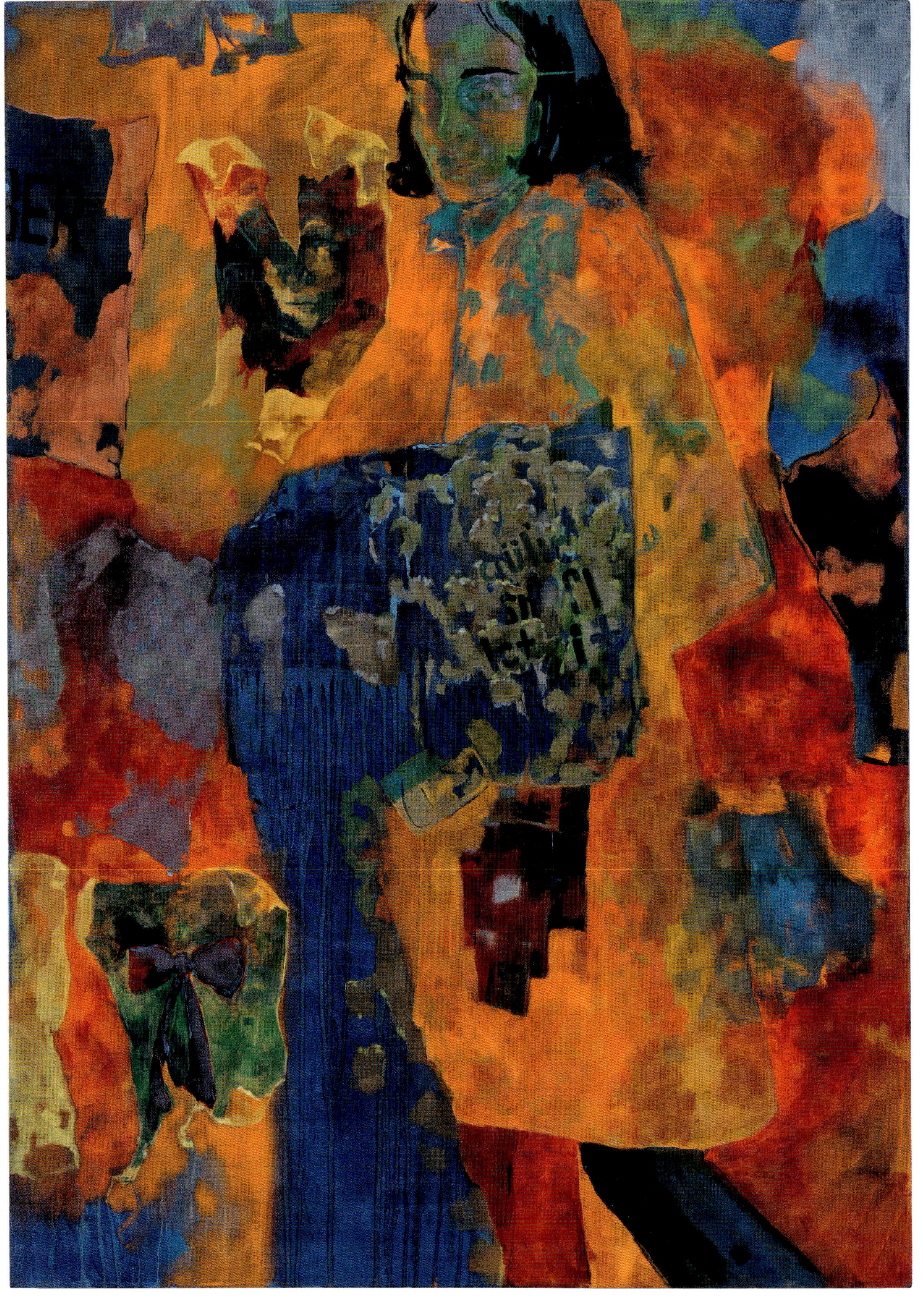

Self-Portrait, 2018

Eye Season, 2018

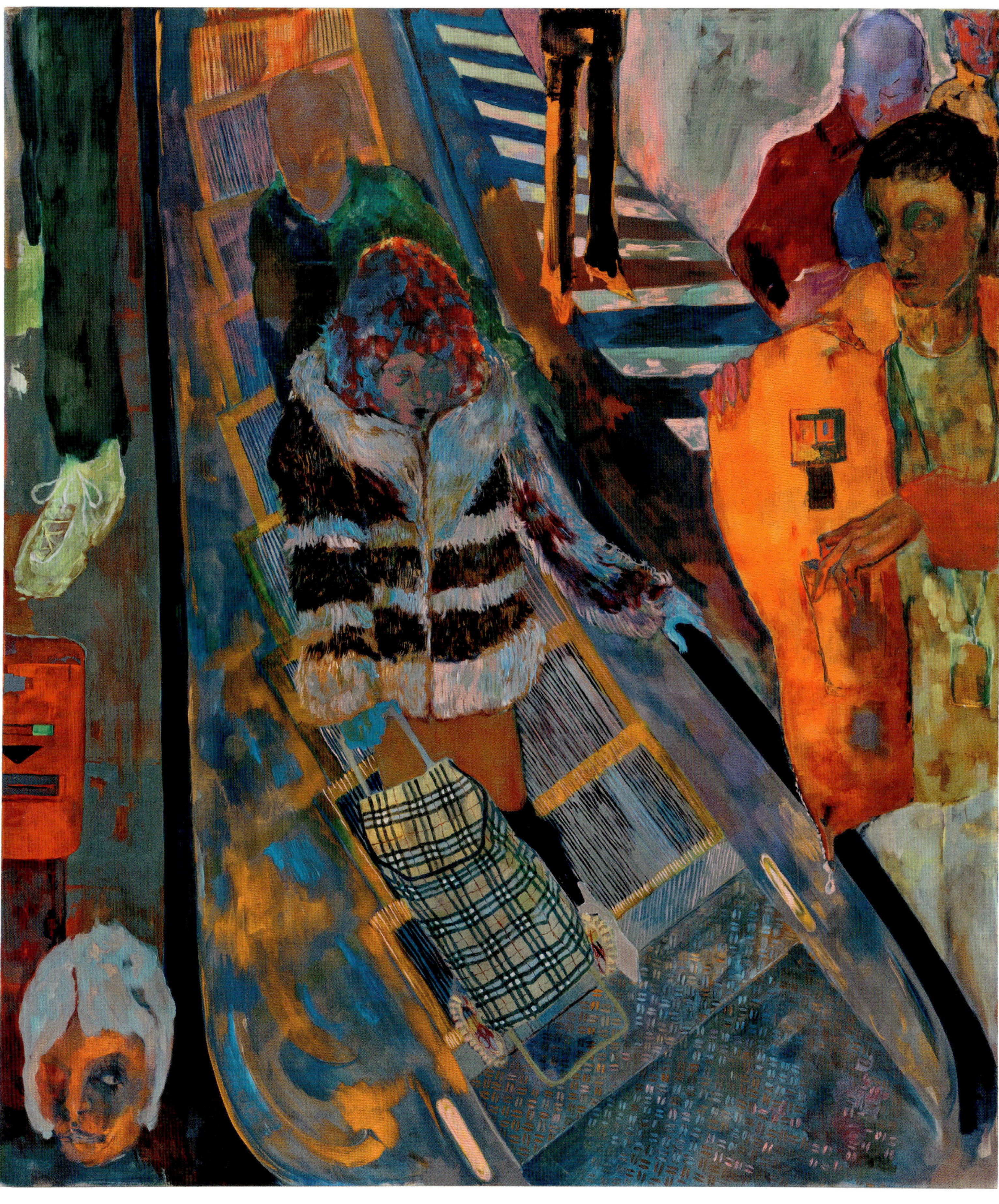

Feierabend, 2018

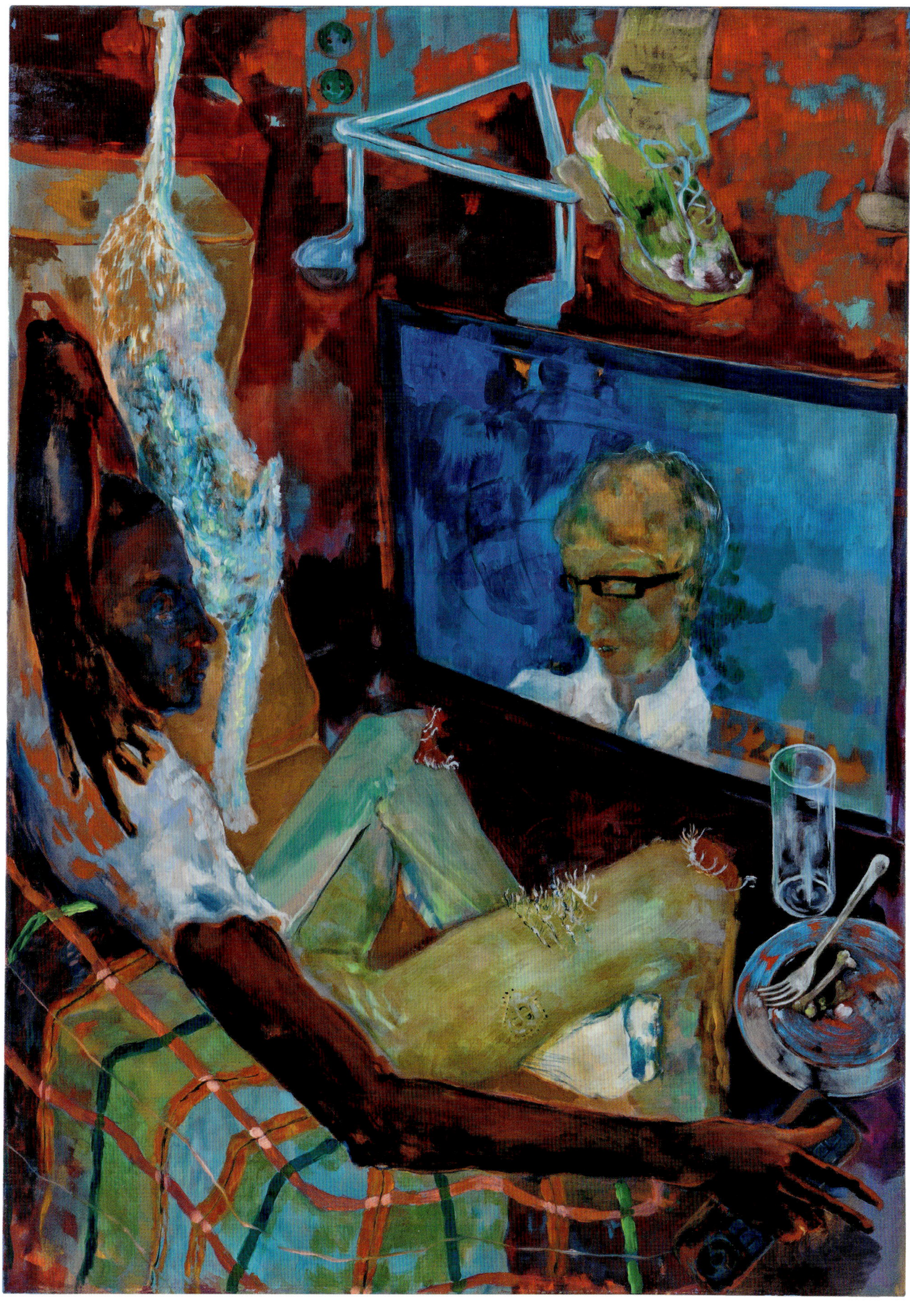

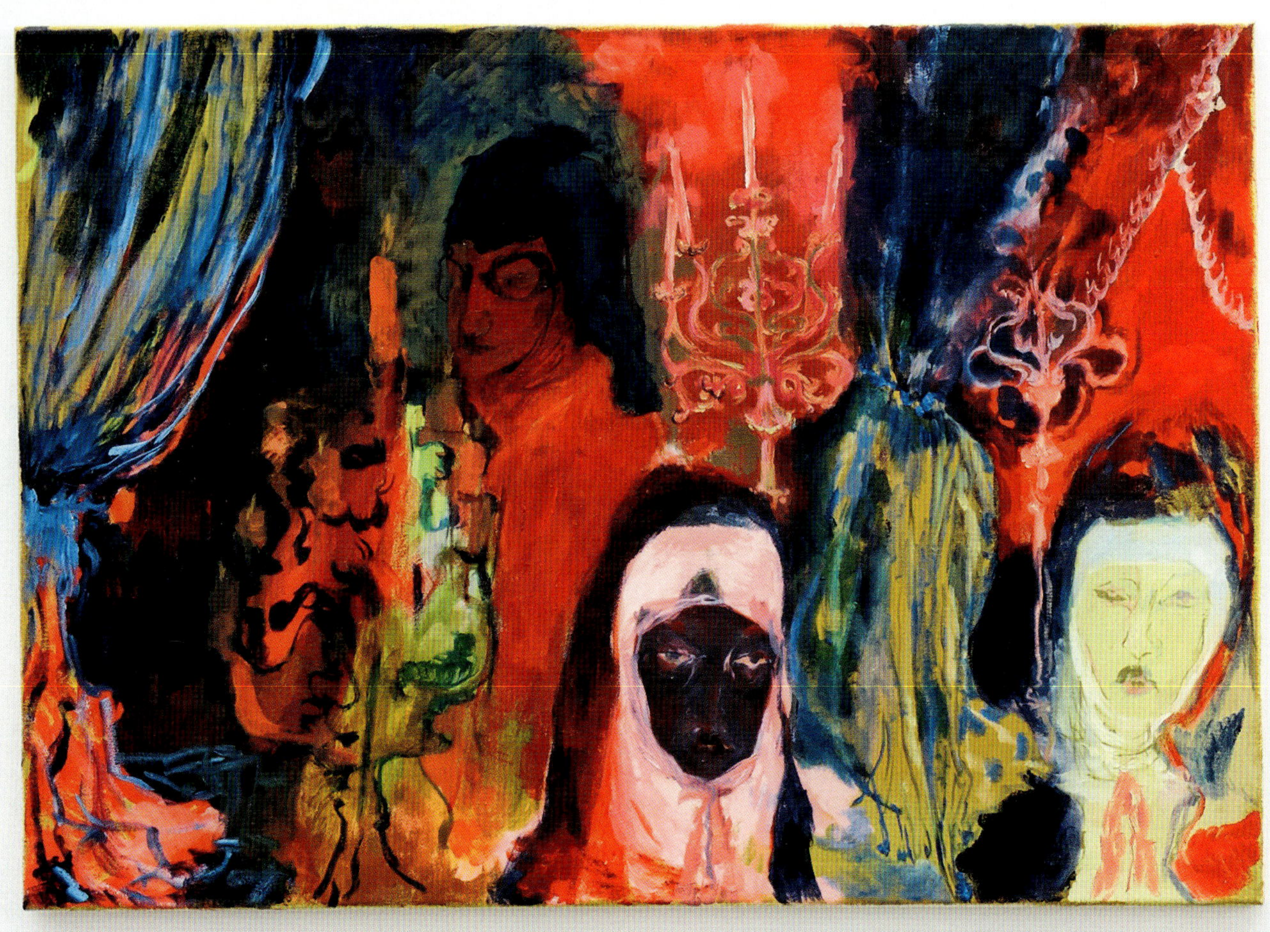

Bad Habits, 2017

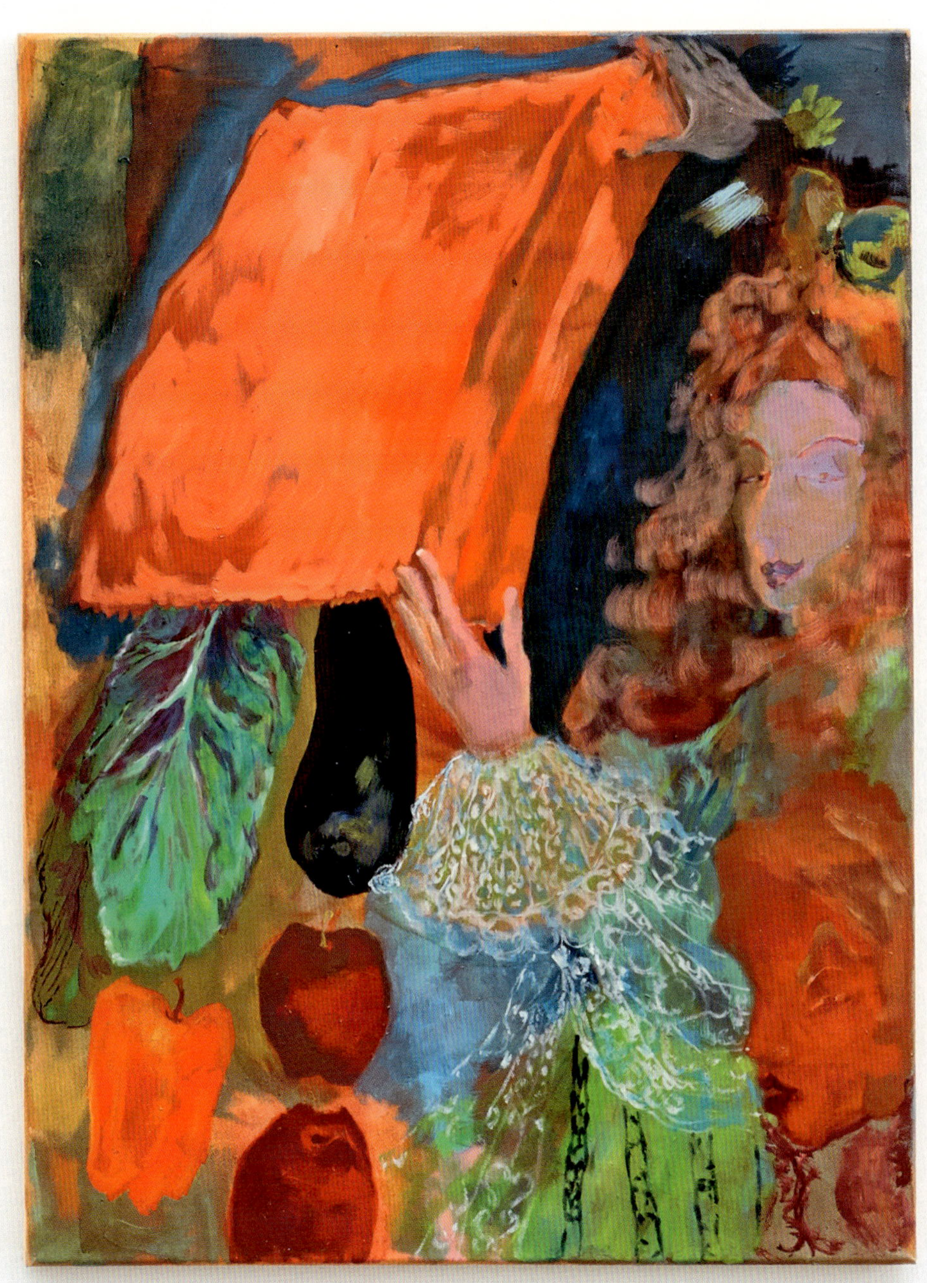

*Dumping the Groceries
(It Slips Out)*, 2016

Ladies in the Toilet, 2016

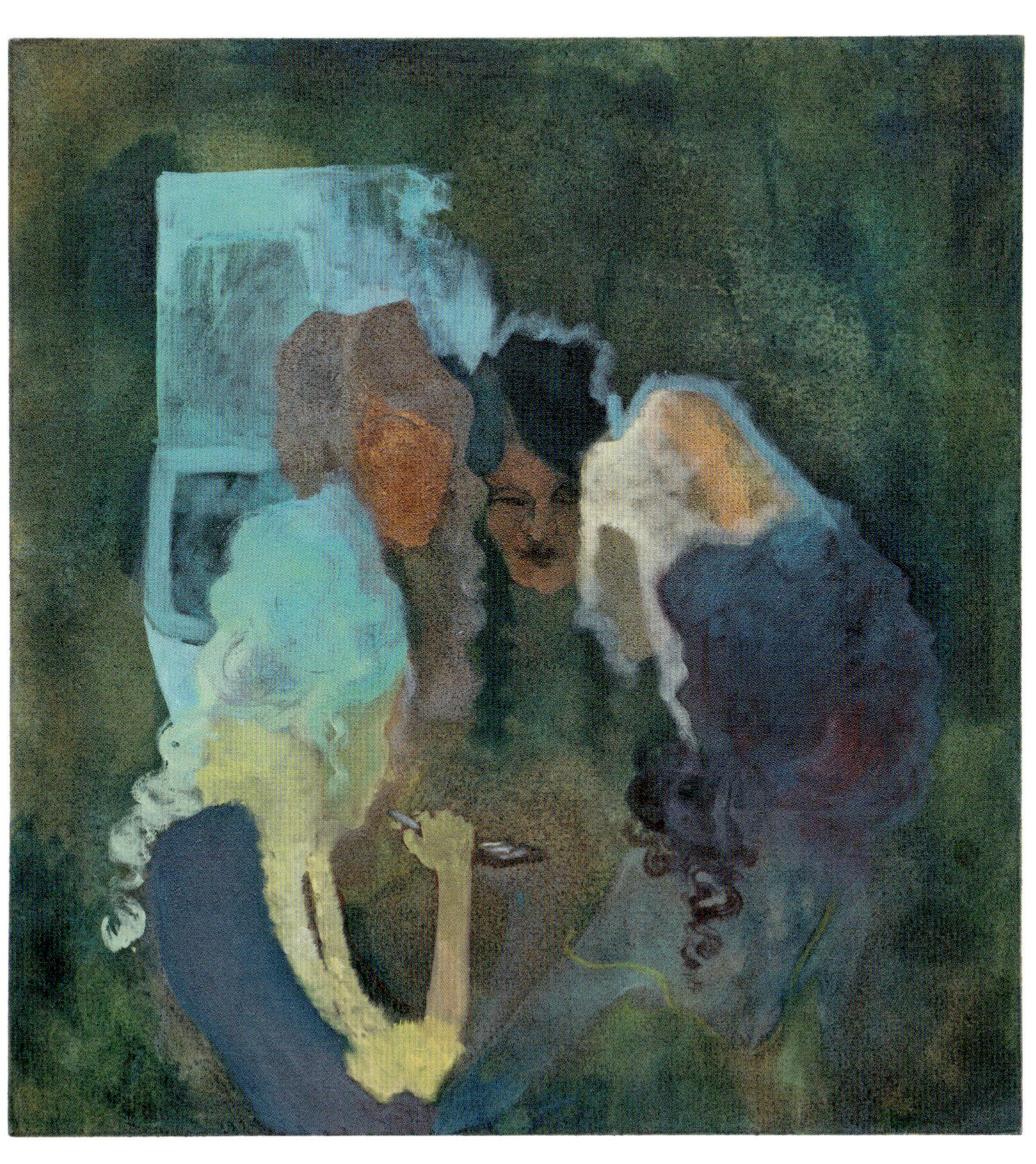

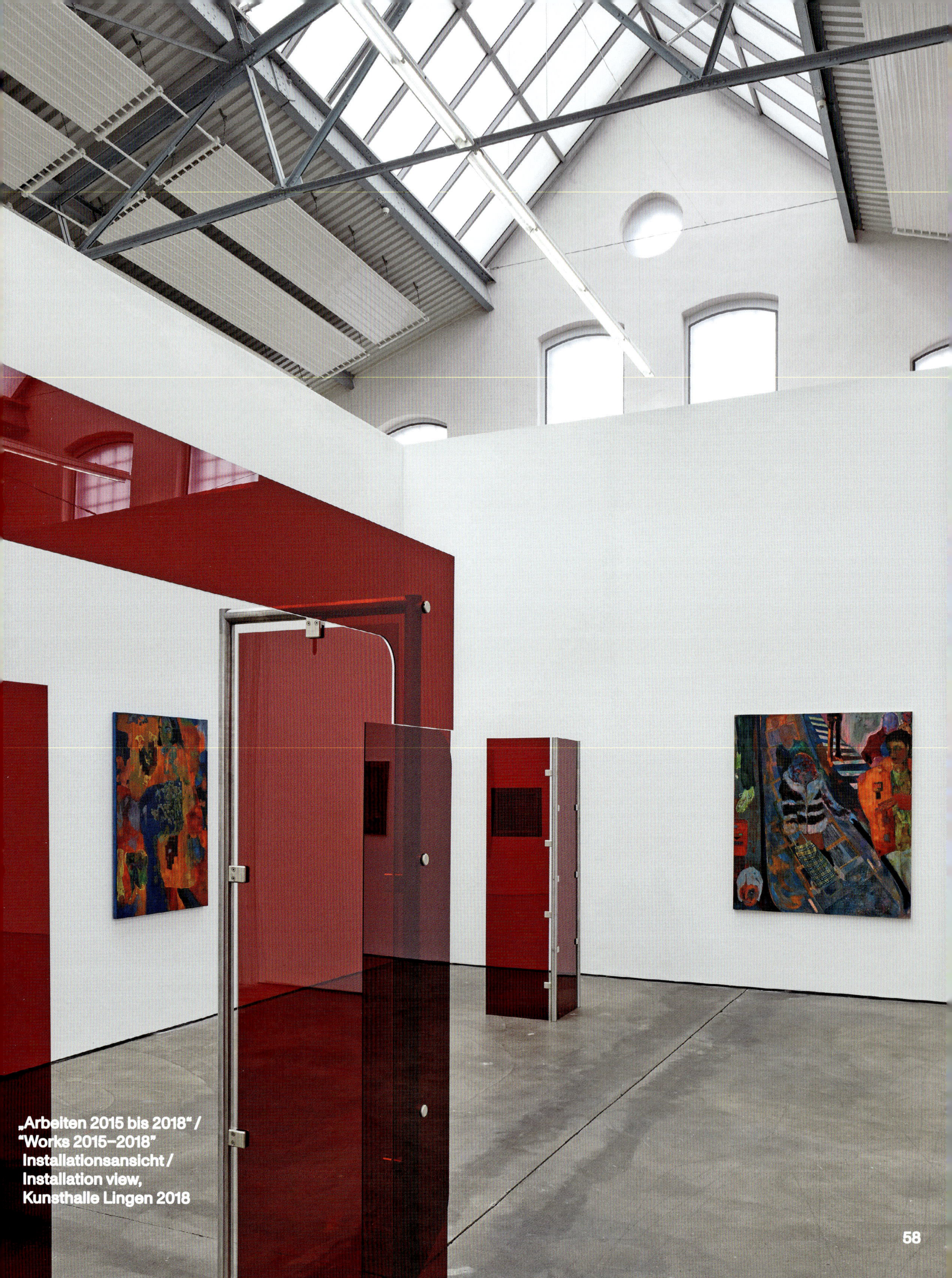

„Arbeiten 2015 bis 2018" /
"Works 2015–2018"
Installationsansicht /
Installation view,
Kunsthalle Lingen 2018

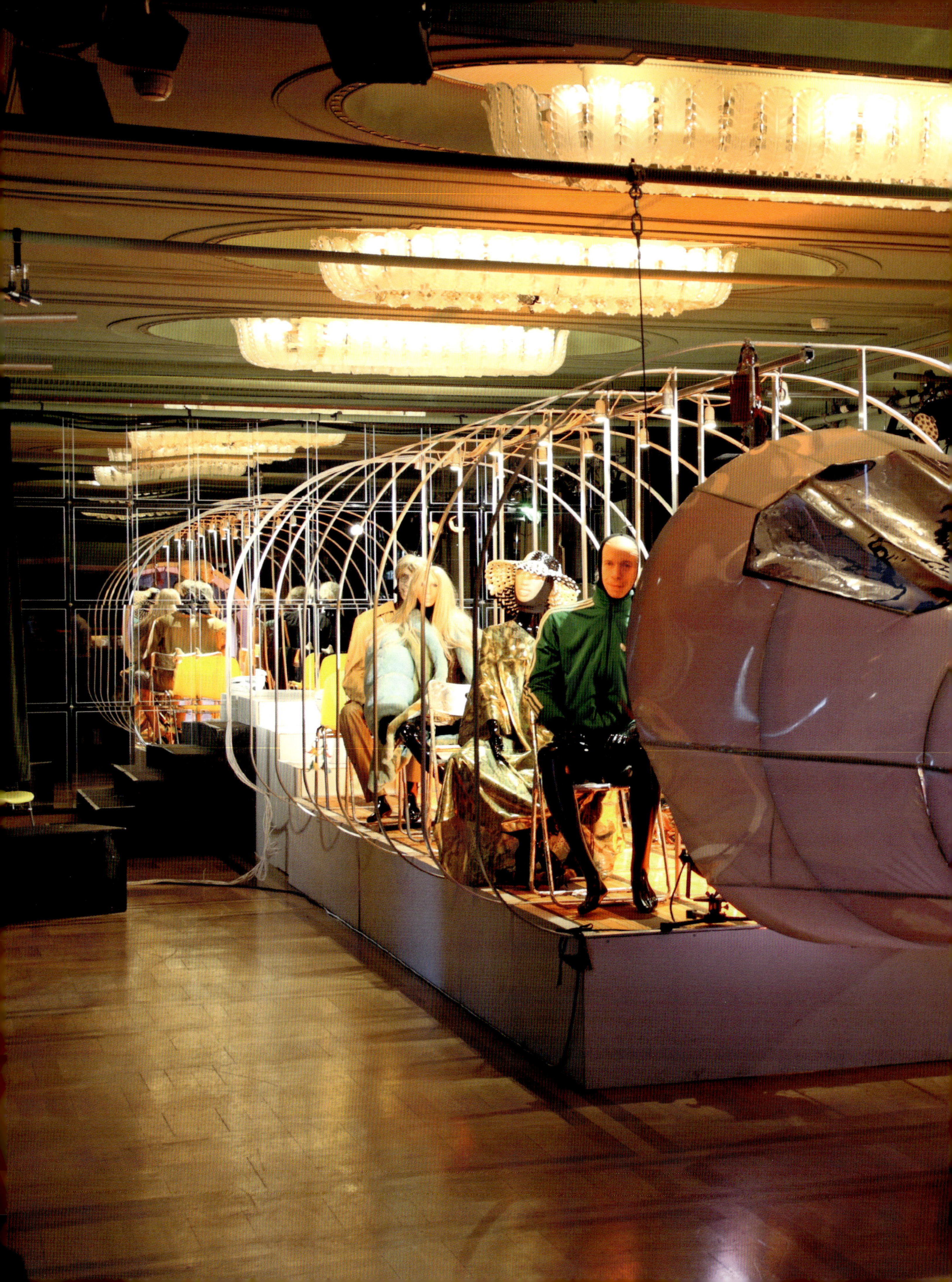

CONCORDE: SATURN RETURNS

Written by Georgia Gardner Gray and Steven Warwick
Originally performed at the Volksbühne, Grüner Salon, Berlin, April 2018.

King Henry VIII—Steven Warwick
Queen Elizabeth I—Britta Thie
Punk—Georgia Gardner Gray
Sir Walter Vapealot—Joseph Geagan
The Firestarter—Tara Khan
The Paparazzi—Max Pitegoff, Calla Henkel
The Ghost of Princess Diana—Michele Di Menna

Set by Georgia Gardner Gray
Costumes by Georgia Gardner Gray

Installed in the room is a giant airplane, the Concorde, with its distinctive white pointy nose. Deconstructed to a skeletal design with brightly orange lit center aisle. The flight attendant, a bald-headed, corseted mannequin without legs, is installed on a runner down the center aisle. Fully clothed mannequin-puppet versions of Grace Jones, Wolfgang Tillmans, Anna Wintour, Queen Elizabeth II, Karl Holmqvist, Karl Lagerfeld, and Donatella Versace are already seated in the aisles. There is a toilet in the back of the plane.
The music begins: 'Reptile' by Nine Inch Nails. Just the aisle floor is lit bright orange. Paparazzi come out, they are slithery like snakes. They take photos of the passenger puppets. Strobes go off like camera flashes.
House lights come up. Sir Walter comes out and strikes a pose, then he throws down his cape in a gallant gesture, making way.
Queen Elizabeth I comes out after him, striking a regal pose and stepping over his cape, she goes to her seat and he follows.
King Henry VIII comes out, posing at the top of the plane and then finding his seat.
The Firestarter on a leash is going mental, followed by the the Punk, holding her leash. They harass all the passengers, giving them the finger. The Firestarter sits on Sir Walter's lap and jeers in his face. They take their seats.
The music shifts to 'Flight IC 408' by State of Bengal. The plane shakes, sonic booms are heard. TAKE OFF

PUNK *(She stands and yells, the commotion suddenly stopping. She has a strong cockney accent.)*: AYyyII OYYYYYYI OOOOOYYYYYY
WHA THA FUCKS GOIN ON
FIRESTARTER: OOOOYYYYYYIIII
PUNK: Pritty wild, innit ... Just a couple a skaliwagsIIII Wut tha fuck they thinkin anywayI? Puttin us on a feckin sticky planeIIII Lik we jus gonna smash tha fuck outta erythn like thye gonna get a fuckin rise outta meII Oh fuck yeaI I got the mergency fuckin exit bitchI Yeaaaa I can stretch me dam stixI Ya babe this is fucking Lit INNIT?
FIRESTARTER: WE GET LIT LIKE NORMSKI INNA DANCE NRG STYYLLEE.
PUNK: Yea u riteI We need a fecking bloody drink its gonna b Bloodyfuckin 3.5 hoursIIII *(takes out a baggy and key)* Reckin aint even nuf time for a bit of chyna white ... Ay babe I got teeny nuf for u too. *(sniffs a bit)*
FIRESTARTER: WYLED UP INNA FURIEIIIII
PUNK: OYY they gonna kick us off the fukkin plane u ball of fat wut u goin round stickin that fluff up ya nose an sickin the shit in tha piss roomII U aint bring a fekkin leaky diaper did u then?? When u scat ... so wut ya thinkin??? Yaaa aint gonna shit me self so just take a scab off like a bloody chint ... nobody 'ere gonna smell Nuttin ... I got me wits bout me then ... *(grumbles and mumbles incoherently)*
SIR WALTER VAPEALOT *(in a strong southern genteel accent)*: Your Majesty, a word please.
I must tell you, your Majesty—the whole land is rebelling against you. Flora and fauna.
Important owls from all over the land been hootin their disapproval.
A crow came to me and perched on my shoulder—squawking in my ear!
CA CAWIIII

A pigeon defecated on me and then it laughed!!!
With my deepest respects, your Majesty ... *(he goes down into a deeeeep bow)*
ELIZABETH I: Walter, do you know what they said to me:
'A woman who doesn't wear perfume has no future.'
But that was not true.
But it isn't.
'It isn't' I said!
I said, 'I won't bathe at all!!'
They said, 'Don't spend time banging on the wall, hoping it will turn into a door!!!'
I went Bang Bang Bang
I went BANG BANG
They said, 'Go find the opposite of being poor' ...
BANG BANG
I knocked in their head
Bang Bang Bang
Jumped out the window!!
They said to me ...
'As soon as you set foot on a throne you belong to some man!!'
They said, 'You will die of boredom.'
I was like BANG
Still alive! And I am still slightly interested in what you may have to say to me, but maybe not because I also have other things on my mind.
SIR WALTER VAPEALOT: Yes, yes I know I am just a turd that you step over on your way to Spain. But I have seen plenty of Goyas and LET ME TELL YOU it may make sense to listen to what I have to say. I have years of experience up and down in and around—I started as a stowaway ... on a big I ship sailin' to the new world ... there, one night sitting the dirt floor—I saw a big ol bundle of stinky brown leaves ... then I started to drift off and the Archangel Willy appeared to me in a vision, and do u know what he said? He said, 'Girl, you better wake up and roll those brown leaves into a doobie!' And I said, 'OOOOO hhaaaaa!! Ok!' And ever since, success has taken me to her bosom like a maternal boa constrictor!!! But! ... I have never been a Queen ... Do you know what the critics are saying, your Majesty??? They are calling you a toad lover! A skiddly tronk!! A Banana Faloozy! A Poodleficker!!!!
QUEEN ELIZABETH I: Some critic called me the Nothingness Herself.
That doesn't help my sense of existence any.
Then I realized that existence itself is nothing, and I felt better.
But I'm obsessed with the idea of looking into the mirror and seeing no one, nothing.
I'm obsessed with ... with the idea of looking into the mirror and saying,
'I don't believe it. How can I get the publicity I get?
How can I be one of the most famous people in the world? Just look at me!'
(strikes a pose on each)
The opalescent child-like naiveté ...
The glamour, rooted in despair! ...
The perfected otherness ...
The albino-chalk skin. Parchment-like. Reptilian. Almost blue ...

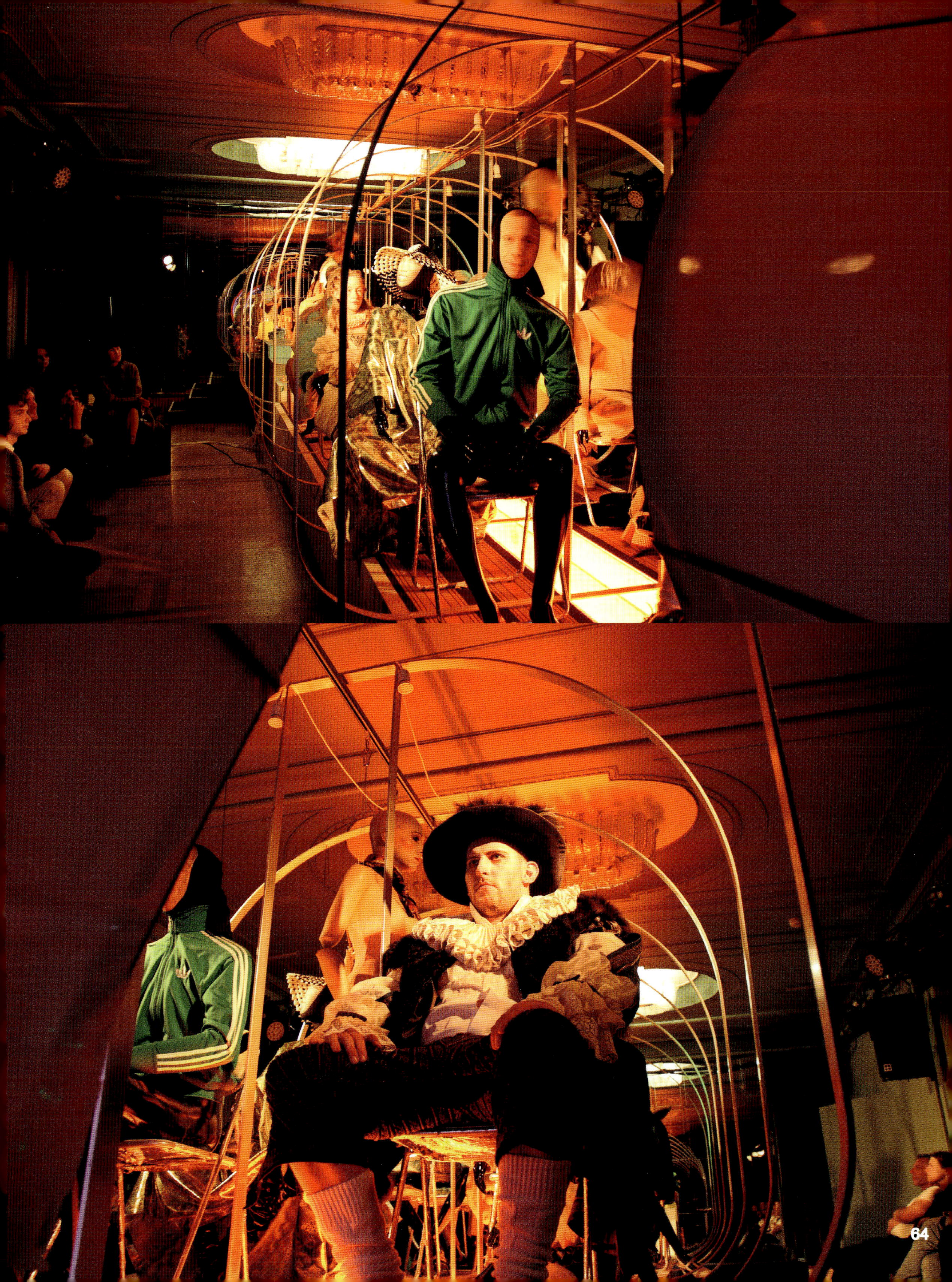

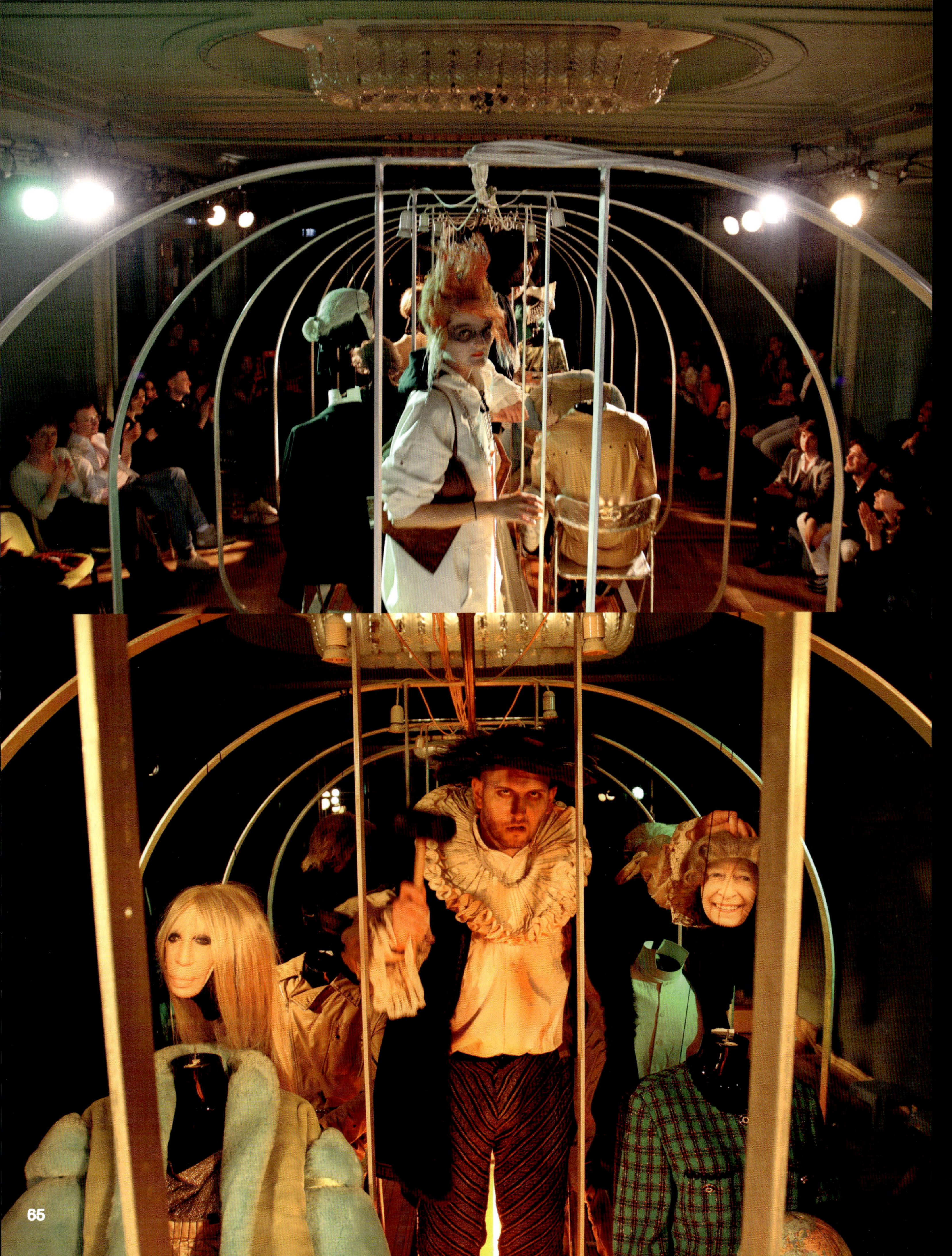

The shadowy, voyeuristic, vaguely sinister aura ...
The pale, soft-spoken magical presence, the skin and bones ...
The graying lips. The copper-bright hair: soft and metallic. The long neck, swanlike, firmly connected. It's all there, nothing is missing.

SIR WALTER VAPEALOT: Oh, Your Majesty ... I would be careful ... They say you're a real snagoo, that you've lost your touch, that you're actually just a mannequin, stuffed full of mince-meat!

ELIZABETH I: I fear for you, Walter. You have what they call ... a chameleon soul ... No moral compass pointing due north ... No ... fixed personality ...

SIR WALTER VAPEALOT: Looky looky, no need for bad mouthing ... I love an argument, I love debate! Look at me, I love to sit around, have a good schmoke *(tokes on his vape)* ... straight from the golden Virginias ... really get into it ... really go into the 'nitty gritty' as they say—takin a microscope and zooooooooooomin in—just gettin all the way into the very nucleus of the matter—peepin all in on the teeny tiny electrons whizzing around!! I looooooove to get all the way out—WAYY out into the nebula of outer space—here we are—flying through the heavens, spankin the upper stratosphere—just getting out into the meta levels of the whole shabang!!!

ELIZABETH I: Look out the window, Walter. Do u see all those teeny tiny little people? Those little teeny tiny ants pitter pattering about, those little flecks of dirt that just bounce around, going on about their day ... on their four little legs? Alllll those little things you see down there—THEY ARE MINE! I AM THEIR QUEEN! So whatever it is that they have to say I can't hear them. All I can hear is you! AND I HAVE HAD ENOUGH OF THIS SCHMEEEEAR CAMPAIGN.

SIR WALTER VAPEALOT: Oh, your Majesty! I swear upon this unearthly airplane to be your true subject! I'll kiss thy foot; I'll pluck thee berries; and with my long nails will I dig thee peanuts. I'll swear to thee great riches!

ELIZABETH I: I don't need more riches Walter! I need ... I don't know what I need Walter! I don't knoooooooooowwww. *(crying)*

SIR WALTER VAPEALOT *(Behind Elizabeth's back he crawls over to the Donatella puppet with some old almost dead flowers)*: These r for u Donatella, I am your biggest fan ... Best to put them in some water ... they are lookin a little dilapidated.

ELIZABETH I *(looks up from fake crying)*: What are u doing Walter!

KING HENRY VIII: That's my wife! Donatella, throw those away! I command youll

ELIZABETH I: Walter! What do u think this is? A bang bang? You're fired!

SIR WALTER VAPEALOT: No, your Majesty, please don't do this to me. You know I would withstand all types of fire and brimstone just to be in your company. The heavens could open up and pour toads on my head—the Lord himself could come down in his infernal glory and take away my whole earldom and I still would be there to see if your feet needed kissin. Chivalry ain't dead, your Majesty!

Elizabeth I turns her back defiantly.

WALTER VAPEALOT: NOOooooooo.

PUPPET FLIGHT ATTENDANT *(as a recording with a very nasal, whiney, posh British accent)*: Would anyone like some teeeaaa??

PUPPET FLIGHT ATTENDANT: Day after day I look into the mirror and I see something—a new pimple. If the pimple on my upper right cheek is gone, a new one turns up on my lower left cheek. On my jawline. Near my ear. In the middle of my nose. Under the hair on my eyebrows. Right between my eyes. I think it's the same pimple, moving from place to place. If I was telling the truth, and someone asked me, what's your problem? I would have to say ... SKIN.

KING HENRY VIII *(He is apparently in very serious conversation with Wolfgang Tillmans.):* SO Wolfy, I got to the bar and I was like, where is my wife?? WHERE IS MY WIFE? Have you seen my wife?? And everyone was like, no no no no no no no ...
What Grace?
Oh yea! Your right!! I cut off her head!! Huh!
Huh, did I hear you correctly, Anna?
Oh no, not today, Satan! Not today!
What Karl??
Get those nuts away from my face!
EXCUSE ME! I would like a Bloody Mary over here!!
(grabs a cup from the flight attendant)
You know, *(sips)*
Oh wow, this is delish! *(He drinks more.)*
Really fantastic, I love the horseradish!
So where was I Wolfy—oh yea ... we are just men and we love the flesh. We are weak for it ... hehe ... Yes ... WHAT!
(whipping around like a madman speaking to voices in his head, addressing each mannequin seated on the plane)
I mean really, WHAT ARE U LOOKING AT?
(turning to each doll)
WHAT!
WHAT!
WHAT!
WHAT DO U WANT FROM ME??
Your beady little eyes imploring me for what!!??
(A strange mood takes over him ... speaking to dolls)
Come, you spirits
That extend immoral thoughts
Unsex me here!!
And fill me from the crown to the toe top-full
Of troll and cruelty!
Make thick my blood;
And quicken my spite
Where I drink blood,
You only drink liquor!
Whilst your thoughts be belabored by booze
I elect myself your murdering minister!!
Whatever with your substances ...
(rubbing globe)
You wait on the wings,
With your featherbrained mischief,
Your heads just eggs asking to be poached.

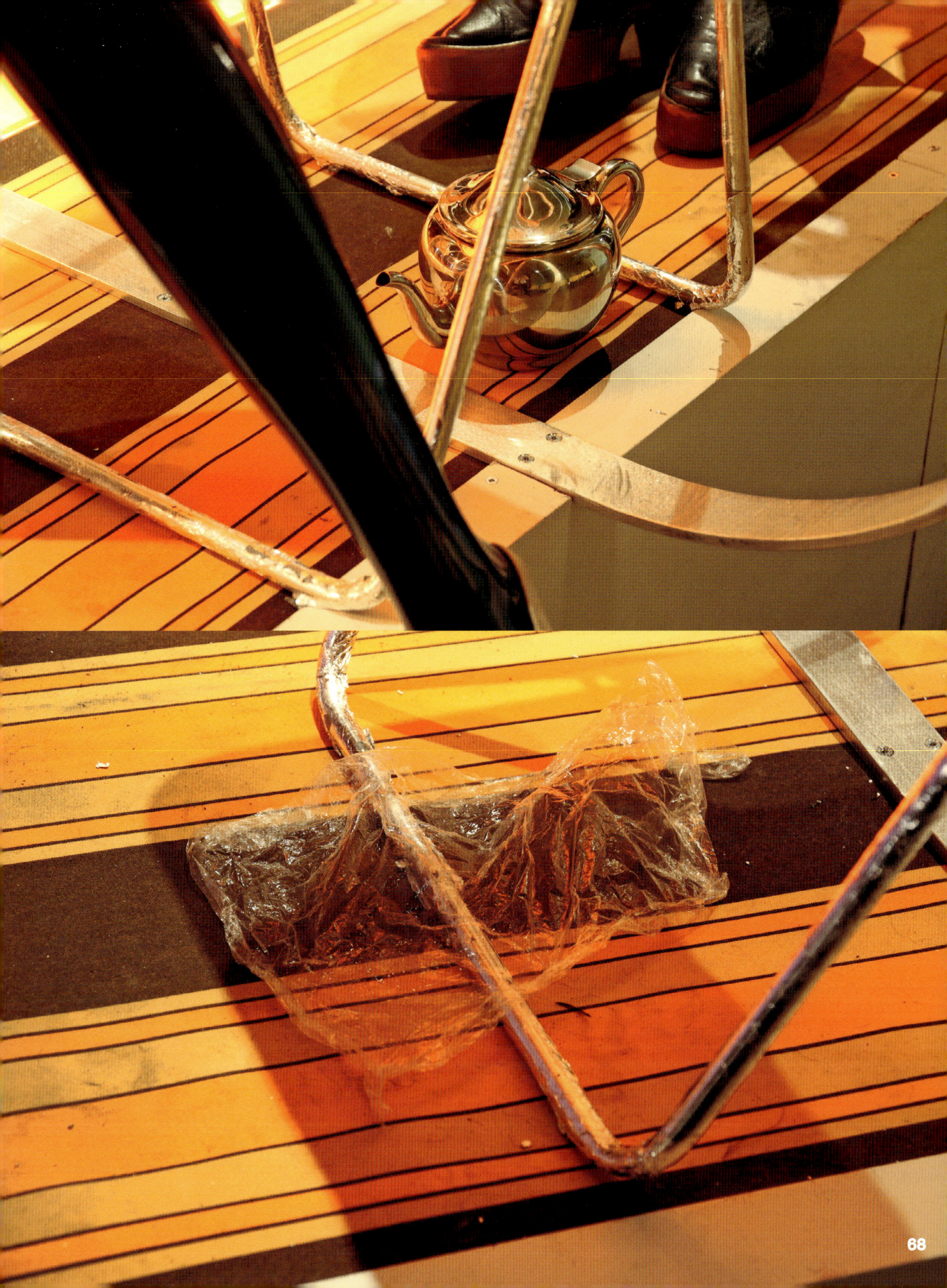

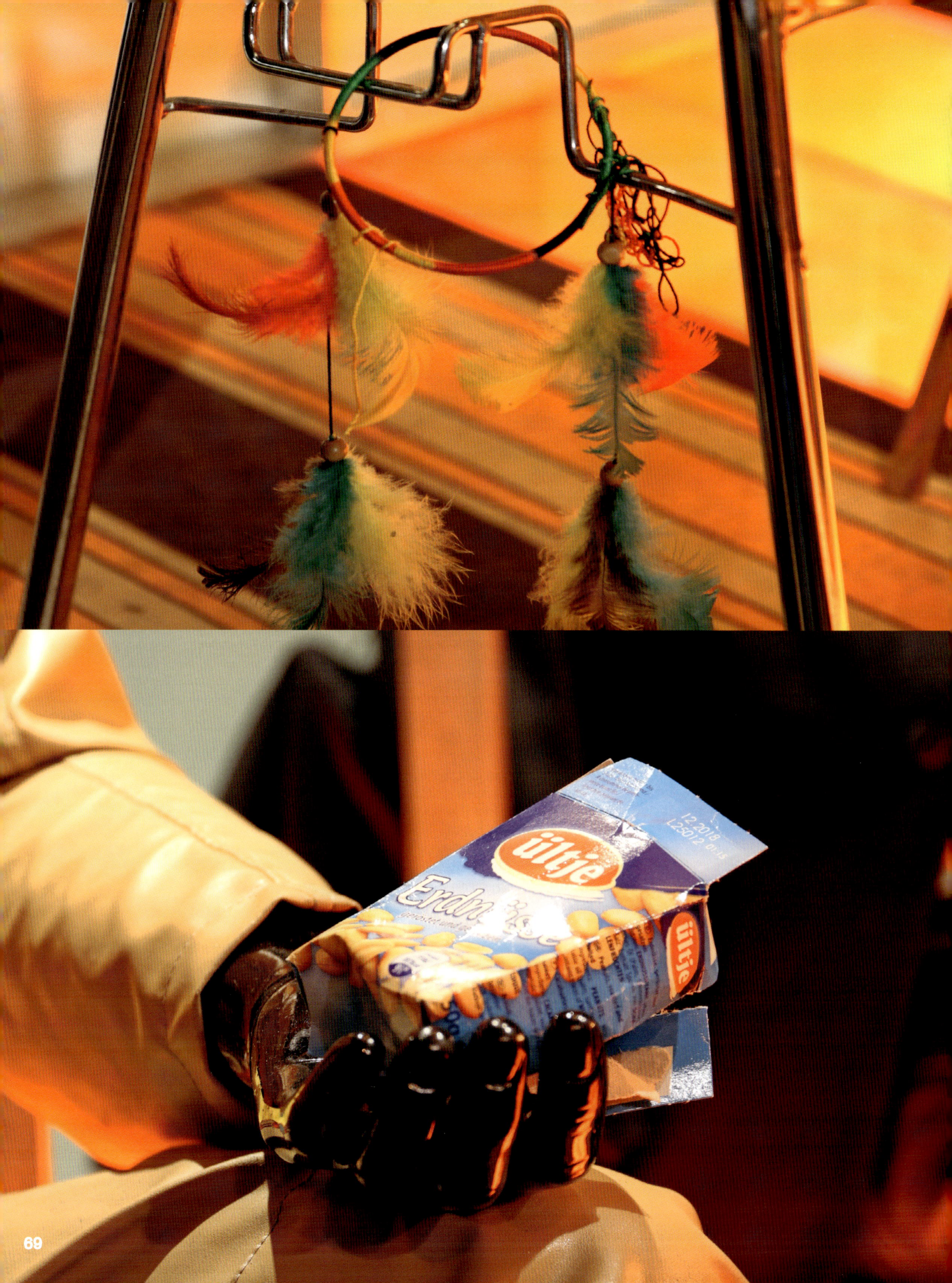

ültje
Erdnüsse
ültje

Yet with only 3.5 hours to carry out the plan
Thine birdie has hatched!!
I pall thee in the dunnest smoke of hell!
My cunning is as ripe as a blueberry!!!
Mine HAMMER sees not the boom it ponches,
And as we slice thru it at the speed of sound,
Heaven does not stop
To cry 'Hold, hold!'
(holding up a hammer)
This is my fist, this is your face! Off with ur heads cuz ur a fuckin disgrace!!!

The song 'This is Life' by Grace Jones comes on—lip sync / Drag King Henry
He smashes off all the heads of the mannequins using the hammer during the music
number, which are connected to a pulley and weight system. The heads dangle,
disembodied. The house lights go off and the 'reading lights' come on above each
mannequin head. They give soliloquies in turn as their light switches on. Henry responds
to each one maniacally.

ANNA WINTOUR: Henry, you are making that same face that a fly makes before it hits a windshield.

KING HENRY VIII: I have as many lives as I have wives!!

GRACE JONES *(strong Jamaican accent)*: Wut is dis weird play? Bring me my oysters! I'll shuck em myself.

DONATELLA *(strong Italian accent)*: Minimalism. What is that? A dead cat in the street with its pecorino full of poppers pulled off the sex room sofa and tossed out into the street with the other torticannoli. AH—MAZE—ING. Versace is the catnip of fashun! THE DOLCE CON LECHE. Madonna! I am the iconic biscotti in bikini sunning me pinsa on the Lido di Jesolo. BASTA!

KARL LAGERFELD *(strong German accent)*: Mein mutter gave me everything I wanted. Mutti was lovely and papa was Arschloch.
We never spoke anyway, and it is good to be traumatized as a child. Otherwise I would never be so famous. When I was a child I loved to bake cakes, and I would sing a little song too when I was making it, it was like this:
(in a singsongy voice, like a happy children's song)
Prepare the dough in a big pot
Three big hands full of flour and what not
But before you start make sure to light the ovennnn
Then get some eggs and put them in too
BUT don't forget a pinch of saalt
And cho-co-late cho-co-late chooooocooolattteeeeeee

KING HENRY VIII: Sounds delicious!!

QUEEN ELIZABETH II *(singing 'Despacito' in a highly affected British accent)*: Despacito, la, la, la, la, la la la LA! Despacito!

GRACE JONES: Corporate Cannibal.

KING HENRY VIII *(picks up a piece of cling film from the ground shocked and afraid)*: WHa, aha ... whhh whhHAT IS THIS???

ANNA WINTOUR: It's a piece of cling film, you idiot.

KING HENRY VIII: Ahh! *(throws it away in fear and disgust)*

WOLFGANG TILLMANS: For the chosen few, flying Concorde is apparently a glamorous but cramped and slightly boring routine, while to watch it in air, landing or taking off is a strange and free spectacle, a super modern anachronism and an image of the desire to overcome time and distance through technology. Because no man is an island ... no man is a plane ...

KING HENRY VIII: O totallyll What a great description of what's happening to me RIGHT NOWI

Blackout.

A green, eerie light lights up the Punk. She's standing on her chair in the back of the plane.

PUNK: U kno it funny, innit, I aint vicious at all. I luv me mum. Yeeeaaa ... really im jus a gooey one—just like a bit o dis and dat on the side, but really im a good won ... oyl A postcard for me MumIII *(starts to write)* Elo MUMI Its ya binbin agin ... How u spell again?? Or INNIT S-H-I-T? But how u gonna spell that then, how u gon spell a damn letter?? It already spelled itselfll

The song 'Beachdrifta' by Rufige Kru comes on. Walter blows smoke and the Firestarter gets up and starts to slowly walk up the aisle, having some sort of strange acid flashback.

FIRESTARTER: WHITE WIDOW ... BLUE NOTE ... TOTTENemCOURT ROAD.

PUNK: BETTA hit the nose-bag twoncel

(*does a bump*)

FIRESTARTER: O MANNNNN YEEEEEA IT WAS LIK THE BOUNCA WAS COMIN ...

PUNK *(not believing her crazy story)*: O reallililly?

FIRESTARTER: YEAaaaaa ... LIK EEs COMIN OVA LIKE a END O LEVEL BADDIE

PUNK: Yeeeeea wu'eva

FIRESTARTER: AN THEN HIS HEAD SPIN ROUND AND THERE'S KATE N MCQUEEN pissin on AN OFFICE CHAIRIII

PUNK: Yea ur just trippinll

FIRESTARTER: Nol

PUNK: Wel, wha is it then?? WUT U GOIN ON ABOU??

FIRESTARTER: ITS THA BATACHANGAAAAAAAAAAAA.

The song shifts to the beat, lights come on in the plane. The Punk jumps out of her seat, getting into the Firestarter's face with a sudden burst of anger, totally mental.

PUNK *(yelling at the Firestarter, edging her backward down the aisle)*: Oh, so now u gettin all IRIE thinkin u a celebrity or somethinlll Ooooooo000 so u wanna be one of em skinny bitches—stickin two pencils and a bit of dental floss callin it a outfit, wipin ya lips all over HELLO MAGAZINE after u vomit on the whoooole front row, hackin it up aaaaaalllllll over the skel'tons front fuckin row at the fuckin fashion showl Wappin ur fanny bout in the back of a taxill Draggin ya tits on the front of some maglll Winnin awards for ur work with the mentally ill lookin alll fuckin unbiasedl

Just some mag filler bouto be recycled vomitl Some recycled snapol Comin back again and again like some regurgitatin ... Stuffin up some mag up their arse n recyclin back to vomit it again ????? Takin a mag n squishin it up stuffin up ya bumb an then vomitin it back up—just vommmmmmitin alllllll over the fuckin fashion show???? Is that wut u thinking then???

FIRESTARTER: Serrrriouuslllyyyyyyyyyy this one time I took the AYA BLACK and I SAW THE FUCKIN PATACHAANGAAAAAAAAAIIIII

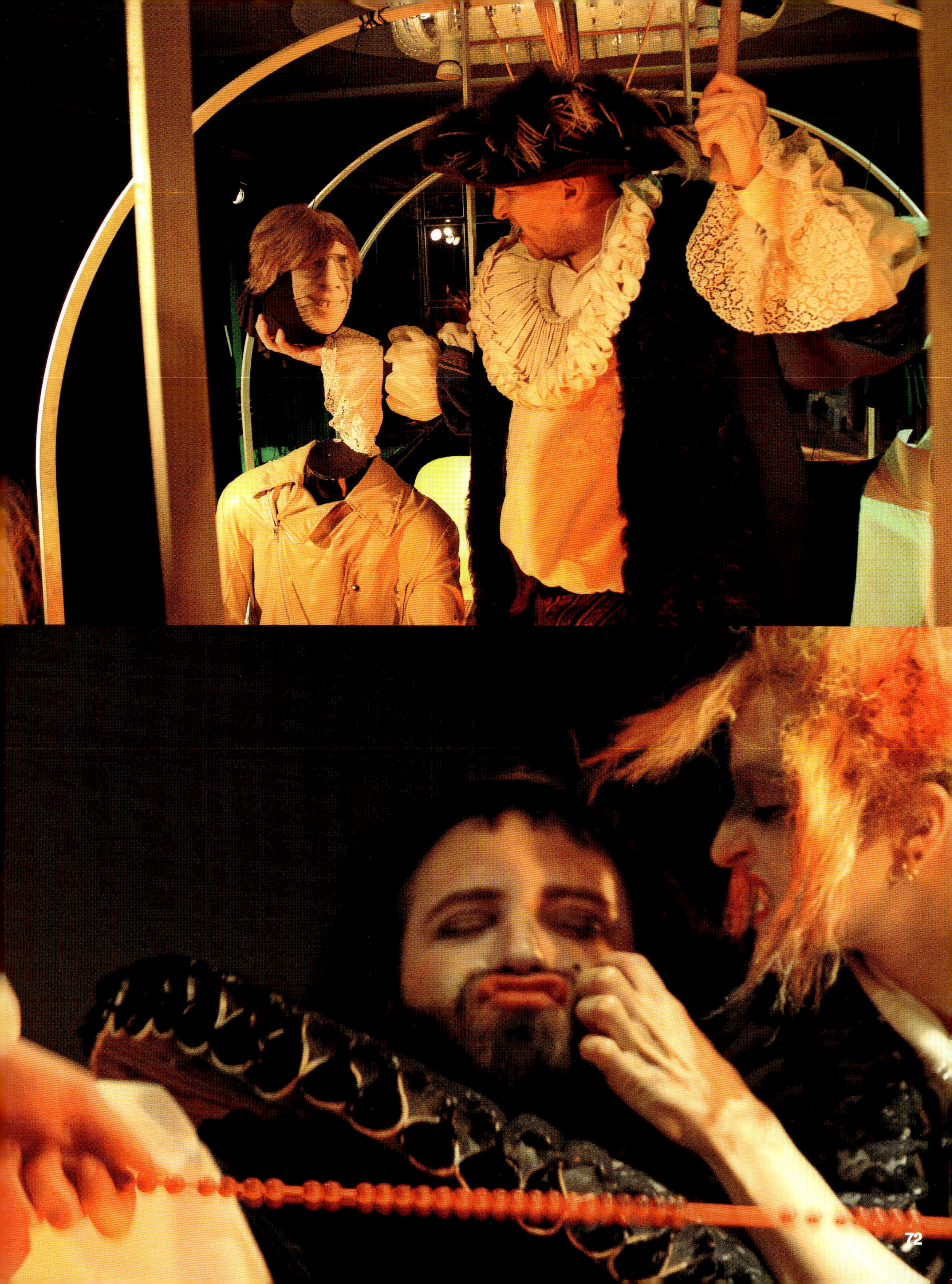

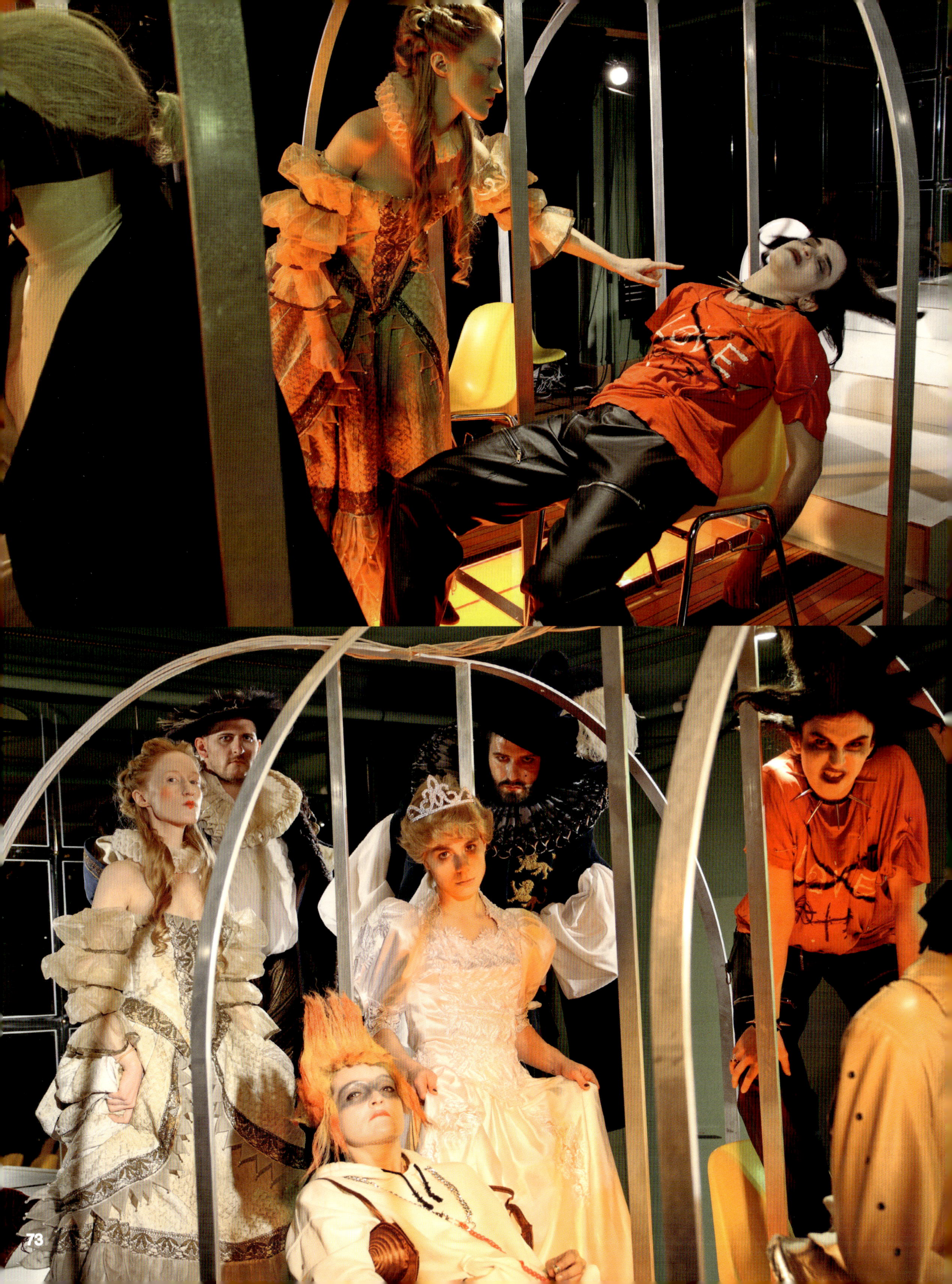

(pushing past the Punk to the back of the plane, where she assumes a Buddha stance)

PUNK *(yelling pointlessly now, not even directed)*: Takin ya wiggly bits and just launchin em!!! Launchin them like a fuckin rocket like a nasa fuckin space mission up on the fuckkin Internet—BREAKIN the fuckin INTERNET with 8 billion fuckin views!!! Pickin up the little glass shards—all the little spiky pieces of the fuckin computer screen—smashin em down ya throat and chewing em like a cake ya Grandma baked for ya fur ya fuckin birthday!!! Blowin a bubble like a lil girl in in the porn hub video and BUSTIN the fuckin Internet all over ya damn face like a fuckin atom bomb!!!!! Mushroom cloud boomin out ur bloody modem like a smokestack—punchin the time clock like u workin in a goddam meme factory!!!

FIRESTARTER: MY HEAD FEELS LIKE A FUCKIN DETONATOR.

PUNK: Takin air force one cuz u been elected President—spreadin your little fanny for the king of the fuckin north!!!!! Snortin all the snow in the north and blowin it out like some feckin celebrity hair do—like Tabitha TAKES OVER gettin up in every salon and lightin up the hairspray like u got a bloody molotov cocktail in ya hand but it's actually a goddam Cuban SANDWICH mixin pork, chicken and beef like u never saw a Jew in ur feckin life! Like u a hacid who runs a fuckin Bra Shop feelin up all the tits in New York City cuz u got kicked the fuck out of Israel for bein a goddam PERVERT!! Sleezin round in Hooters Gettin ME TOO'd until u go to the GRAVE with it fuckin inscribed on ya tombstone—TITTY GRABBAAAAAAAA!!! *(Punk starts getting IRIE too)*

FIRESTARTER: THA PATACHANNNGGGGUUUUAAAAA.

PUNK: Smokin YA tits til they bust open LIKE A FeCKIN BABY GETTIN BORN OUT YA FUCKIN CHEST GETTIN REINCARNATED LIKE YOU hadda a fuckin epiphany that the only thing left in this fuckin world is ya tits hangin off ya damn chest!!! Gettin born and reborn like is that a baby or a FAT ASS FUCKIN BUUDDDDHHAAAAA??????

SIR WALTER VAPEALOT: SILENCIO!!! THE QUEEN IS TRYING TO GET SOME REST!!!

Music cuts.

He tucks her in tenderly, goes into the bathroom and sits on the toilet.

As if singing a lullaby, while on the toilet he sings 'Candle in the Wind' by Elton John.

The ghost of Princess Diana drifts onto the plane in her wedding dress.

After the first chorus, he pulls out his journal and starts to scribble aloud.

SIR WALTER VAPEALOT: Dear Journal,

Today we are flying Concorde to attend the Biennial. They seem endless these days. The Queen once again showing face so as to remain indubitable to her lowly subjects. The people here are just horrible. Utterly unwoke … Once I was in the bathroom, dropping a deuce and scribbling away in this very journal—and some guy opened the door right in my face, trousers around my ankles. Obviously I had forgot to lock the door. I sat there staring at him—and he staring at me, nobody budging. Finally I exclaimed, 'I'm sorry!' And this man, with a superior air, closed the door again to let me finish my business. I ASK MYSELF WHAT IS THE MEAN-ING OF THIS! It was he who should have recoiled at the sight of me!!!!! Luckily we arrive with great power and superior ambition. I now realize what my purpose will be when we get there … TO DESTROY THEIR CULTURE!!

Diana opens the door to the bathroom and he screams.

    SIR WALTER VAPEALOT: AHHHHHIIII

He shuts the journal all flustered, pulls up his pants, flushes, the music abruptly cuts,
FLUSHING SOUND

    ELIZABETH I *(waking up with a yawn and a stretch, walking over to the Punk, who is*
        nodding out like a junkie): Darling! *(poking the Punk's shoulder)*
        Darrling!! *(pokes her again)*

The Punk wakes up and looks incredulously at the Queen.

    ELIZABETH I: Doesn't it ever make you sick? Doesn't it just make you sick sometimes
        to have to be made up to look like you were just ... dragged out of the gutter, as
        if you've just been shooting horse in some toilet like some, some soiled 'Agent
        Provocateur' with some, some, ripped up T-shirt!

    PUNK: Wha tha hell U just say ya bumbag? Are u jolly well fuckin with my teet?
        Ay babe, didya hear that!?? Said I got ta cut me bits and toss em out of the tree!

    ELIZABETH I: But really, I mean, don't you get tired of it all!!

    PUNK: Wha tha snicket? Who gives a fuck wha this fuckin cricket gotta say with er
        fuckin chirping!!! I'll fucking choke er out n tie err up to the gibbon with a snick
        tally dee!
        FUck U u fuckin snaggy log with a Pimple on er arse!!!!

    ELIZABETH I *(utterly disgusted)*: Uh! What language are you speaking anyway? I AM
        the commonwealth! ... WALTER!!!
        WALTER!!!!!

An alarm sounds, like analog cell phone ring comes on, everyone looks bewildered, cover-
ing their ears, cowering.

    ELIZABETH I: Walter, Walter ... what is it?

    WALTER: I, I don't know ...

BEEP BEEP BEEP

    ELIZABETH I: What, what ... Is it a BEE?

    SIR WALTER VAPEALOT: I don't know, your Majesty, I don't know what it is!!

    ELIZABETH I: Is it a BEEE Walter???? Find it! Kill it! Kill it!!

    KING HENRY VIII: What is that infernal sound?? Make it stop! Make it stop!

    SIR WALTER VAPEALOT *(takes an old phone out of his shirt)*: It's here!!! It's on me, it's
        on me!!
        (He throws it away and the ringing doesn't stop.)
        It's here ... it's there ... it's a bee ... *(He very gingerly picks it up again.)*

    ELIZABETH I: Oh ... oh ... it's a ... small shoe

    KING HENRY VIII: Tell it to stop squeaking!!!

    SIR WALTER VAPEALOT: Yes, yes, your Majesty, I believe it is ... a squeaky little shoe ...

A voice is heard, disembodied, coming from the phone.

    VOICE: HELLO??

    SIR WALTER VAPEALOT: AH!!! What? It speaks!! It speakss!!!! *(He faints.)*

    VOICE: Helloooo??

    ELIZABETH I: Walter, Walter, it's speaking ... What is this savagery? *(nearly in tears)*
        Walter, Walter!!

    VOICE: Hello!!

    ELIZABETH I: Ah, eh, mmm ... *(picks it up strangely)* HELLO!

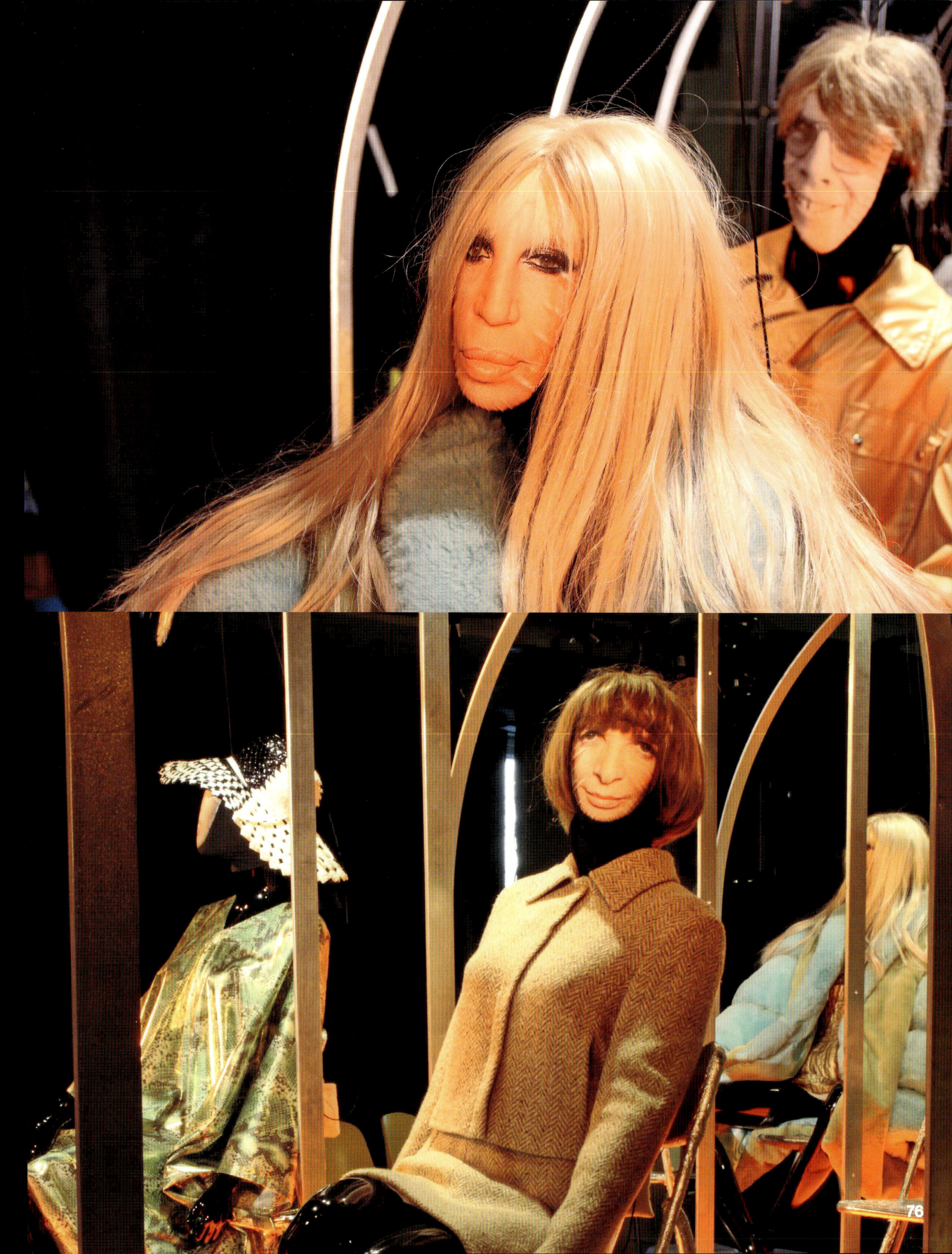

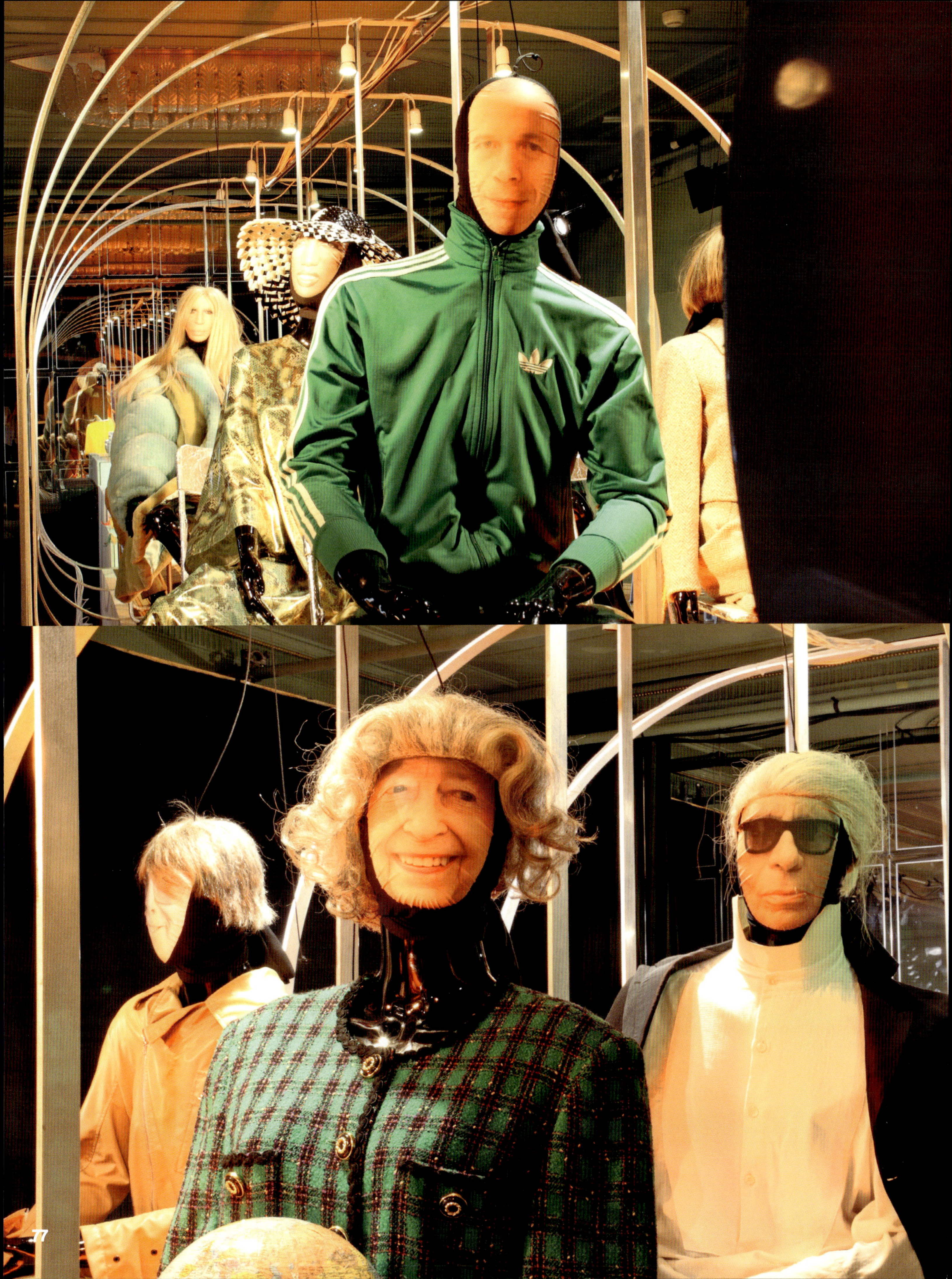

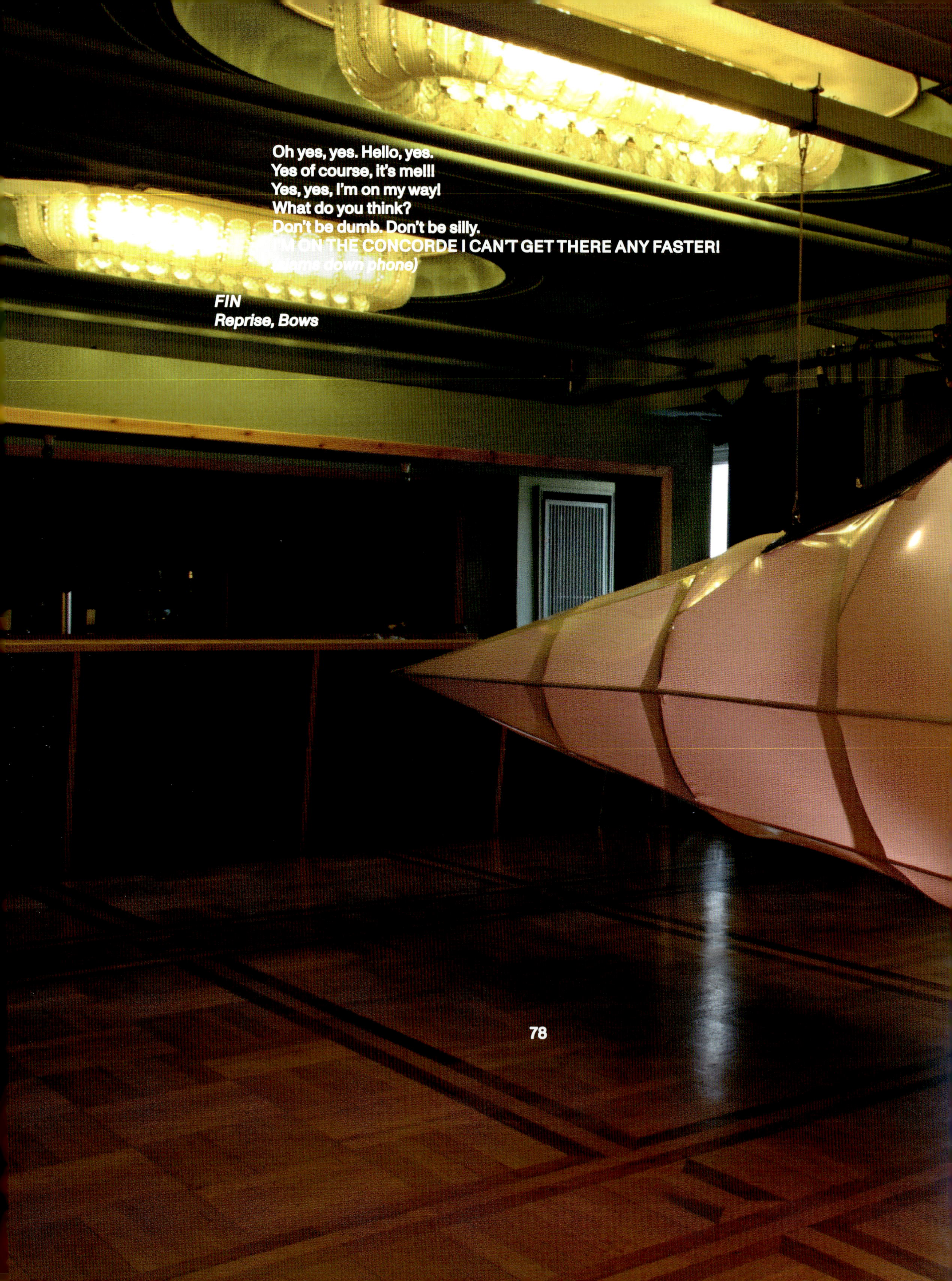
Oh yes, yes. Hello, yes.
Yes of course, it's me!!!
Yes, yes, I'm on my way!
What do you think?
Don't be dumb. Don't be silly.
I'M ON THE CONCORDE I CAN'T GET THERE ANY FASTER!
(slams down phone)

FIN
Reprise, Bows

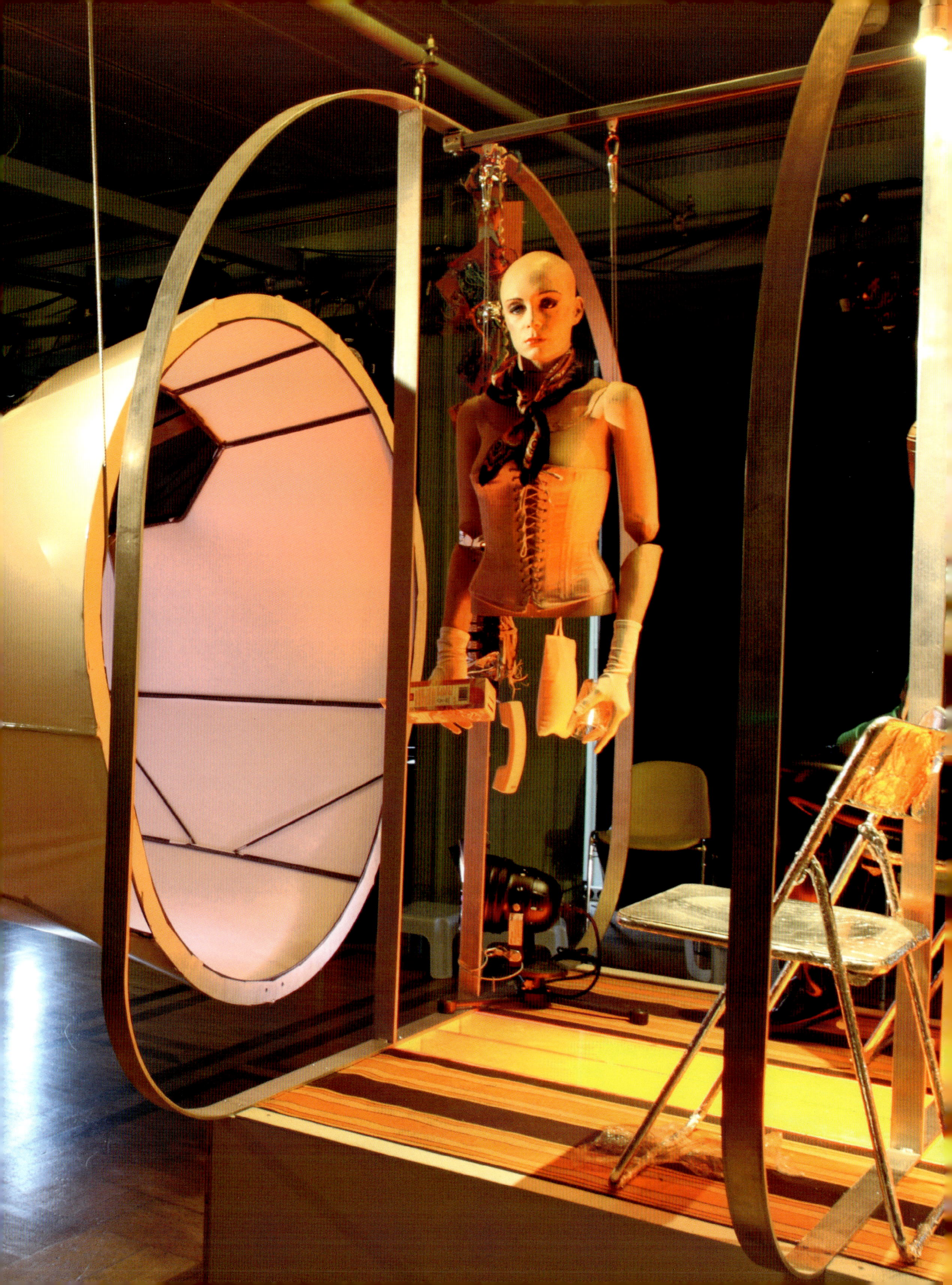

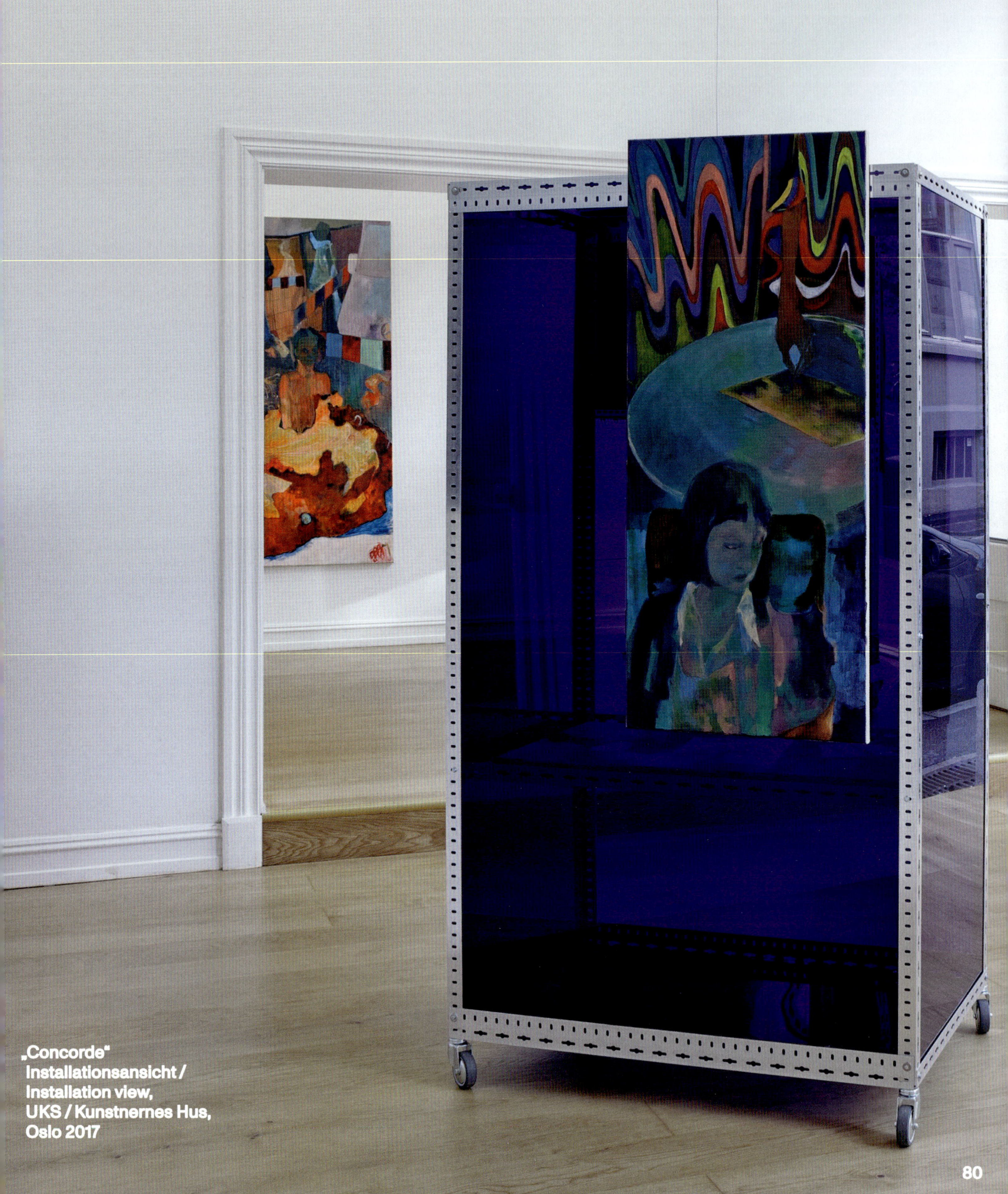

„Concorde"
Installationsansicht /
Installation view,
UKS / Kunstnernes Hus,
Oslo 2017

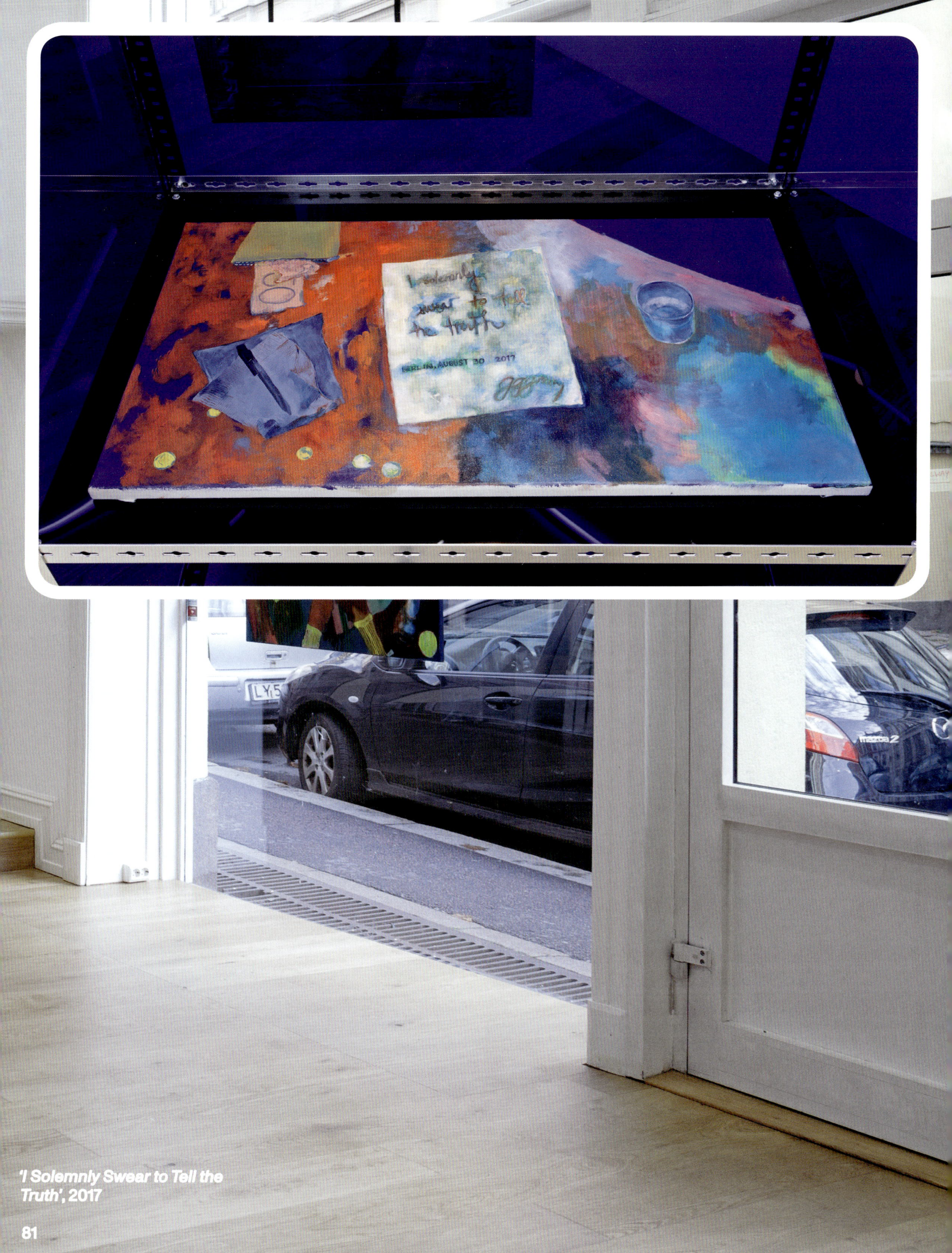

'I Solemnly Swear to Tell the Truth', 2017

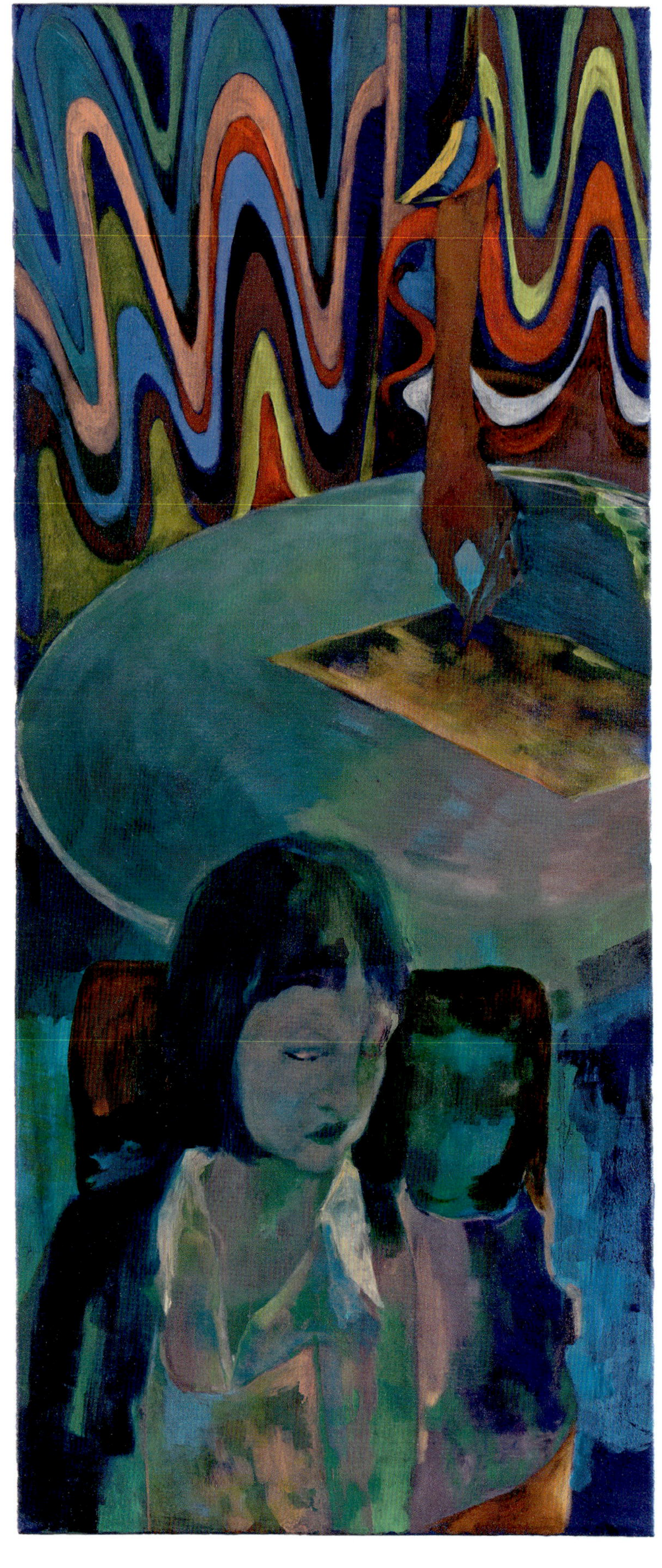

Kontrakt LXIX, 2017

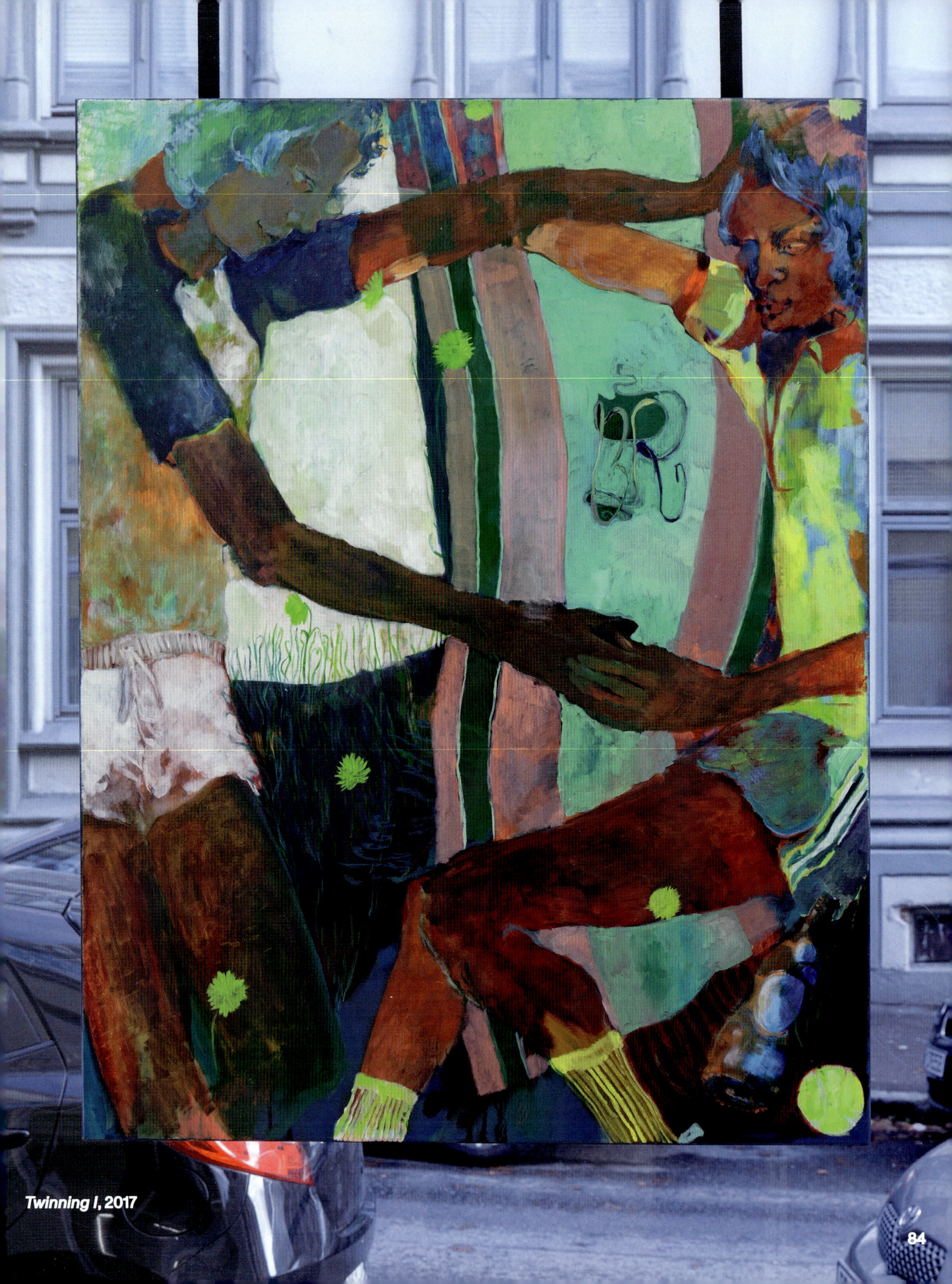

Twinning I, 2017

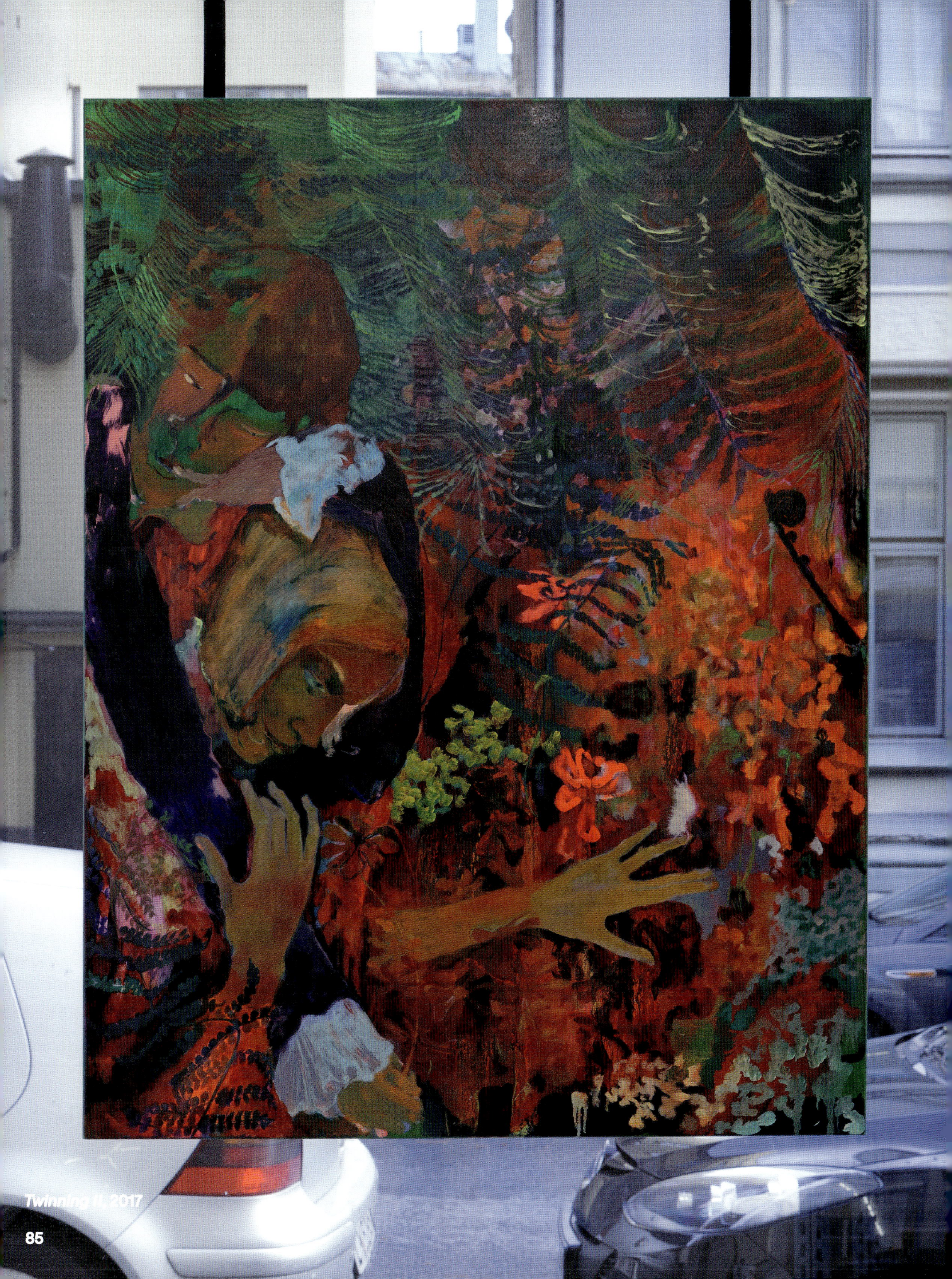

Twinning II, 2017

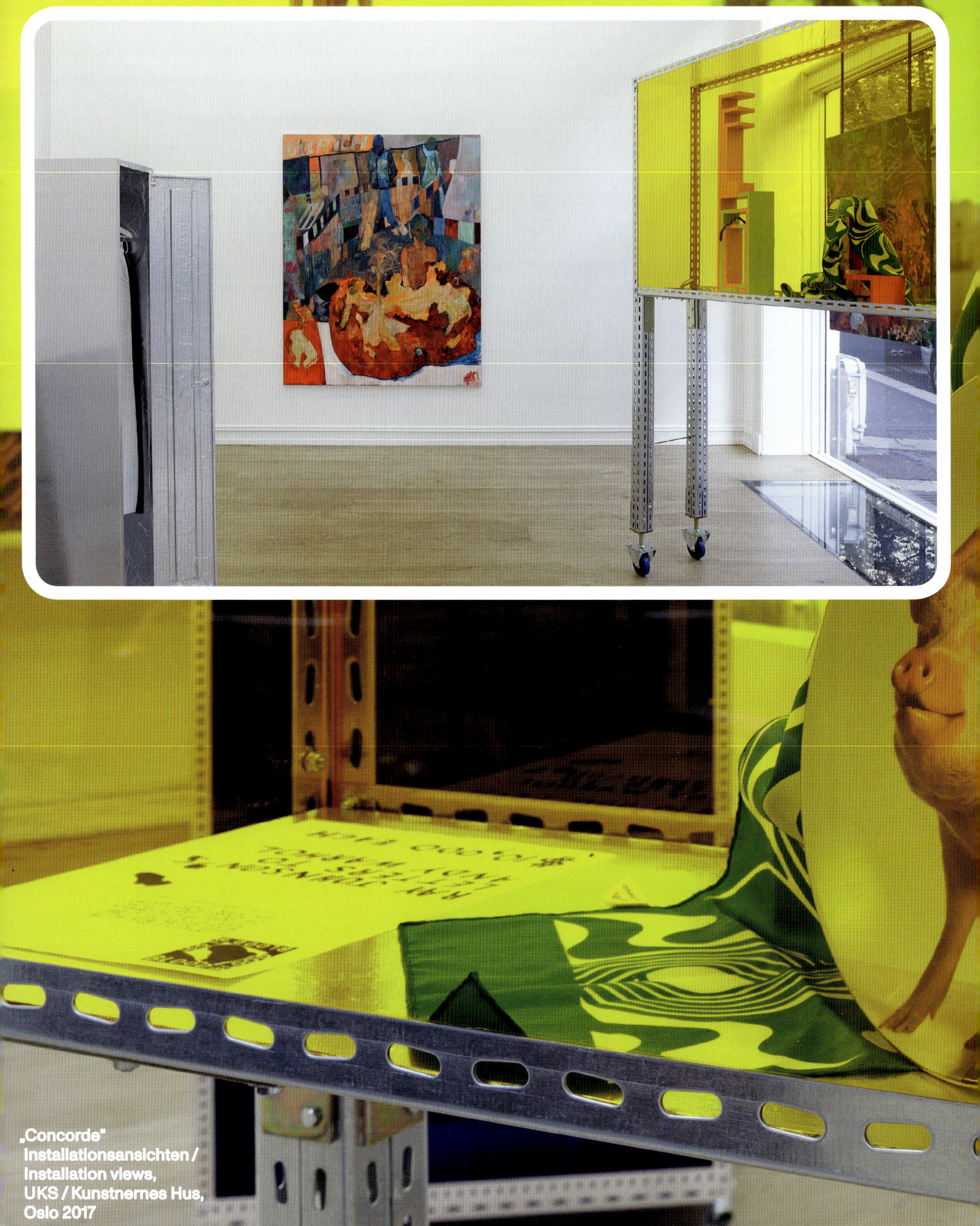

„Concorde"
Installationsansichten /
Installation views,
UKS / Kunstnernes Hus,
Oslo 2017

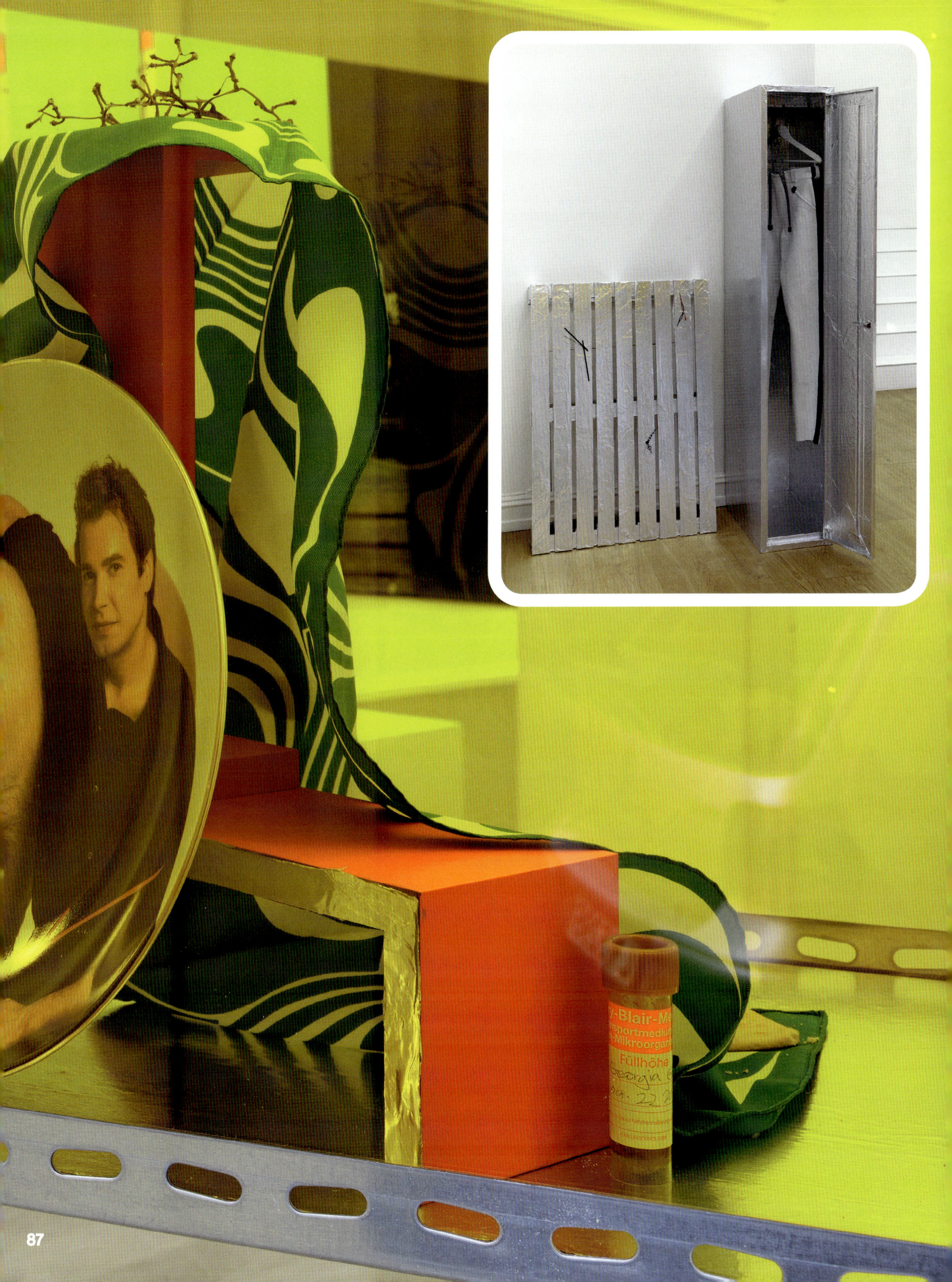

y-Blair-Me
sportmedium
Mikroorgani
Füllhöhe
eorgia
22.2

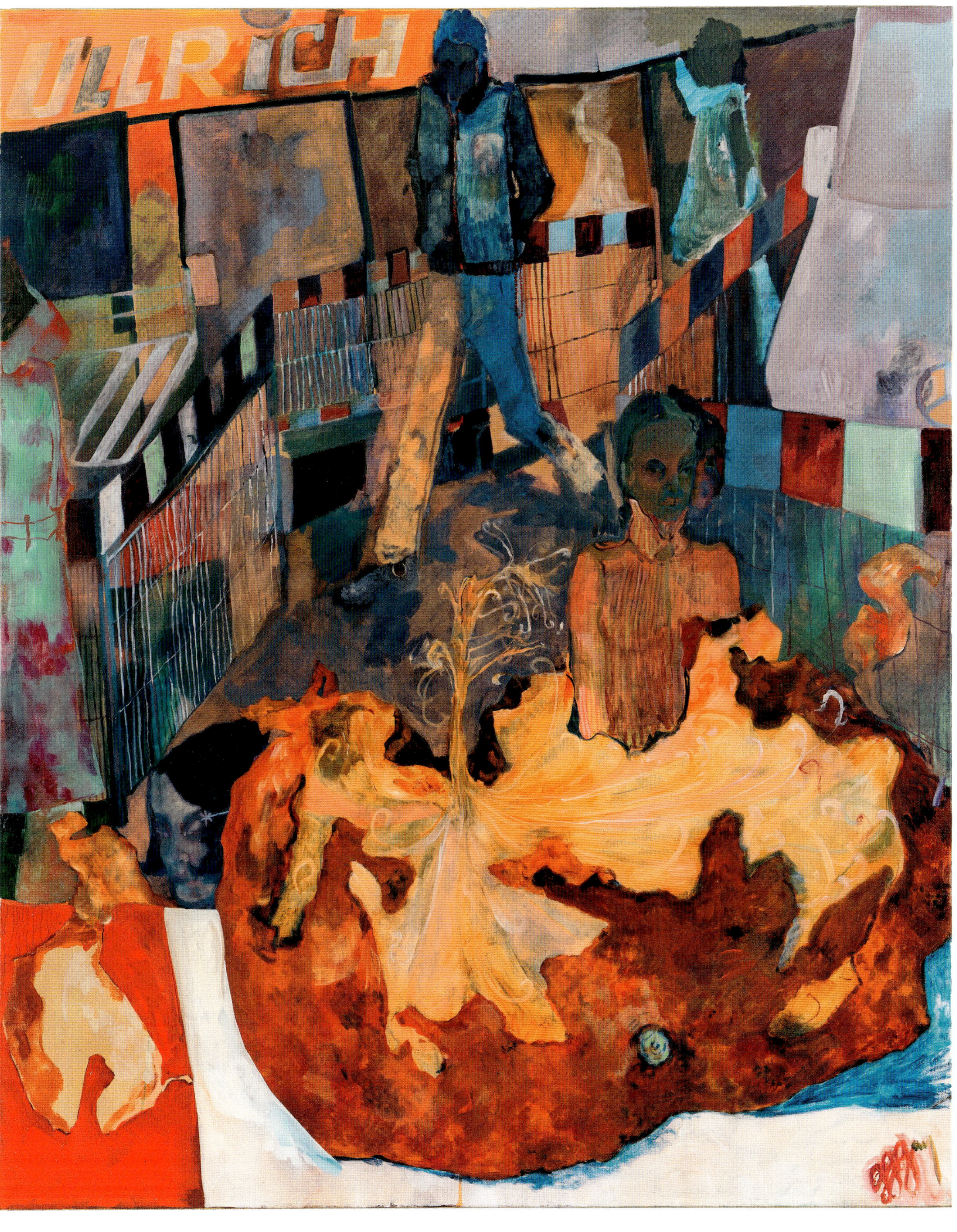
ULLRICH

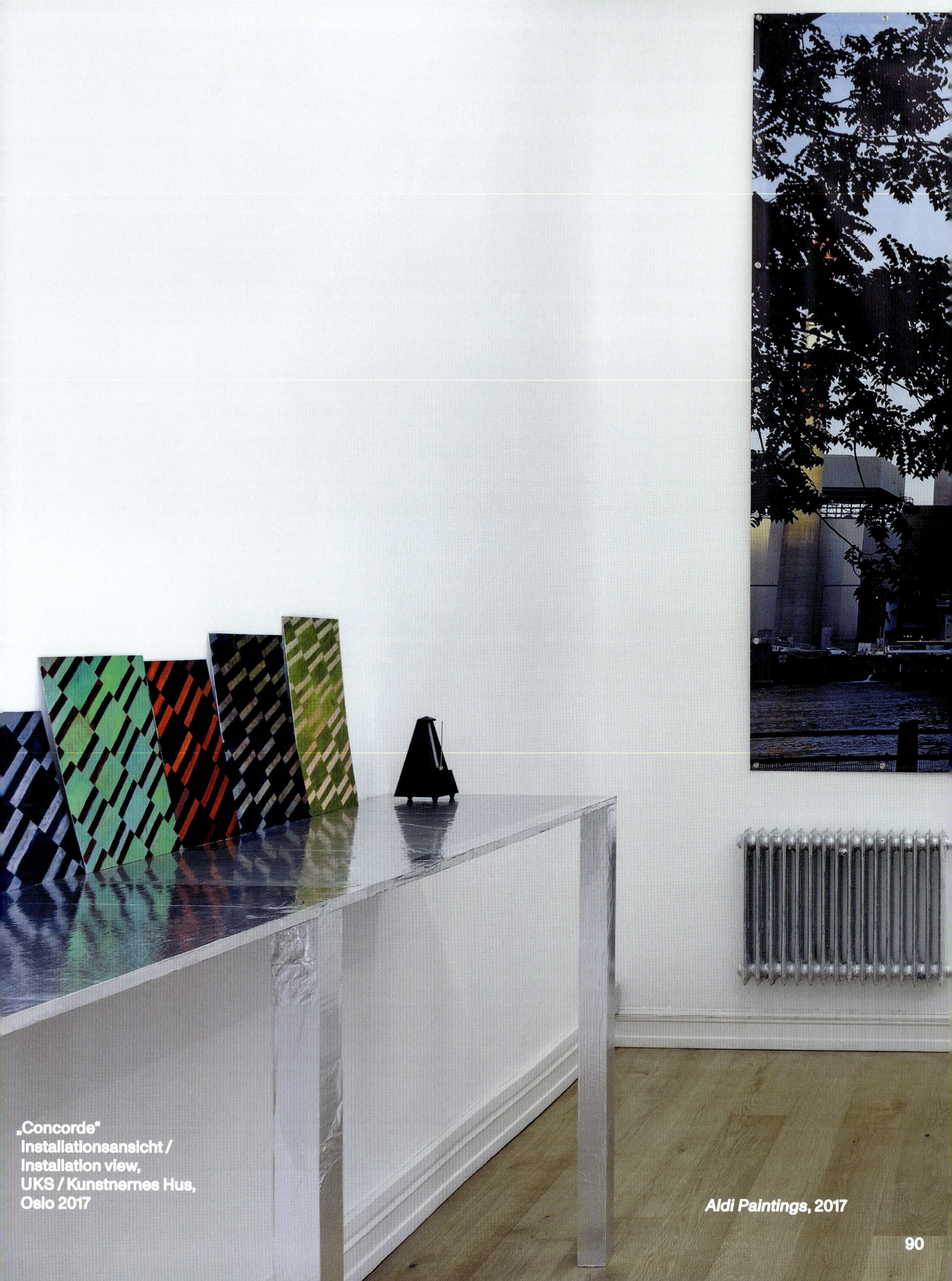

„Concorde"
Installationsansicht /
Installation view,
UKS / Kunstnernes Hus,
Oslo 2017

Aldi Paintings, 2017

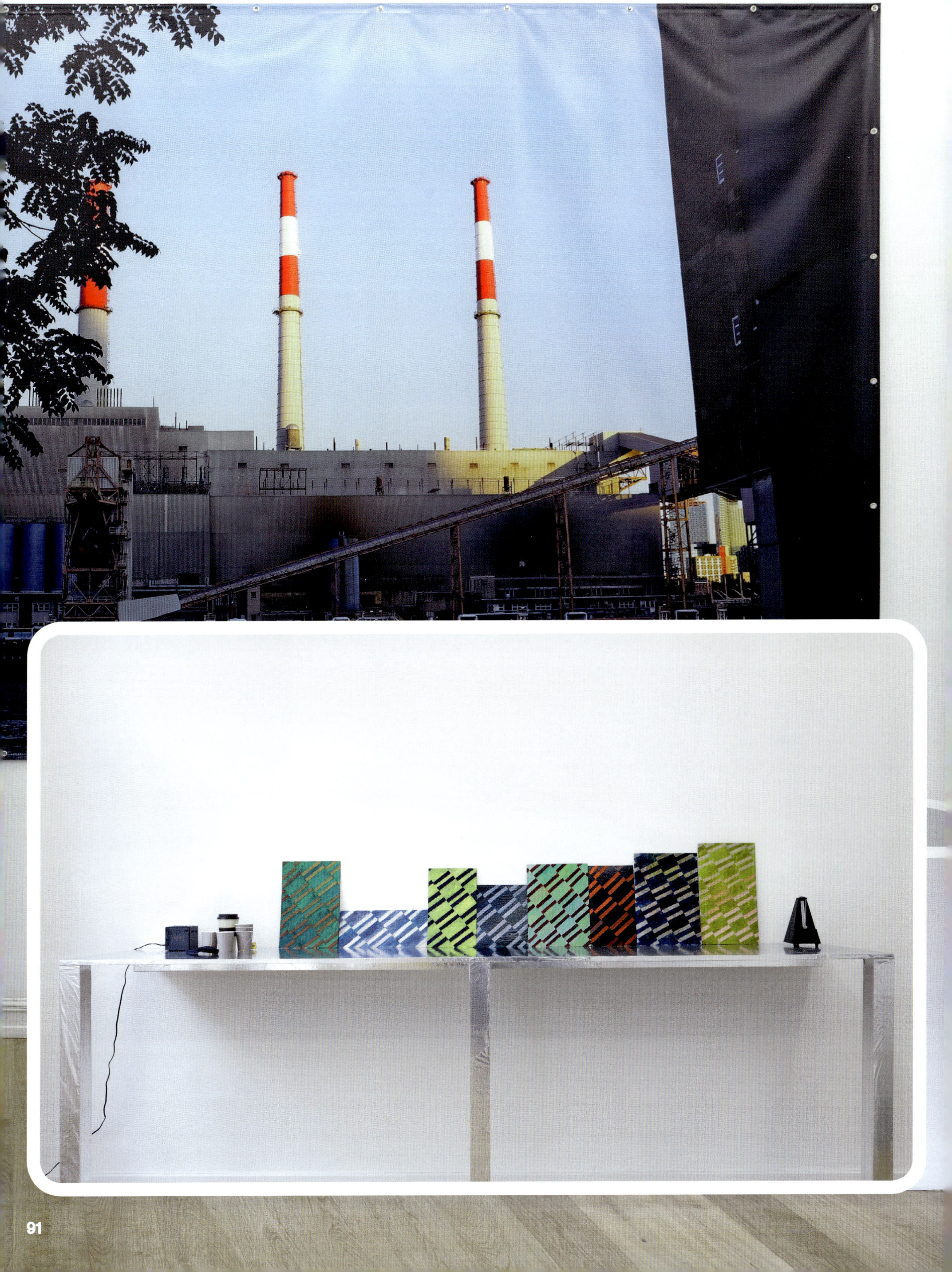

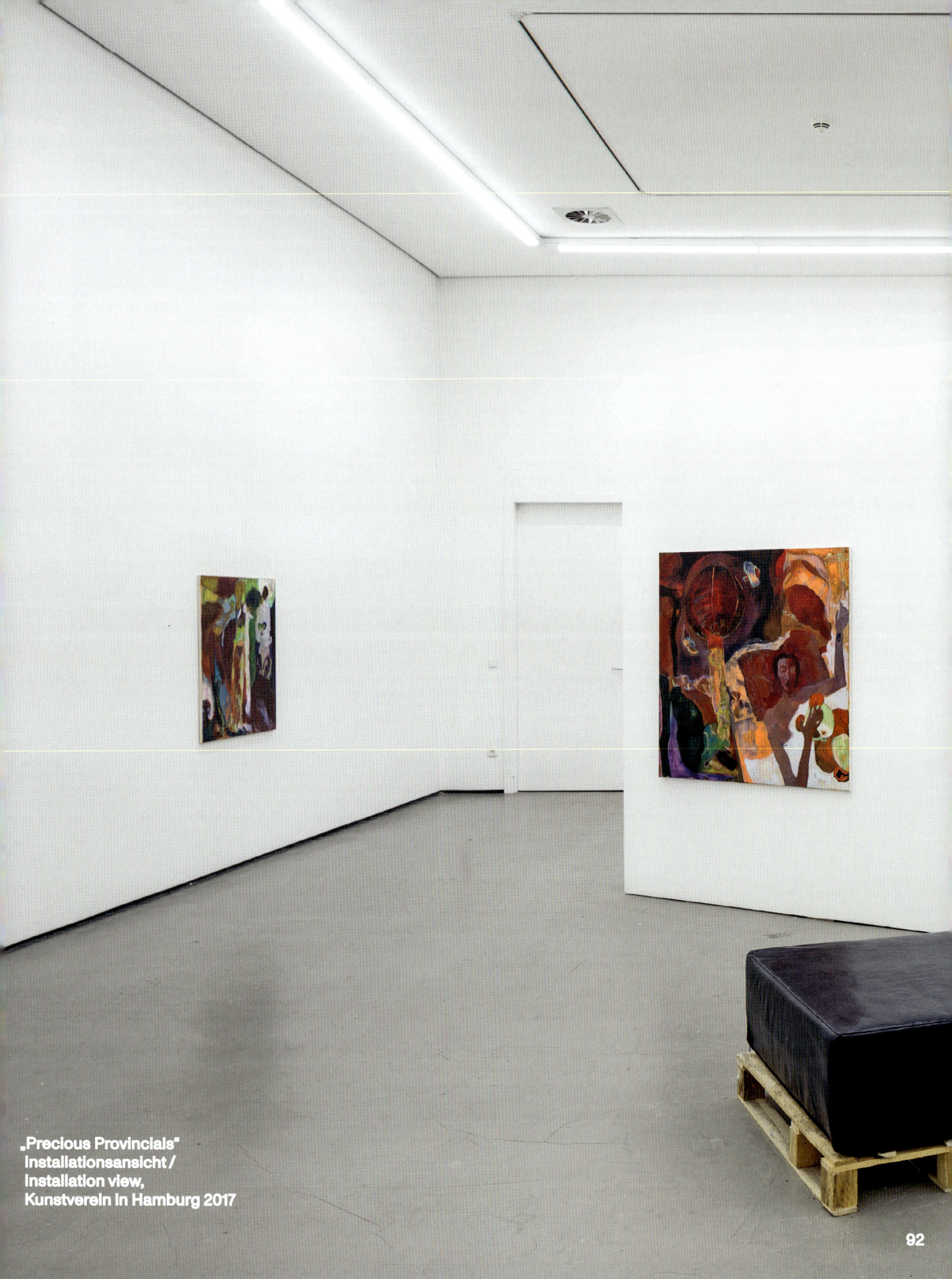

„Precious Provincials"
Installationsansicht /
Installation view,
Kunstverein in Hamburg 2017

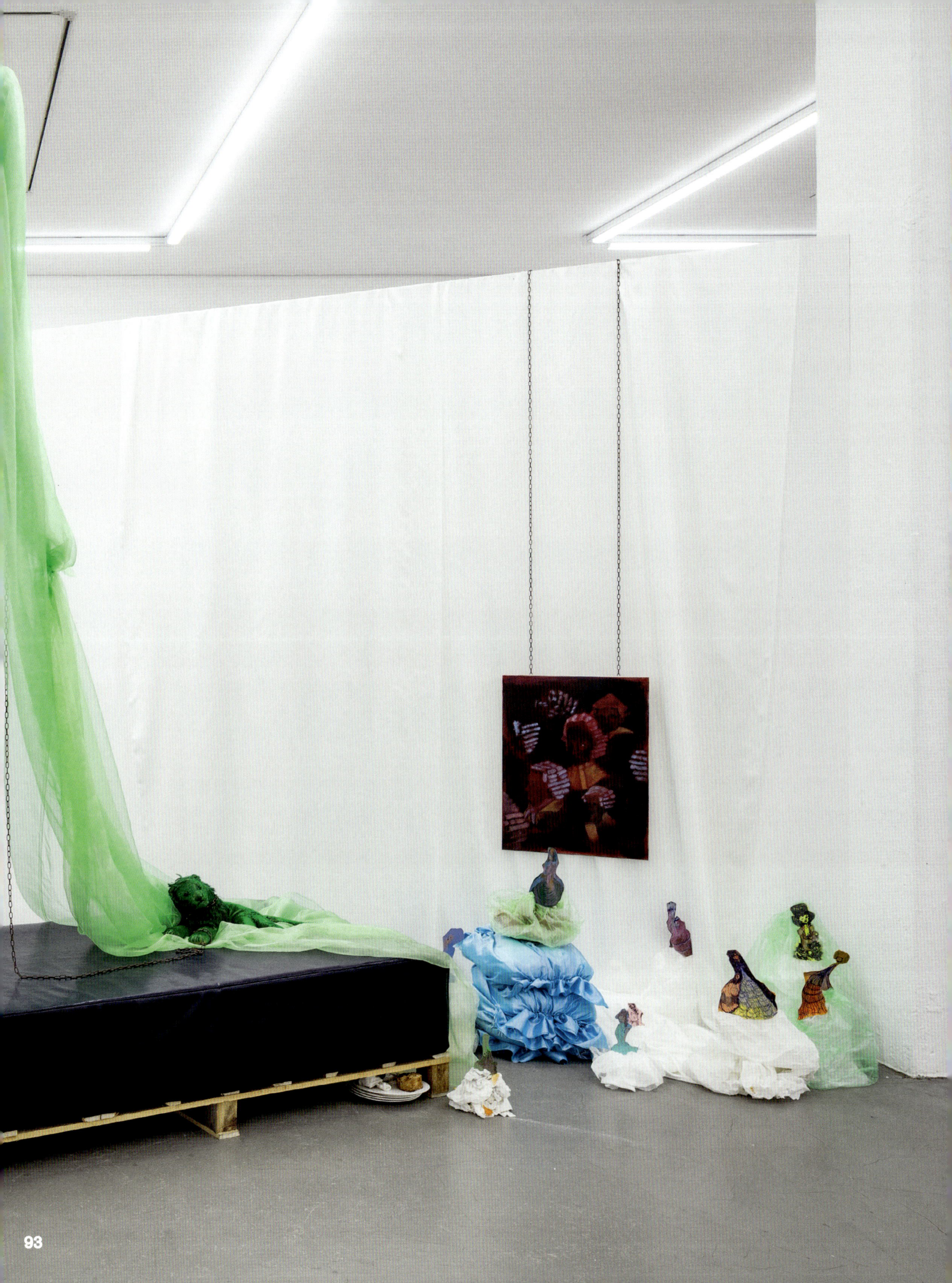

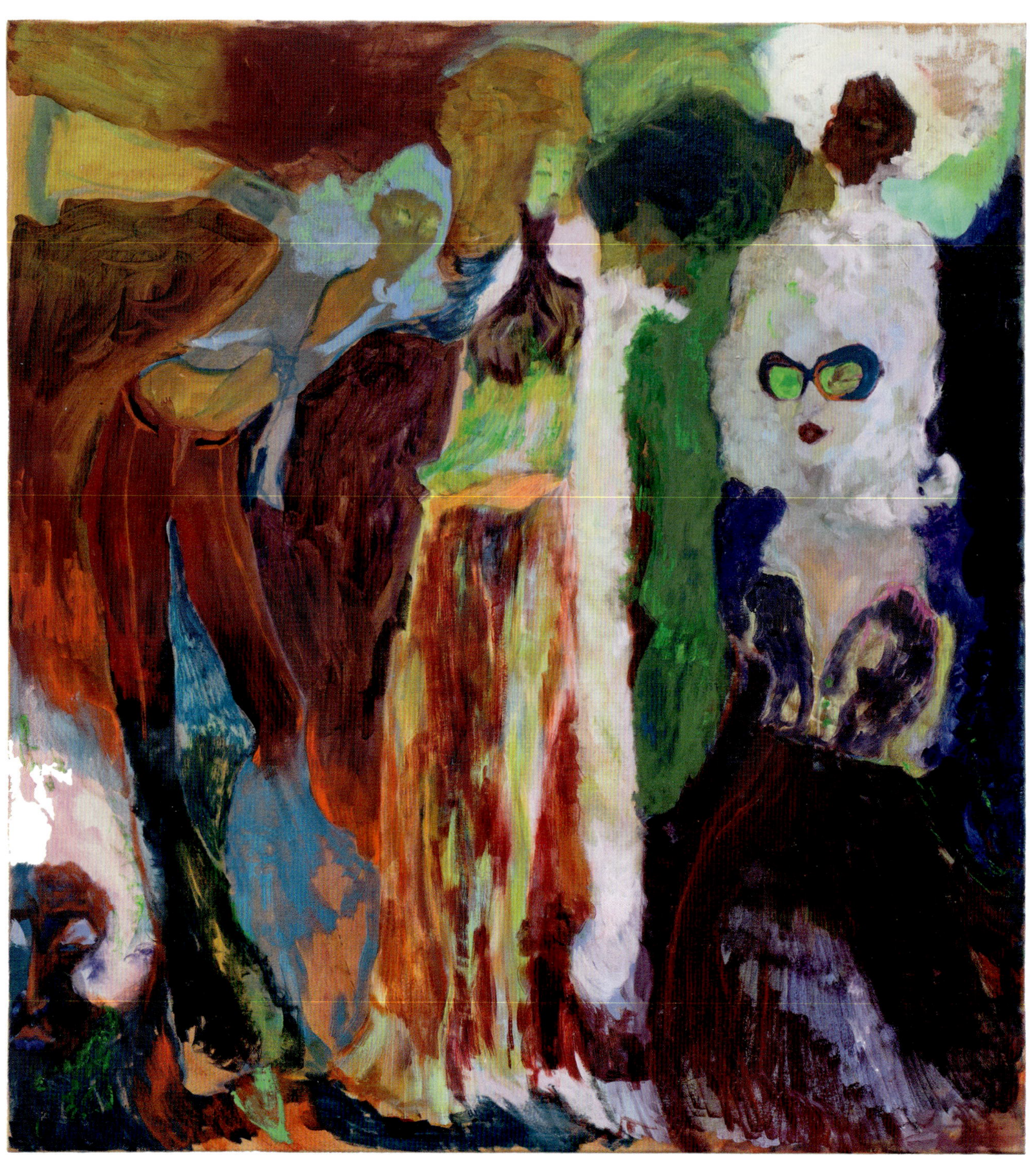

Grouples in a Green World,
2017

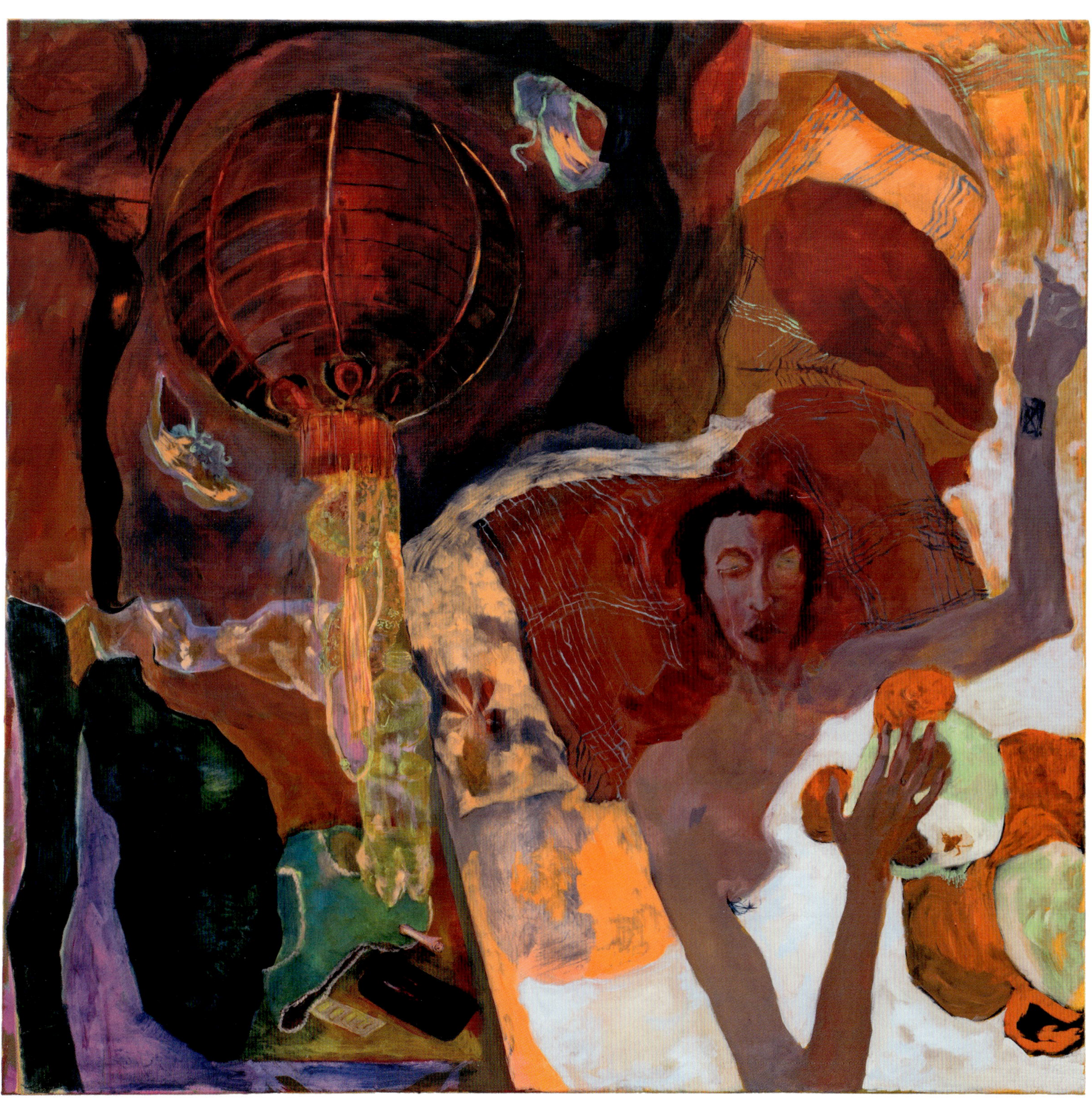

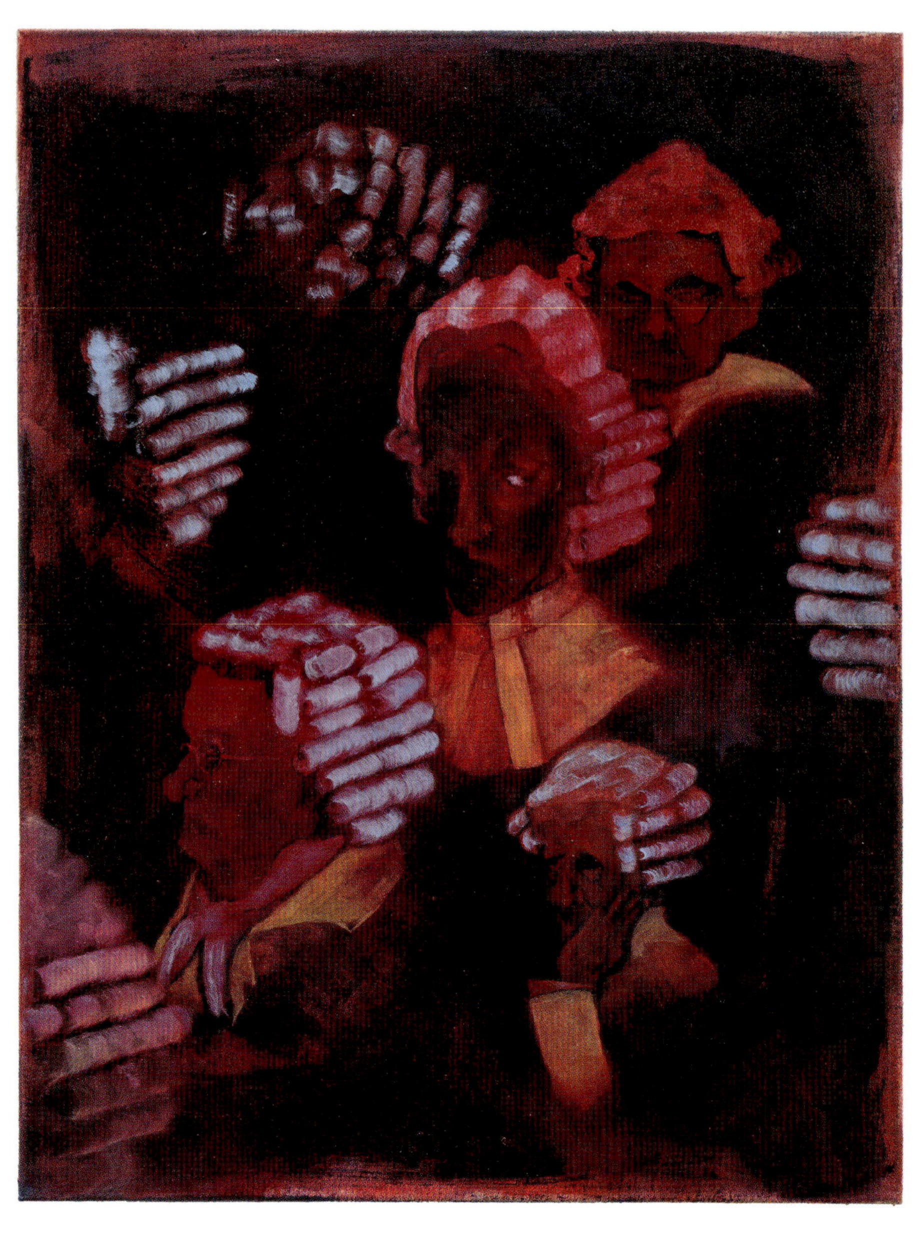

Die Richter, 2016

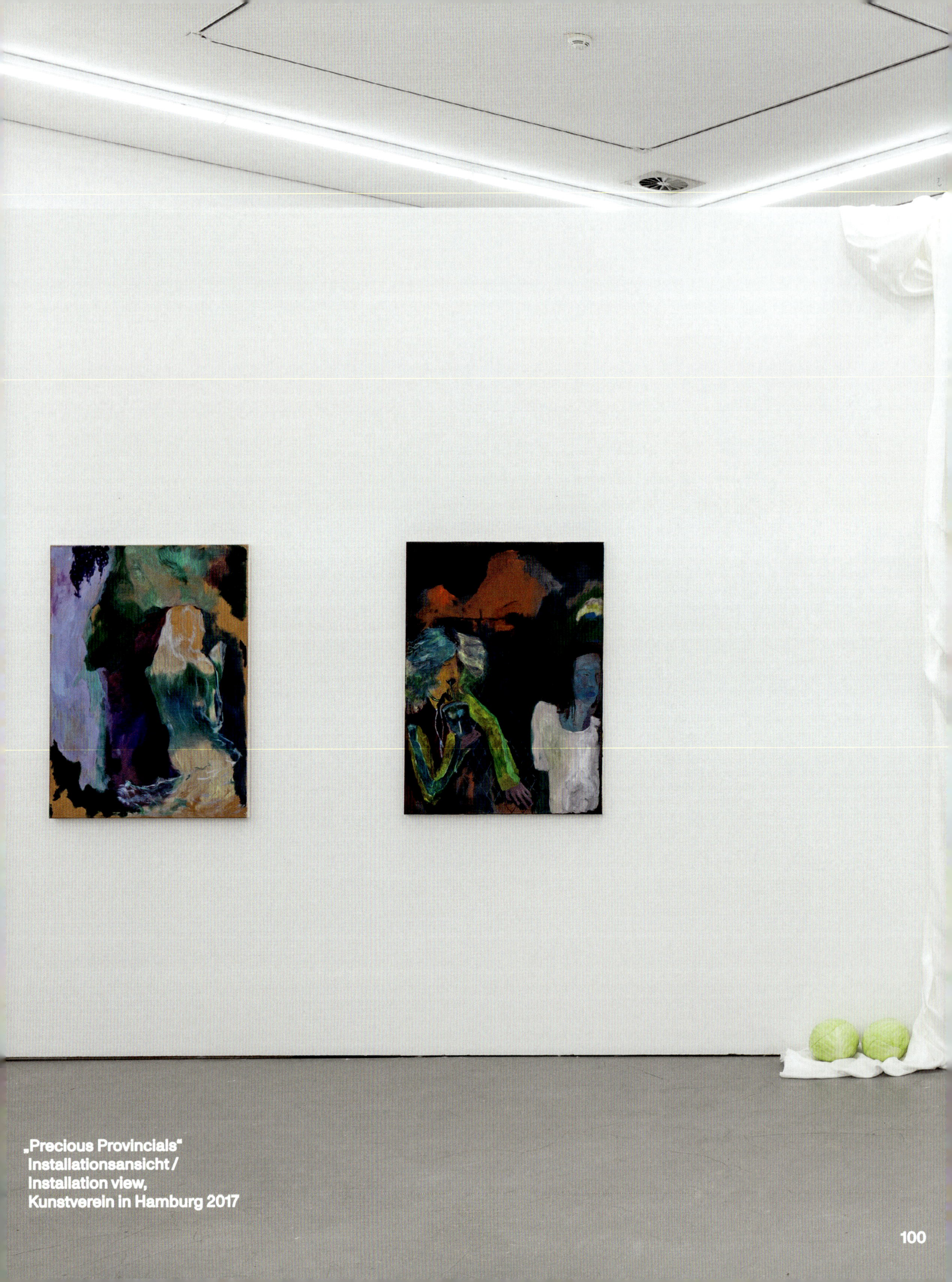

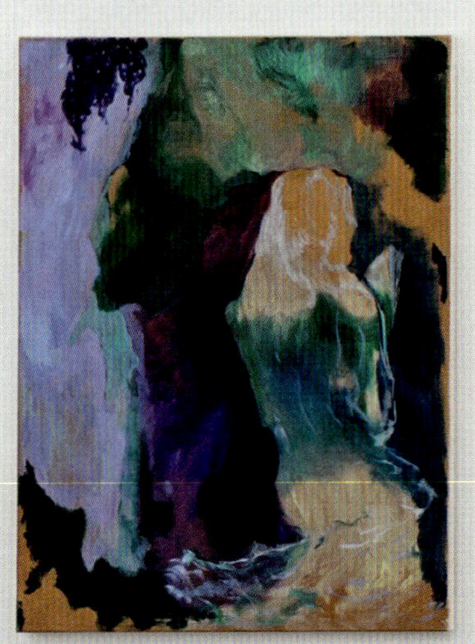 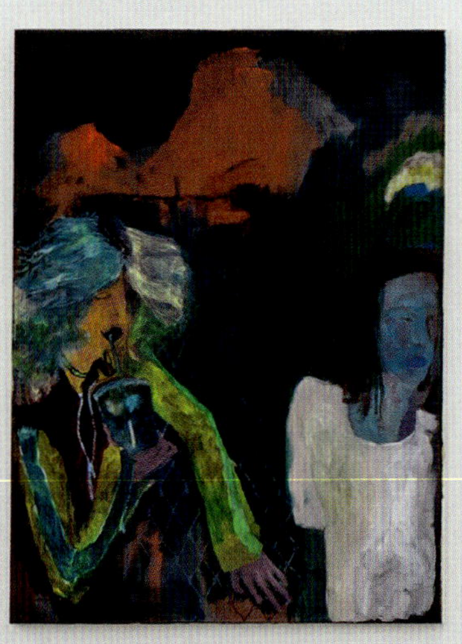

„Precious Provincials"
Installationsansicht /
Installation view,
Kunstverein in Hamburg 2017

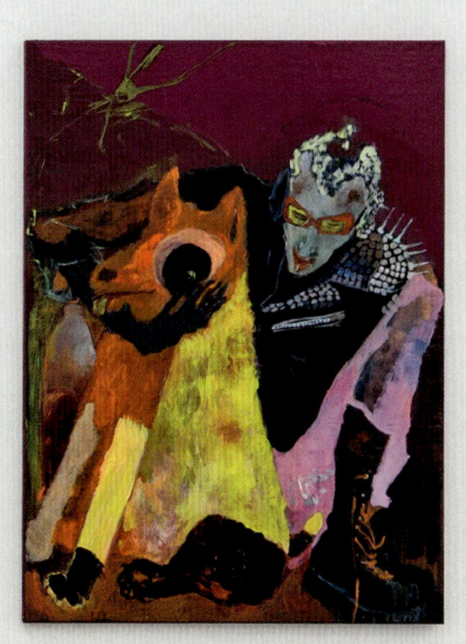

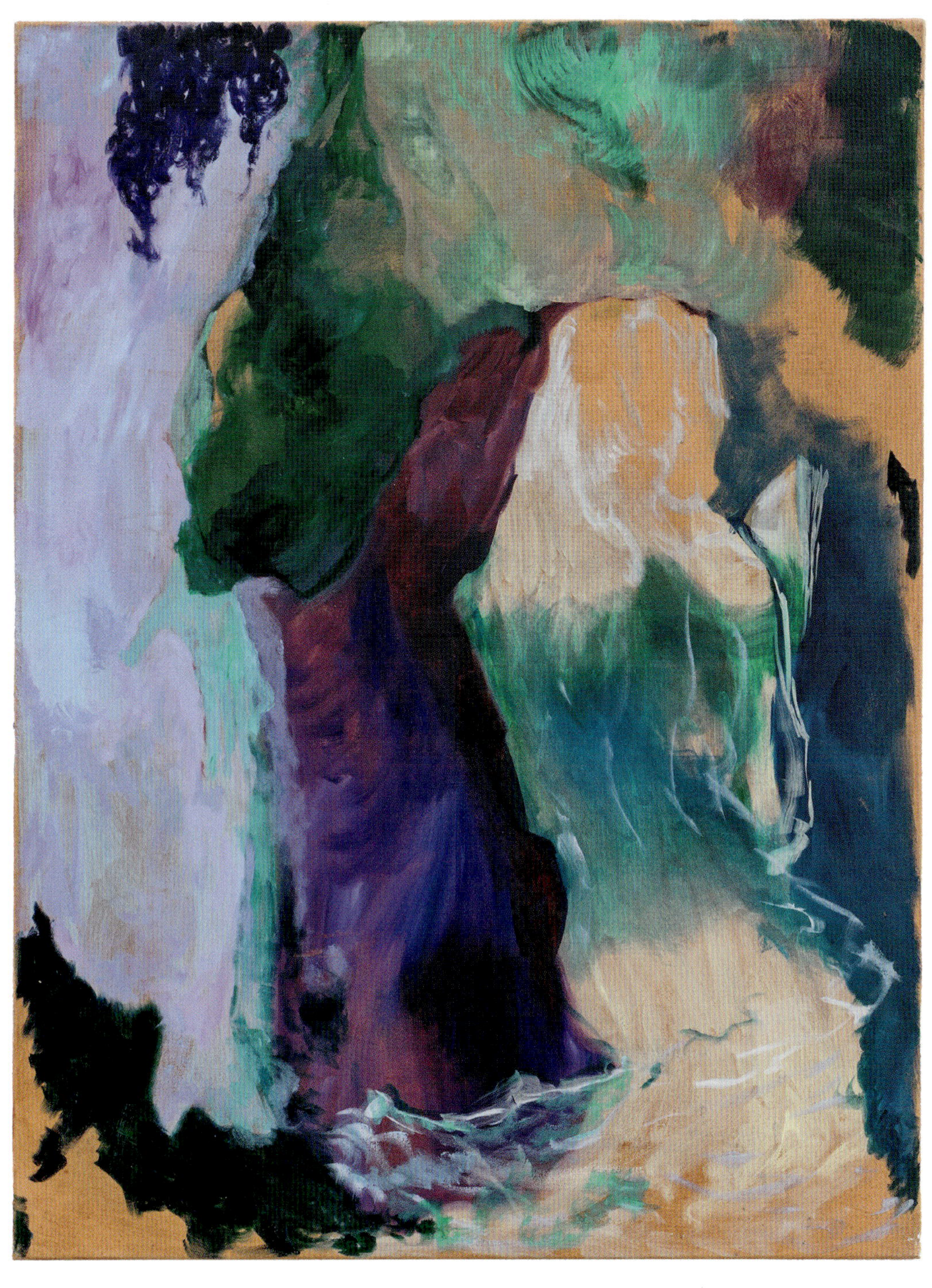

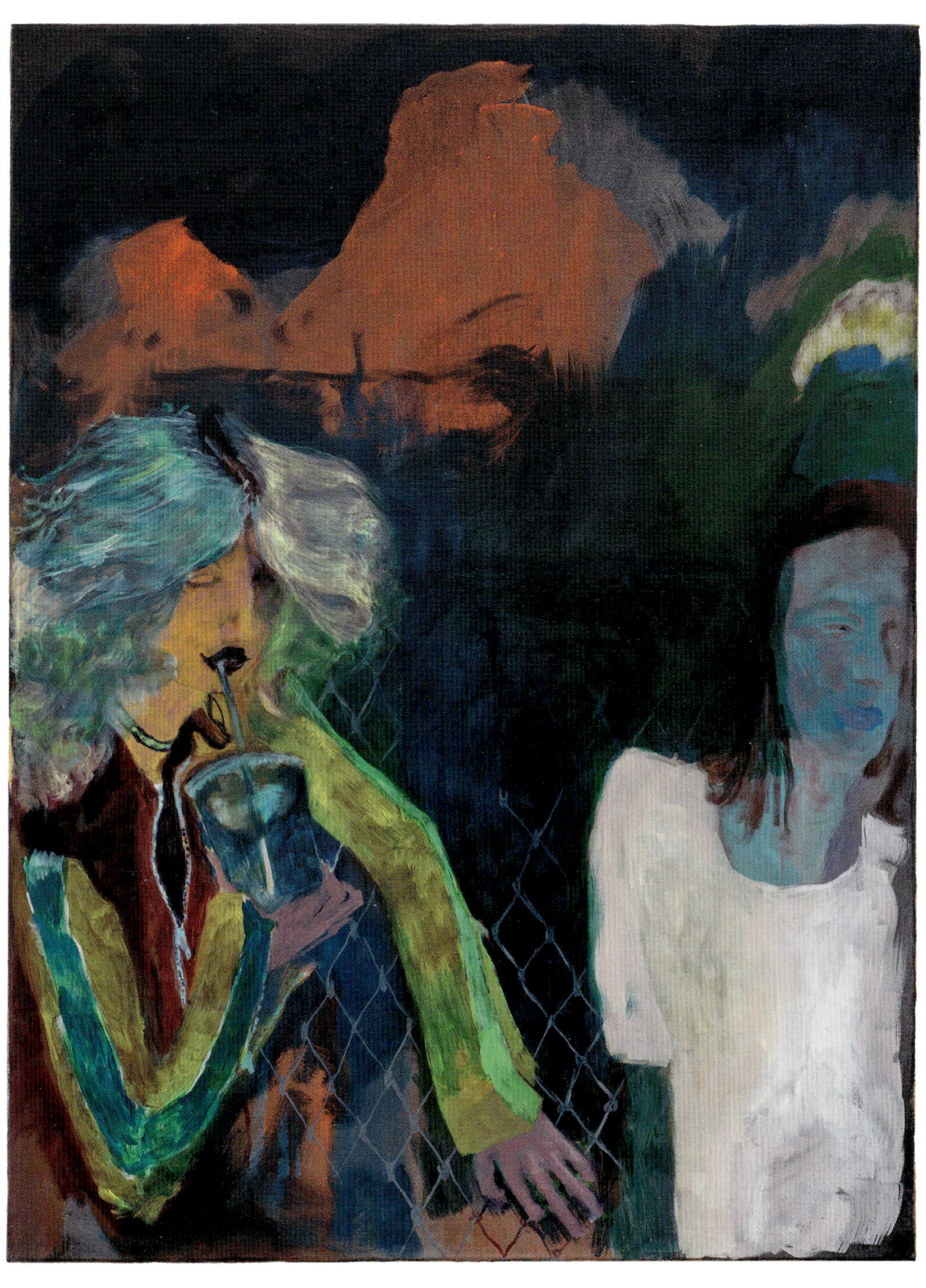

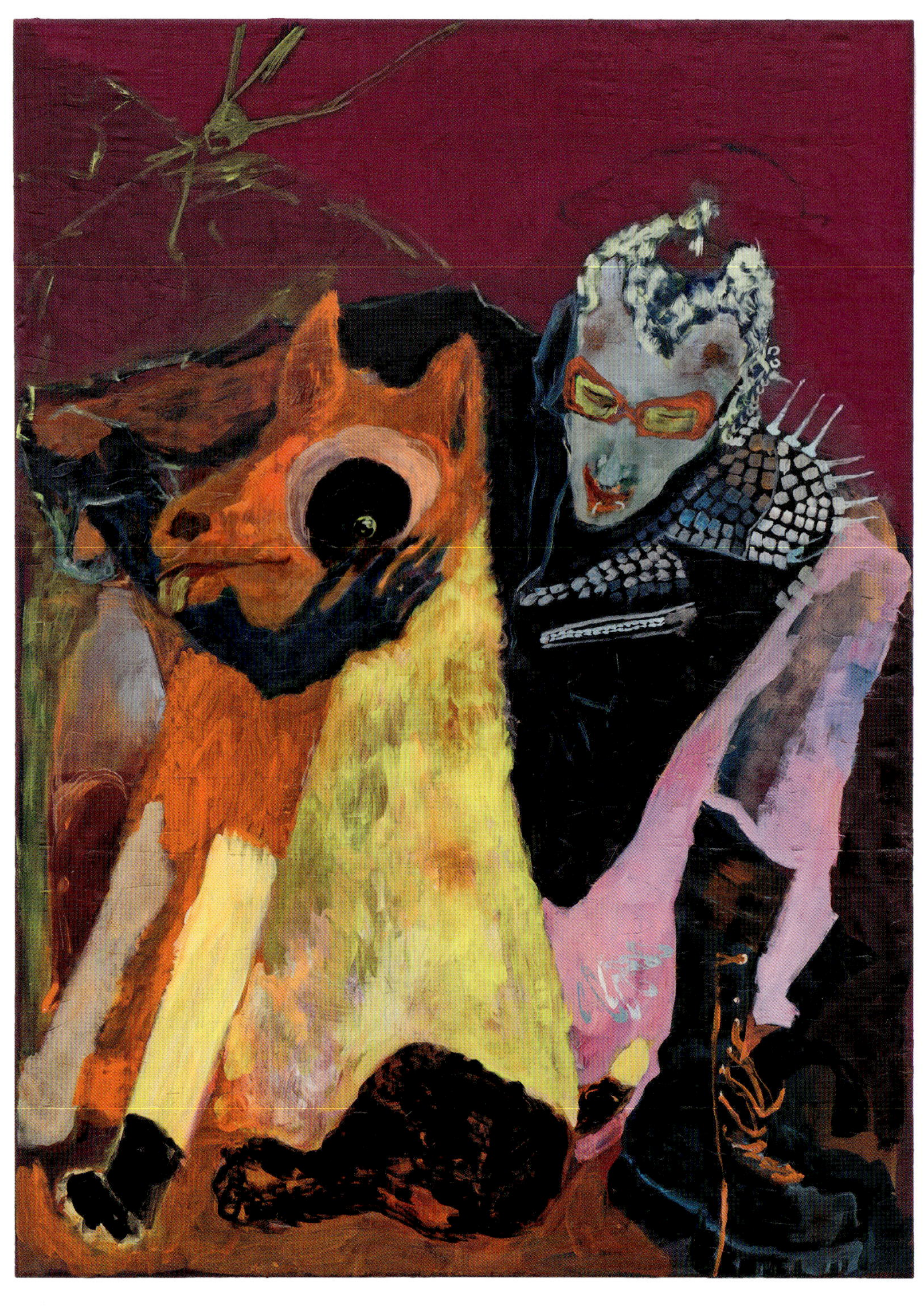

Clingy Punk, 2017

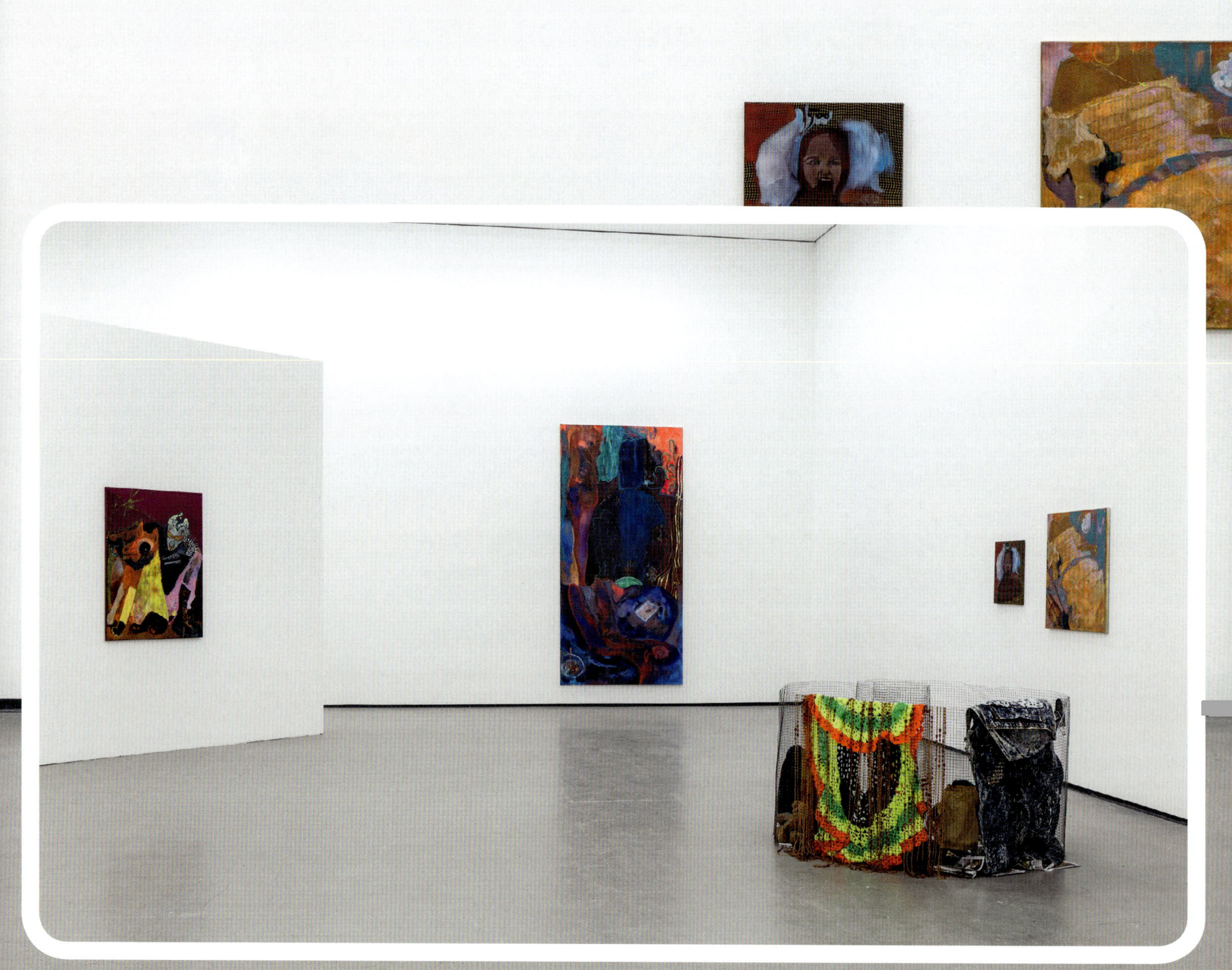

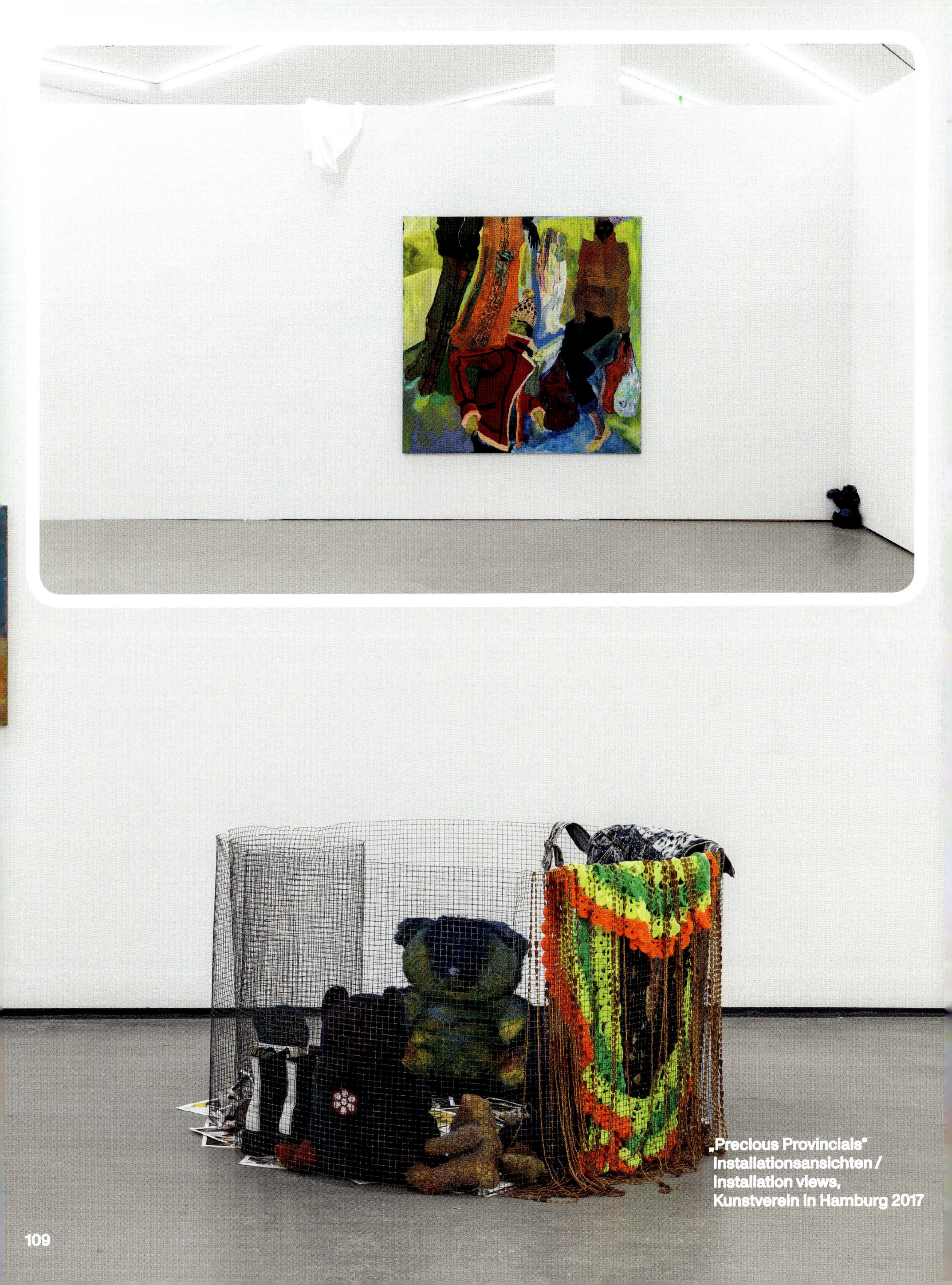

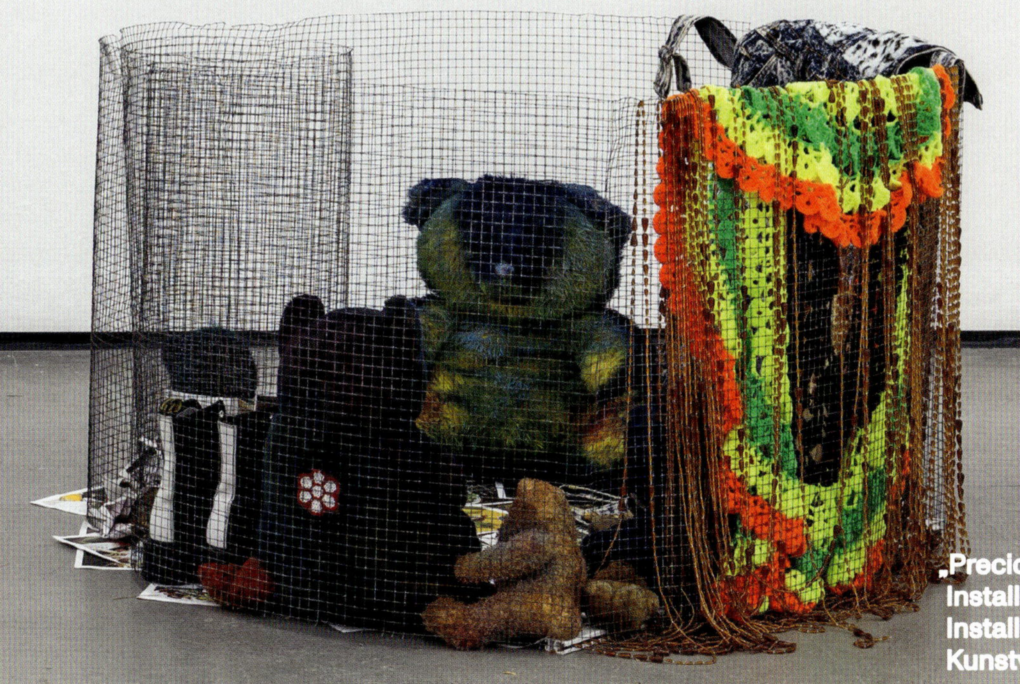

„Precious Provincials"
Installationsansichten /
Installation views,
Kunstverein in Hamburg 2017

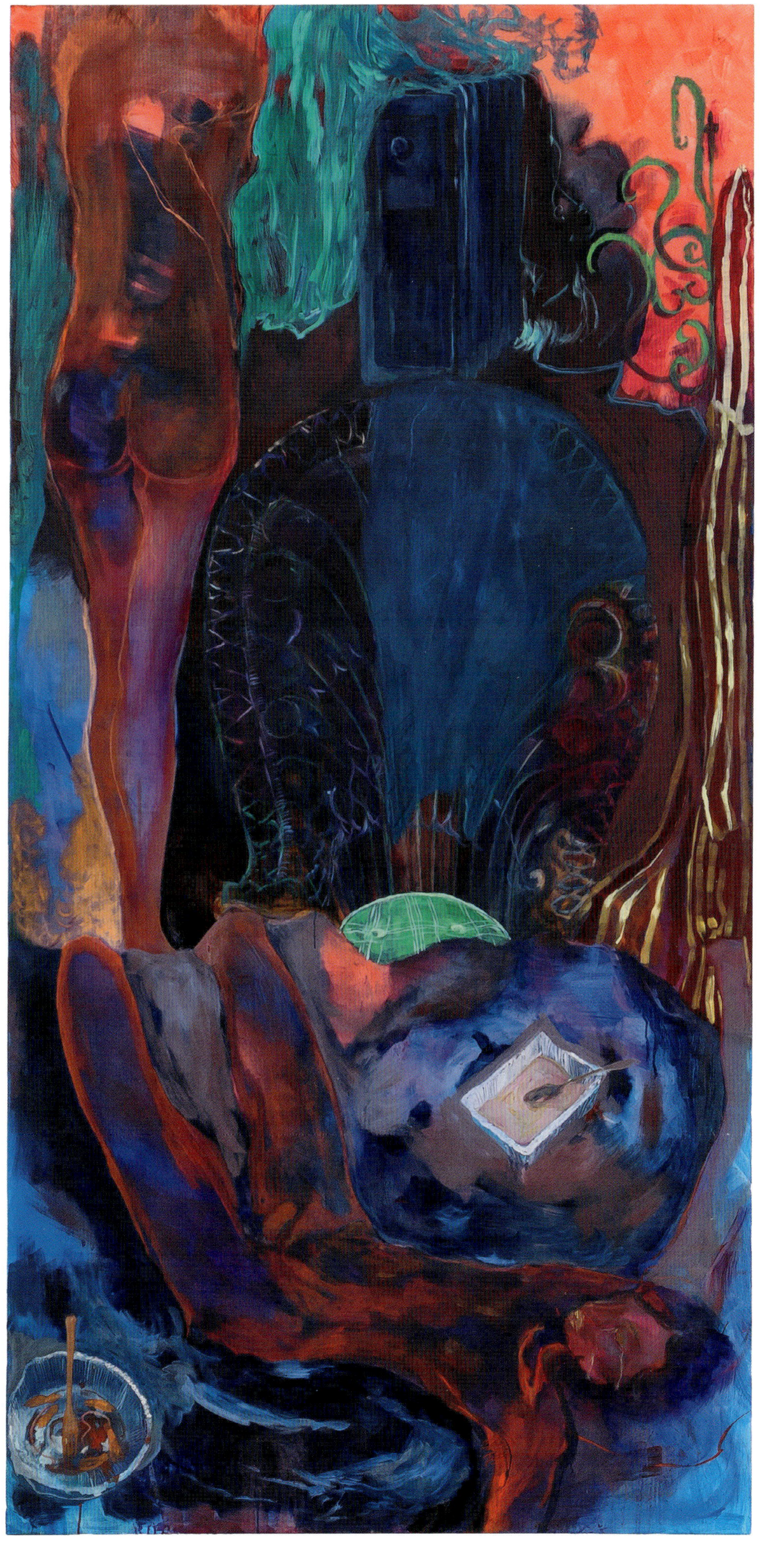

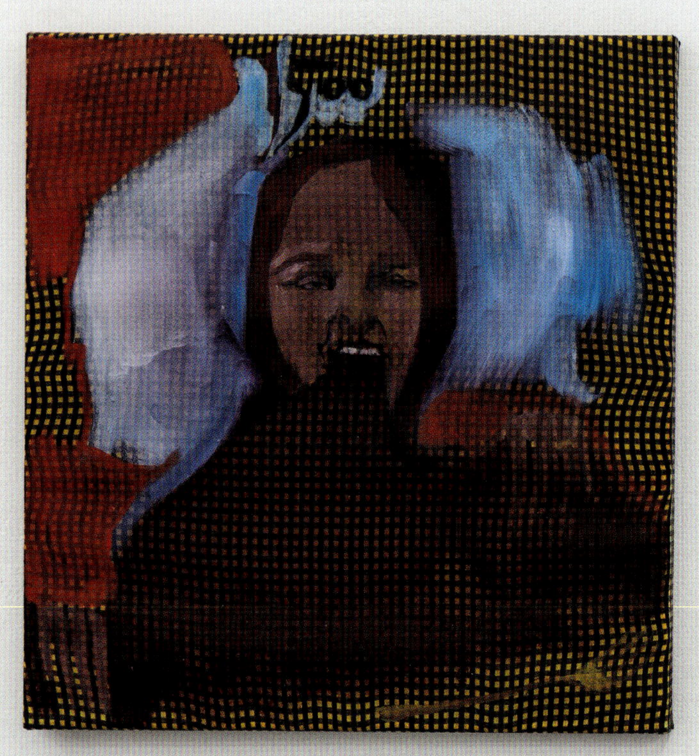

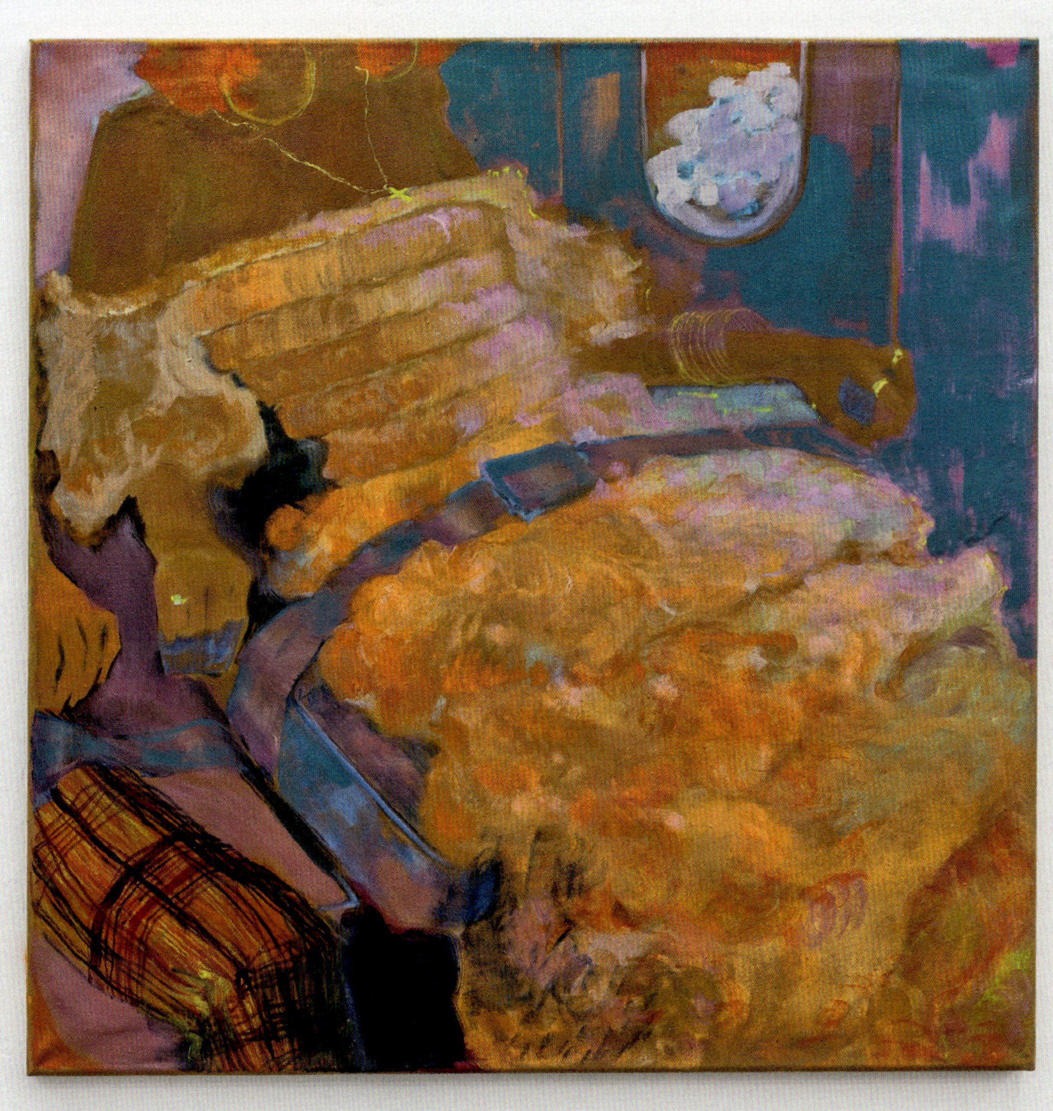

Turbulence, 2017

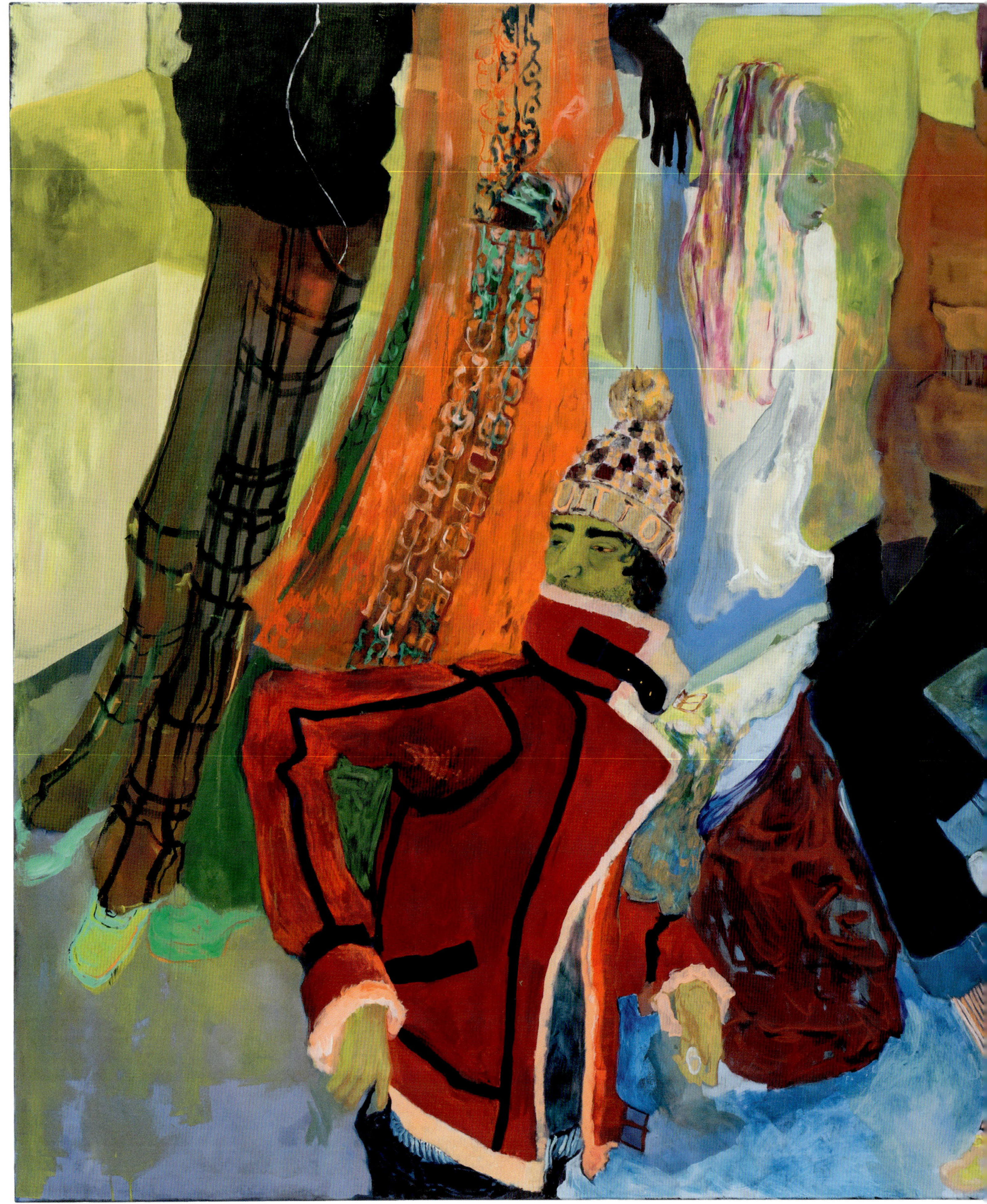

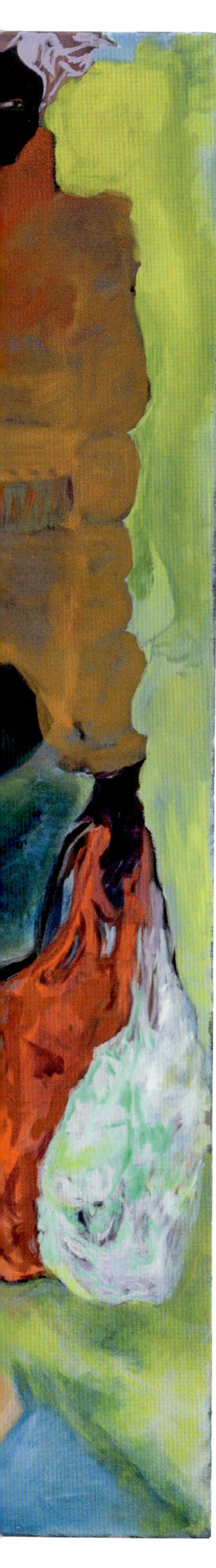

The Paris RER Regional Train,
2017

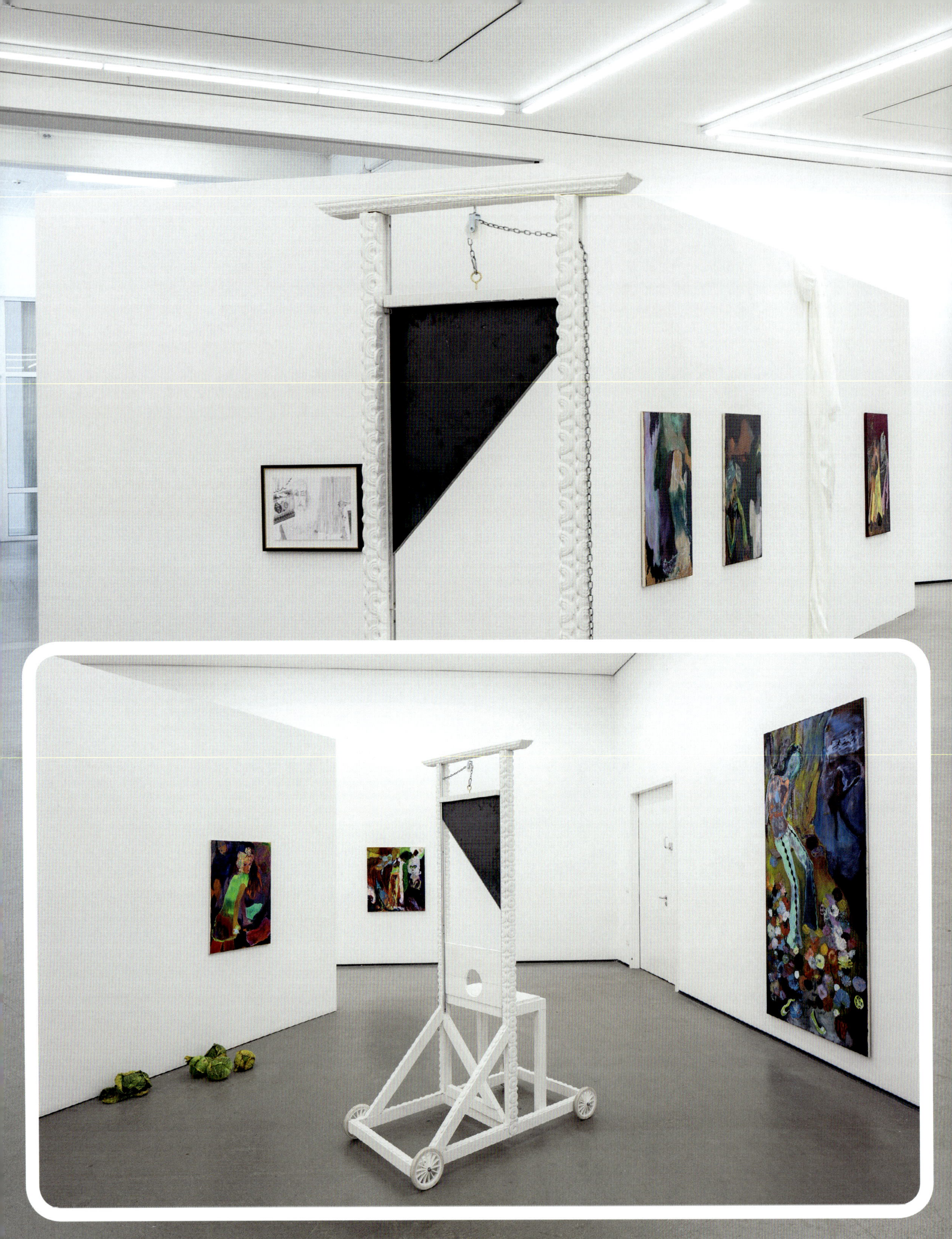

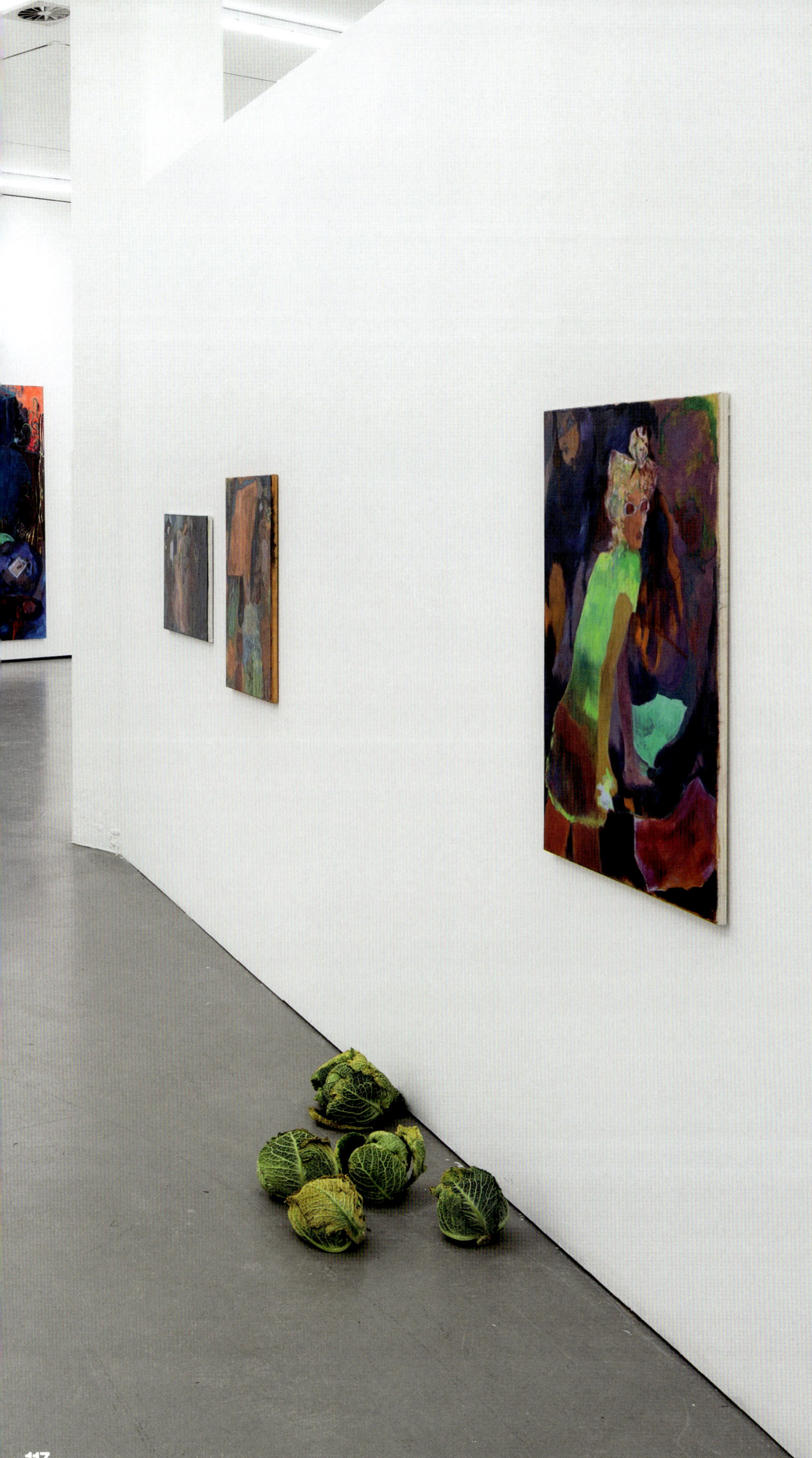

„Precious Provincials"
Installationsansichten /
Installation views,
Kunstverein in Hamburg 2017

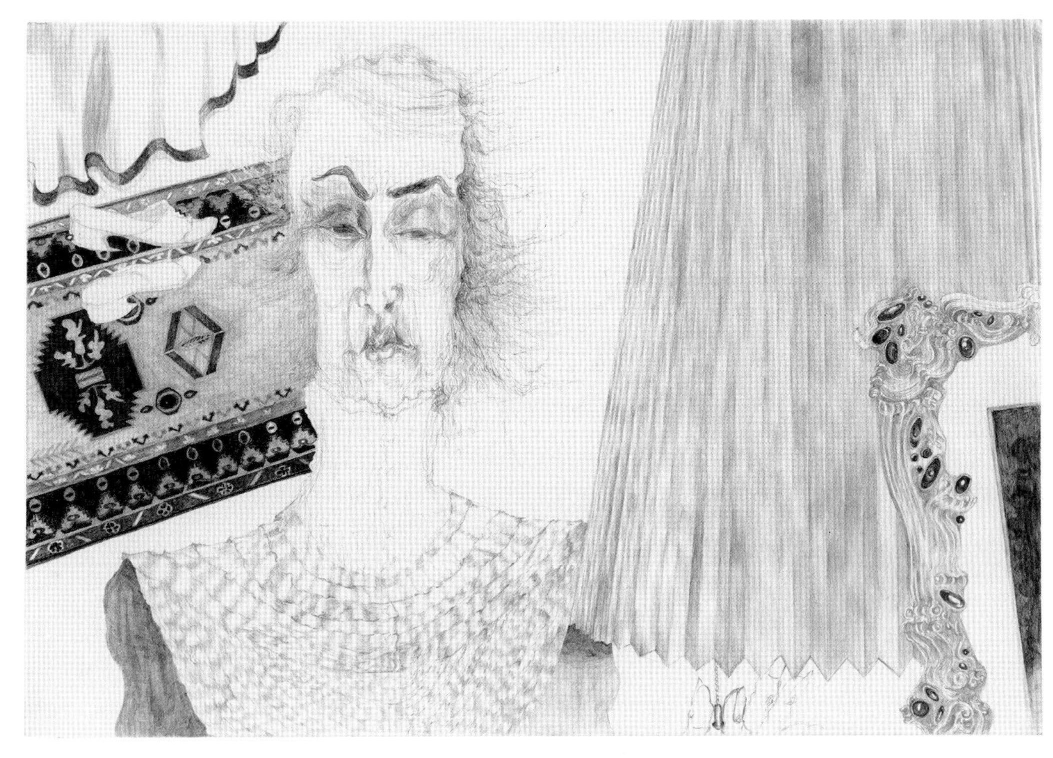

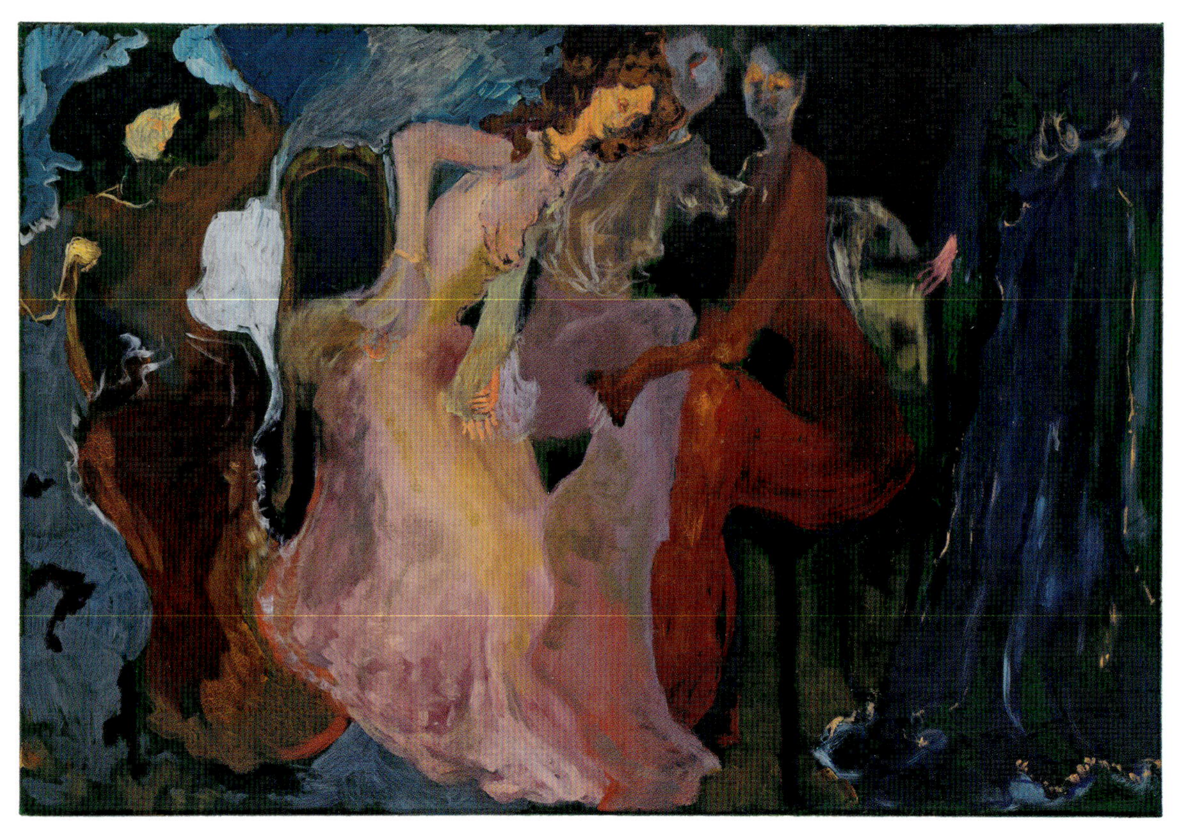

Private Meeting, 2017

Crumpling Your Stupid Idea,
2017

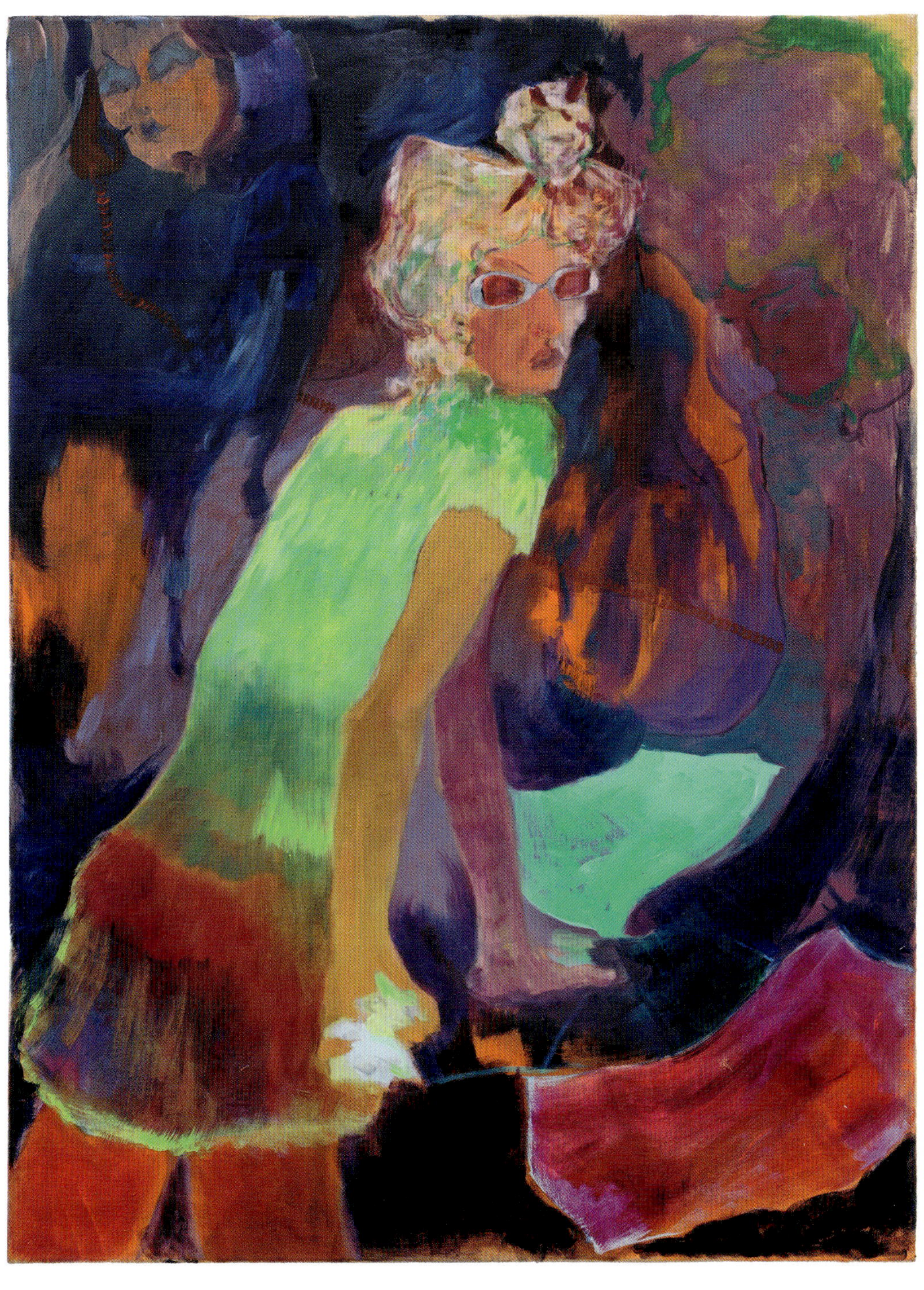

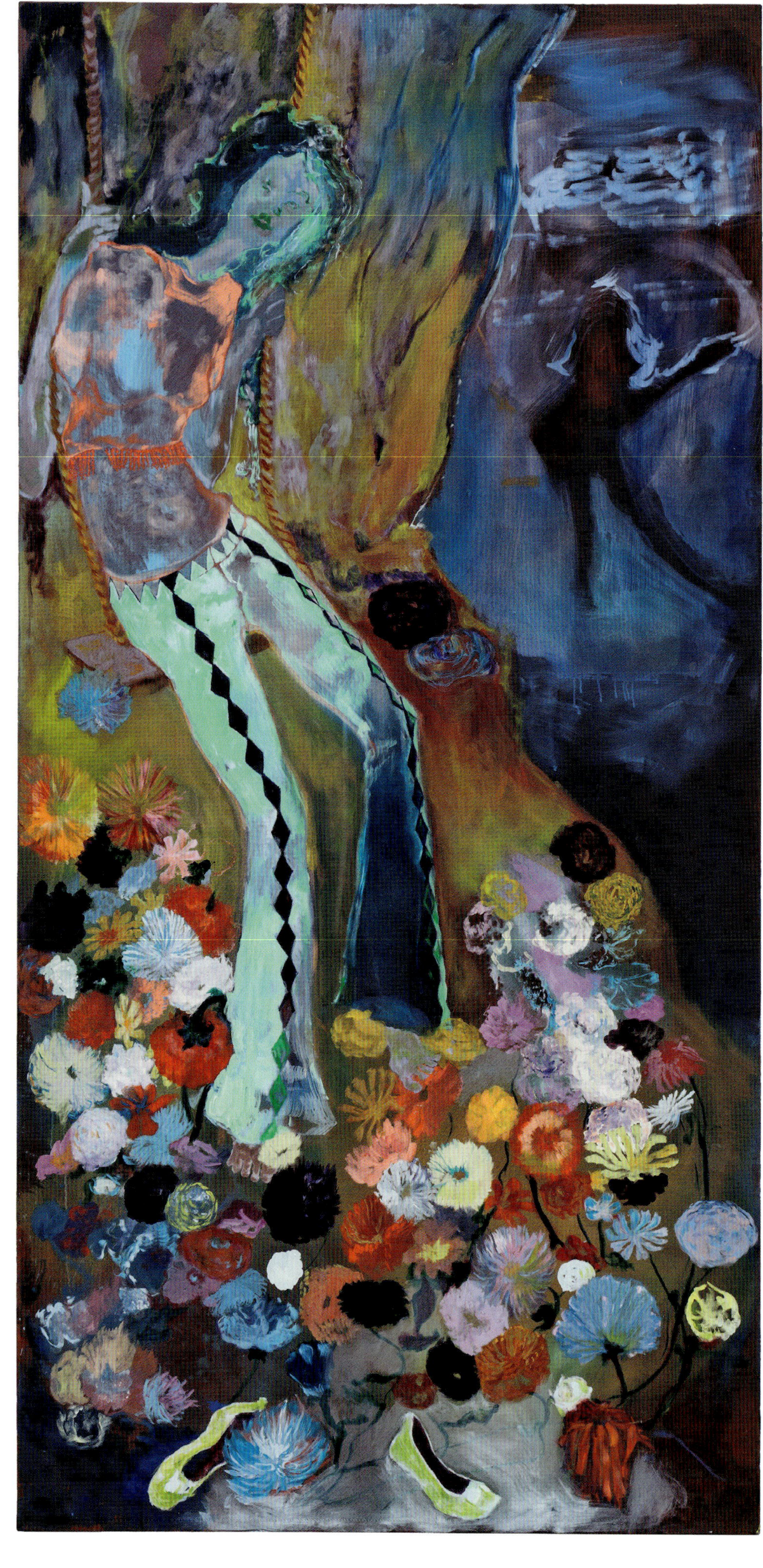

Backstage, Still Alone,
Swinging from a Hippy Tree,
2017

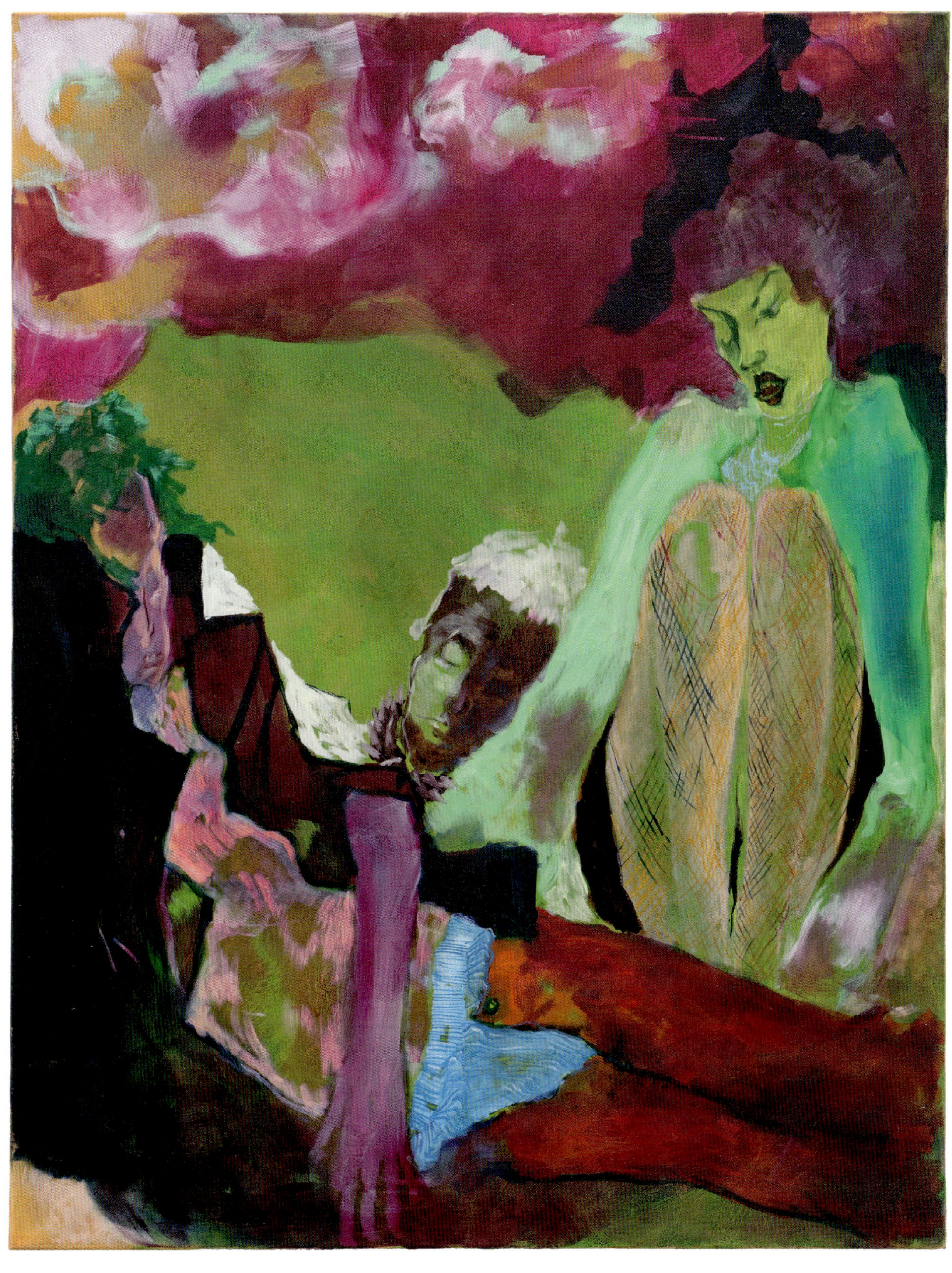

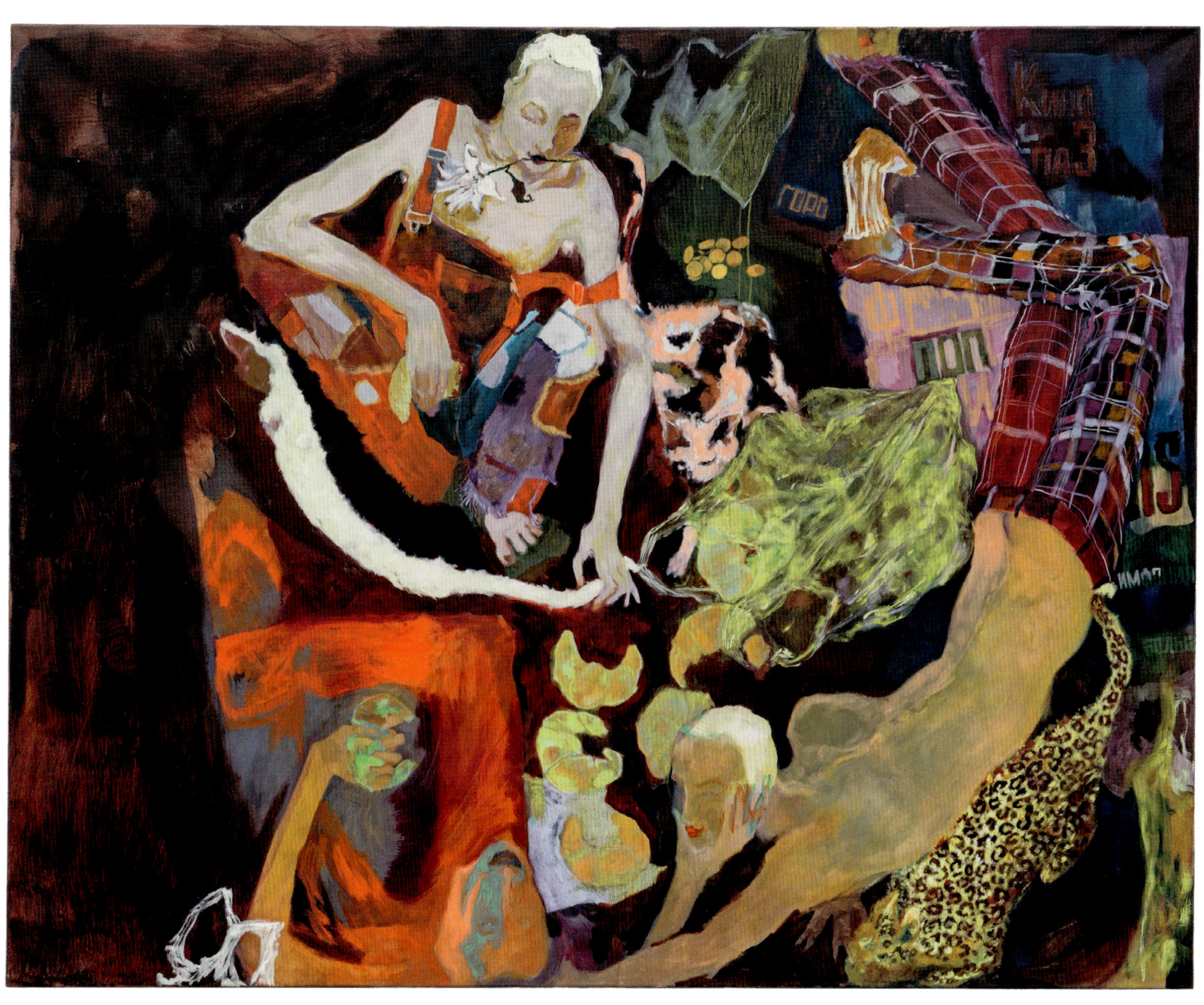

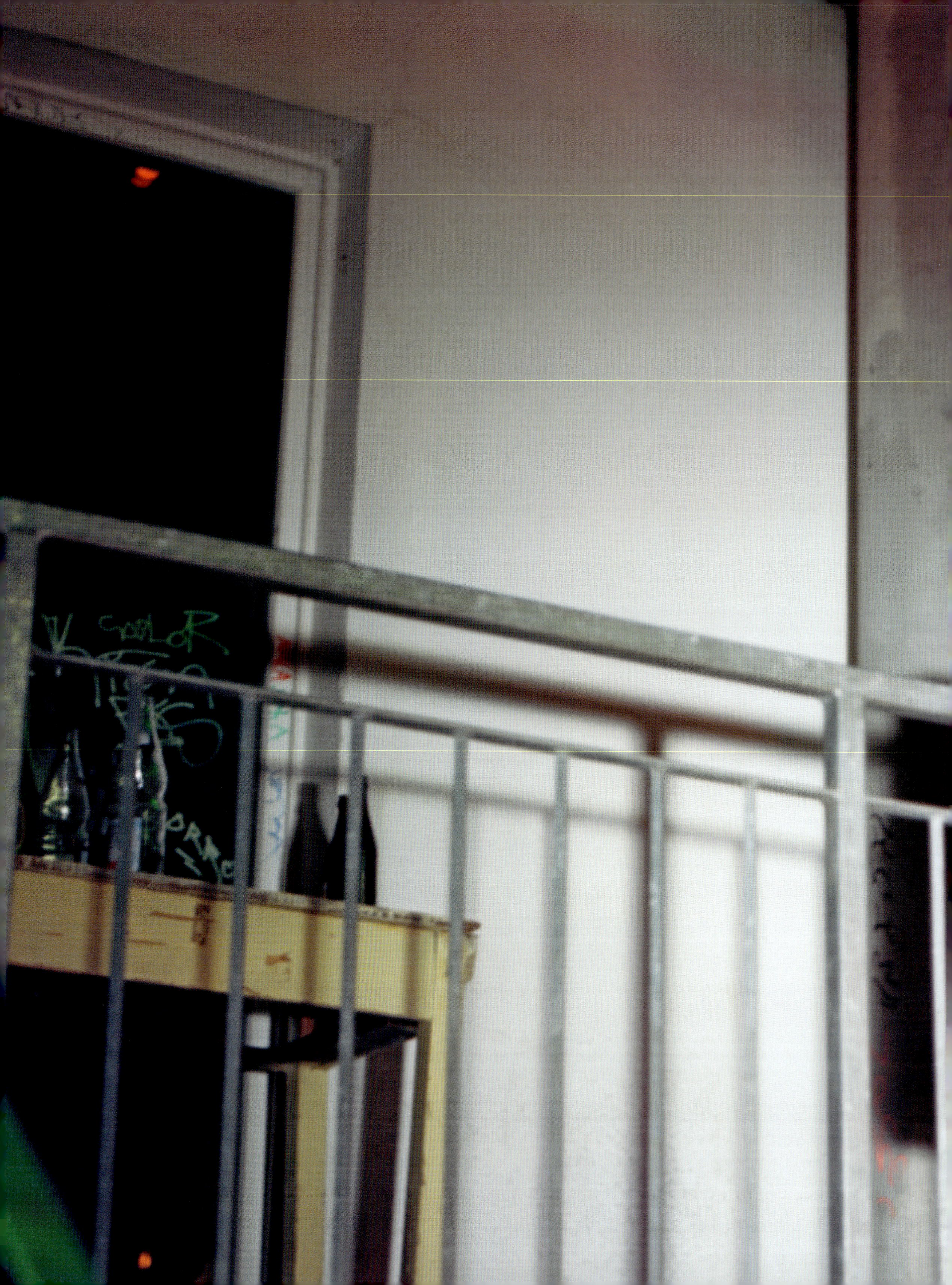

SCHAUMSTOFFLADEN (FOAM SHOP)

Written by Georgia Gardner Gray
Originally performed at ACUD, Berlin, September 9, 10, and 11, 2016

Schaumstoffladen Owner—Pablo Larios
Butty—Patrick Armstrong
Penny—Preston Chaunsumlit
Repair Man—Kyle Joseph
Penner—Patrick McGraw
Telephone Pole—Dan Bodan
Poodle Man / Chimney Sweep 1—Julian Garcia
El Coco / The Mother—Elias Pitegoff
The Baby—Max Pitegoff
Delivery Boy / Chimney Sweep 2—Isaac Penn
The Jew / Chimney Sweep 3—Felix Mura
Drunk Man—Tobias Spichtig
Bubble Boy—Billy Rennekamp

Produced by New Theater, Berlin, and Elodie Evers
Set by Georgia Gardner Gray
Costumes by Leila Hekmat and Mia Von Matt

Schaumstoffladen sits on the ground floor of a two level sidewalk starting on the balcony level. Gritty, '70s NYC vibes. A big telephone pole is next to the laden and reaches up to the balcony level. A bright neon lit yellow sign spells Schaumstoffladen. The shop interior is draped in fabrics, the foams are lining the walls. On the counter there is a telephone. To the right of the counter, there is a messy bathroom into which we can see. There is a toilet, a mirror, messy stacks of clothes and magazines with a clear shower curtain. Outside of the laden in a grassy spot beneath the telephone pole is a Penner's lair. It is dirty and oil stained with messy blankets. There is a tall stack of cans in a pyramid that the hobo has obsessively built. We see his guitar, Strassenmagazin and Vietnam veteran jacket. A large campy flower grows next to the pole where the Butterfly lives.

The song 'Miss Broadway' comes on by Belle Epoque. The Schaumstoffladen sign lights up. Penny enters onto the balcony and struts down. She is looking rough, she had a long night. Her headscarf on she walks haughtily to the beat of the song. She unlocks the laden and goes inside. She goes into the bathroom and starts freshening up in the mirror. Next, a man walks down the sidewalk with a briefcase, the Schaumstoffladen owner. He walks behind the counter, starts setting up for the day. Penny sticks her head out, half made up. Pablo just looks at her. She yanks shut the curtain.

     PABLO: If I had five of you Penny, I would have a nickel. *(laughs to himself)* Hey Penny: How much money does a skunk have?? One scent!
A telephone repair man comes onto the stage carrying a hammer.
     REPAIR MAN: Hello, telephone repair.
     PABLO: Oh, hello. Yeah, the phone is broken. I have been trying to call Penny—I wanted to ask her if we could get together and make some cents, if know what I mean ... hahaha.
     REPAIR MAN *(very serious)*: Well, sir. Let's have a look.
He inspects the telephone that is on the counter. Tests receiver, etc.
     REPAIR MAN: It appears the problem isn't your telephone, therefore it's gotta be the line. I'm gonna have to go check the pole.
He walks outside and climbs up the pole. He starts banging it with the hammer.
The Penner wakes up.
     PENNER *(sighs)*: AHH!
He rolls over in bed. Lying on his side, he has a little strum on his guitar.
The Butterfly flies over to him.
     PENNER: Oh good morning Butty. How's it shaking today?
The Penner starts playing his morning medieval jig song. Butty does his morning tai chi. Butty seems happy.
     PENNER: Yea Butty, I'm in a good mood today too. I got lotsa things I wanna do today.
     PABLO: Penny? What do you call a blonde with a dollar bill on the top of their head??? All you can eat, under a buck! *(cracks himself up)*
Penny sticks her head out of the curtain and blows some smoke.
     PABLO: Let's get this day started right, Penny! Get all shined up in there!
'My Forbidden Lover' by Chic comes on. Penny is ready and feeling herself. She spins around the laden in a pink kimono. She dances out to the Penner, he is captivated by her. Butty flutters over to her and they dance for a moment. She struts down the sidewalk, it's a beautiful day, she dances back up to the laden and leans against the pole. She lights a

cigarette. The music fades.
Telephone Repair Man comes down.
>REPAIR MAN: Well, well, I think the problem should be all fixed, Madame! If you need
>>me again, just give me a call!
>>*EXITS*

Penny is not really interested. She slinks over to the Penner.
>PENNER: So, Penny. How are you today? You look nice.
>TELEPHONE POLE: Yeah Penny, you look reeeaal nice today. MMMMmmm.
>PENNER: You think you could sneak me a little stack from in there?
>I'm getting a little sore.

Penny pretends not to hear. She prunes herself, picks lint, smokes.
Shows off her legs to the Penner.
Enter Poodle Man. 'Nice & Slow' comes on by Jesse Green (with barking sounds). The
poodle is on wheels, it is his puppet. He throws a ball, the poodle chases it, etc. It barks, he
pets it, etc. Eventually, they arrive at the Laden. Penny loves the doggy, she pets him.
>PABLO: Hello sir, how are you today?
>POODLE MAN: I'm good, looking for something for my pup.
>PABLO: What a beautiful animal. What sort of a thing did you have in mind for that
>>special doggy?
>POODLE MAN: Well, I need something that he can lie on for his naps. Something for
>>good dreams.
>PABLO: I think I have just the thing!

He goes to the foams and fuddles around a bit, throwing things in the air. He comes out
with a foam.
>>Here it is! The Barkstoff 300. Made for animals, but with a human touch, I think you
>>will find it perfect for him. Let him smell it!
>POODLE MAN: Ok!

He goes out to the poodle and lets him smell the foam.
>>Look! He loves it!!
>PABLO: What did I say?
>POODLE MAN: I will take it. How much?
>PABLO: 44.50 or three installments of 15 with our schaum plan.
>POODLE MAN: That's nothing! I will pay it all now.

He lays down stacks on the table and walks away with the foam.
Reprise of 'Nice and Slow'. Penny follows the poodle out of the laden, sad to see it go. She
leans against the pole and lights a cigarette. Poodle Man exits. MUSIC FADES.
>PABLO: First sale of the day, Penny! Just like that. Penny, we gonna get some cash
>>today!!

The telephone rings.
>PABLO: Penny!

Penny ignores it.
>PABLO: PENNNYYYY ... !
>PABLO *(answers himself)*: Hello SCHAUMSTOFFLADEN
>>*(VERY SERIOUS)*
>>Ah, yes. Mr. El Coco.
>>I am well, thank you.

Ok.
Ok.
So, squishy or not squishy?
Fat or skinny?
Thin or thick?
Modern or old-fashioned?
Fluffy or ...?
Yes. Yes. Come immediately. I've got just the thing.
(Hangs up the phone.)
PABLO: Get ready Penny, we gotta biiiiig client coming in.

'Oh, L'Amour' by Giorgio Moroder comes on. El Coco comes out.
Penny snaps to attention. She goes into the laden. She takes off her kimono. She ties on her apron. She clips a flower in her hair. She sprays on some perfume.
Enter El Coco, the music fades.

PABLO: Well hello my good man. How are you today?

EL COCO: HM. Good. I just called, I need some schaum.

PABLO: Well, I can tell you that you have come to the right place!
I have soft schaum, firm schaum, long schaum, short schaum and anything in between.

EL COCO: I need something real soft, like I told you man!!

PABLO: Well let me show you our sleepy schaums! I have many! Here is the soft-and-good schaumstoff mehrschlaf, and here we have the fluffy-and-nice schaum-max, and here we have the schaum xx feeling and pleasure. All top of the line schlafschaum!!

EL COCO: Hm. Lemme try em.

PABLO: Oh yes, by all means!!

Pablo lays out the foams on the counter and the man begins to lie on them hornily.

PABLO: Penny! Can you please bring Mr. El Coco here some jasmine tea over here? It aids in relaxation.

Penny comes in with her tea set, acting extra sexy, hands El Coco a cup of tea, then slowly pours him a cup. Staring into each other's eyes, El Coco takes a sip. He puts the tea cup back down on the tray and Penny walks back over to the toilet.

EL COCO: Nah, hurts my knees! You know I can't have my knees hurtin in my business! *(He throws down the foam off the table.)*

PABLO: Ah yes, the knees are very sensitive. Try the others!

EL COCO *(lays down on the next foam)*: Nope. How am I expected to get freaky on this?!!

PABLO: Well, please do not hesitate to try them all!

EL COCO: Yesssss, ahhhhhh. Now this is one is Allll Riight.

PABLO: Yes, yes the schaum xx feeling and pleasure. An excellent choice.

EL COCO: Oh yeaaaaa. This foam is bangin!!! Hey foxy lady, *(gesturing towards Penny)* wanna come ova here and lay with me for a sec?

PABLO: Why absolutely, Mr. El Coco! Penny, please help this man with his schaum!

Penny goes over to El Coco. She hops up on the counter and they spoon for a moment.

EL COCO: Ohhh yeaa! I can get down to this. I'll take two!
Thanks Lady, you are lookin fly today. How bout I come pick you up after you get off work?

Penny swings her legs back over, abashed.
El Coco jumps down off the counter. Reprise 'Oh L'Amour'.
> I'll come pick you up at six. I know a little spot where we can get down!

Penny drifts over across the stage as he exits, waving goodbye to him. Music fades.

PABLO: Penny! Get over here! We are getting rich today!!

PENNER *(lying on the ground all nonchalant)*: You really gonna let that guy take you out Penny? That drug slingin' asshole? He's just gonna break your heart ... leave you pregnant with nowhere to go! I ain't got much Penny, but I gotta heart of GOLD, Penny—and you I'm paackin heat!!! (gestures to his own reclining self) I'm gonna get you pregnant and you're gonna move you and that baby in right here to my lil lair. Gonna get you a high on a nice healthy dose of Vitamin F!! And let me tell you ... that F doesn't stand for foam ...

Penny goes inside, shuts her curtain, slumps on the toilet, knowing that the Penner is right.
The Bee Gees' 'Love You Inside and Out' comes on.
Penny snaps out of her funk, changes into her cleaning lady outfit and cleans.
The Jew enters, takes his time. He walks, throws glitter down from the balcony, throws a big gold coin at the Penner ... The Jew exits and the music fades.
Baby crying track is heard offstage for a few beats.
George McCrae's 'Rock My Baby' comes on.
A mother enters carrying a fake baby. She tries to hush it. As she makes her way down from the balcony, a life size baby enters alone. She stands and screams.

BABY: MAMAAAAAA ... MAAAMAAAAAA
WAAAAAA
WAAAAHHHH

Mother rushes in after her.

MOTHER: Shhhhhhh baby mama is here!!

BABY: WAhhhhhhhh :(:(:(:(

MOTHER: I know, I know, it's ok. *(takes her hand)*

They arrive at the laden and open the door.

PABLO: Hello! What a beautiful child! How old is she?

MOTHER: Oh, thank you, she just turned two.

BABY: WAAAAAAA

MOTHER: I think it's almost naptime!

PABLO: Well let's get her a good schaum, get her real comfy!!

MOTHER: That's exactly why we are here!

PABLO: Well, I have many great baby schaums. *(He pulls out a box of little foams and holds them in the air.)*

PABLO: Here is the Bambi Baby, the Dolce Baby Angelina, Dolce Baby Nico ...

MOTHER: Well, shall we try them?

PABLO: Please, go ahead!

The baby sits on each and then screams because she doesn't like them.

MOTHER: Nope!!

They go through about four, then finally,

BABY: GAGAIIIII :):):)

MOTHER: Oh perfect, she loves it!! We'll take it. THANKS!!

BABY: GAGA

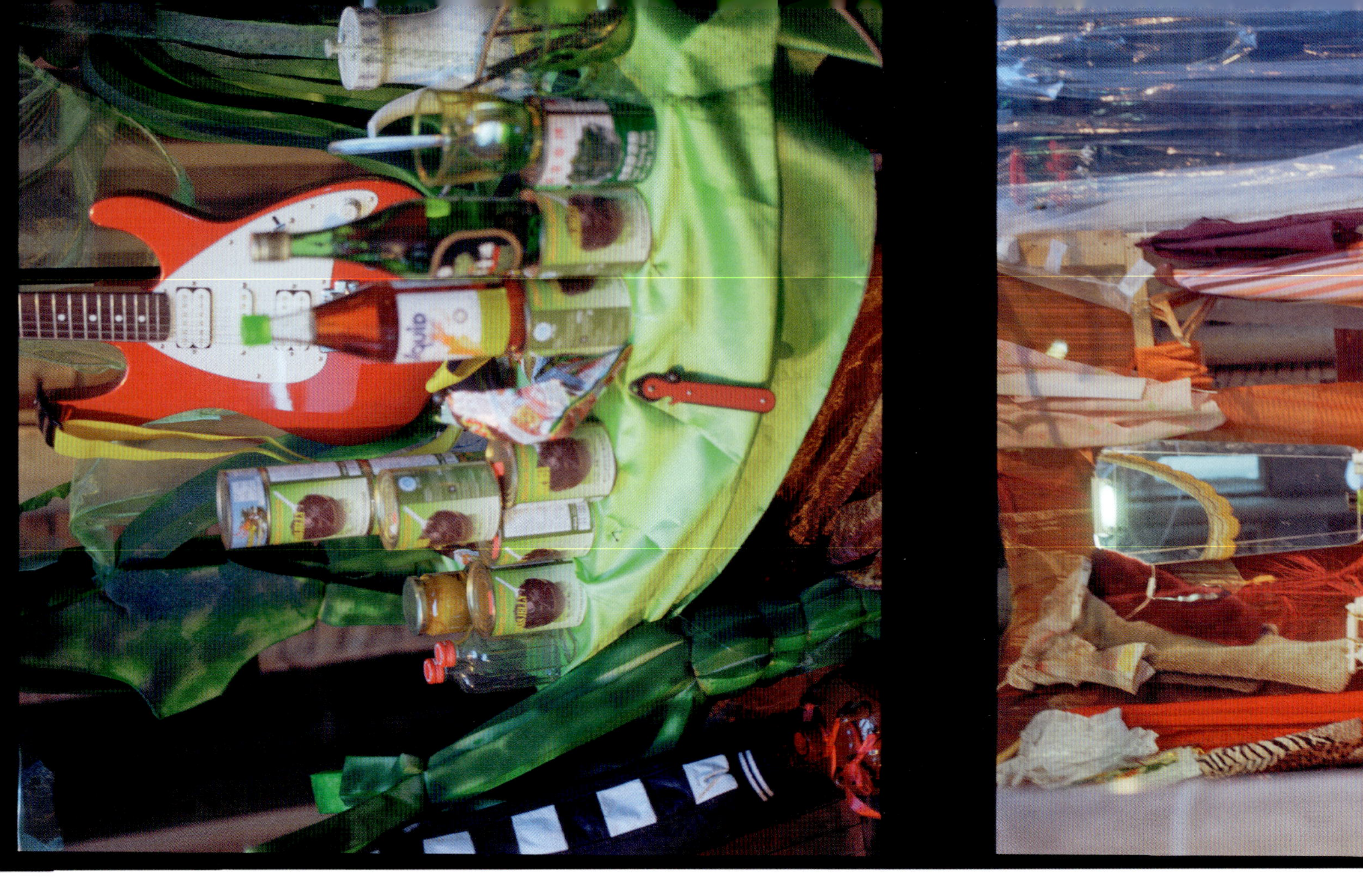

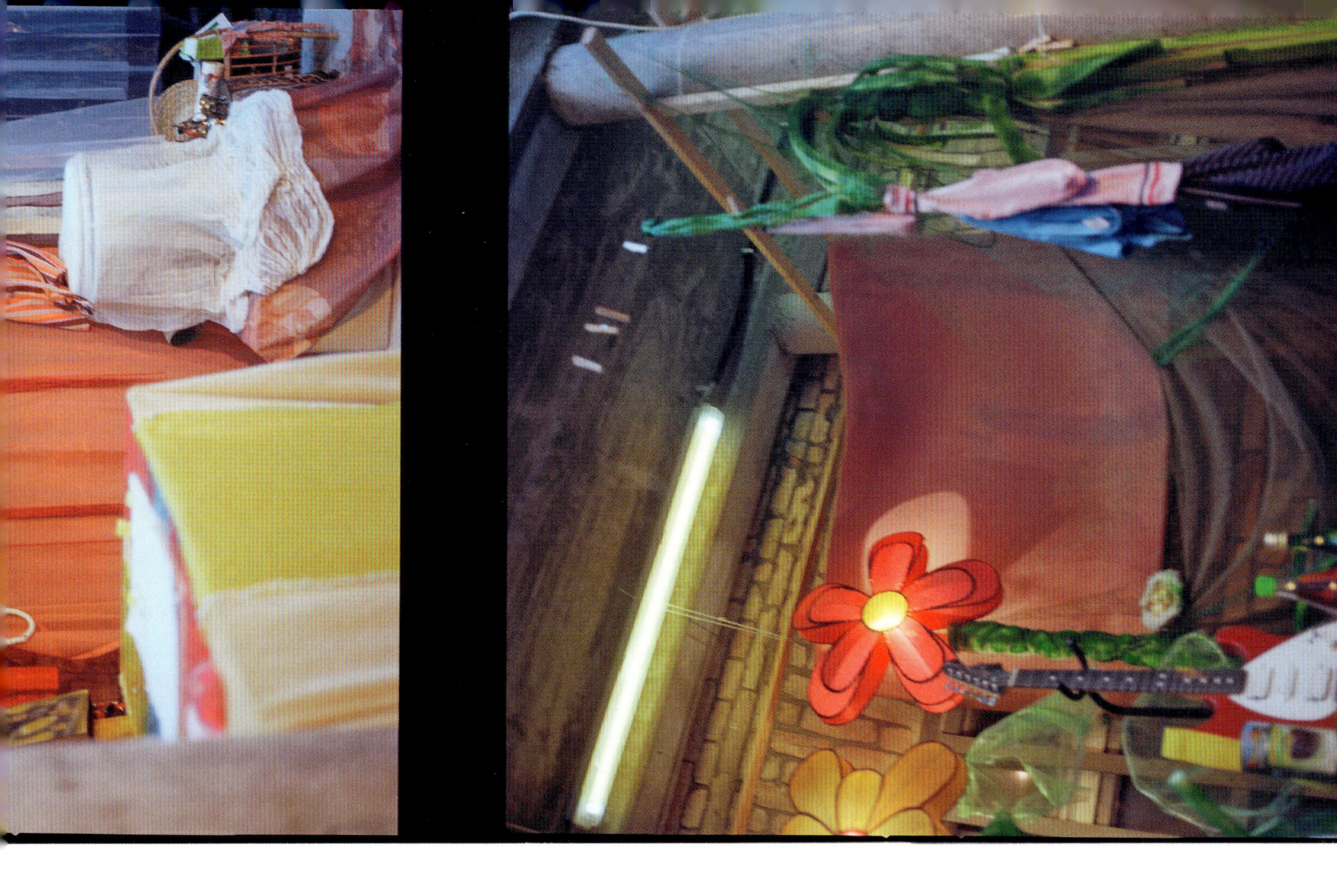

PABLO: Perfect!

MOTHER: Goodbye! Wave goodbye to the nice foam man, honey!

BABY: WAAAA

They take the foam and walk off the stage.

LUNCH TIME

PABLO: What should we order for lunch Penny? Did u bring any cash today?? Hey Penny, what happens when you give 61 dollars to a blonde?? She wants 8 more!!

Penny scoffs but not too phased.

PABLO: *(dials up on the phone)*: Hi, yea, let me get two of the specials, please. Yea the lunch special. Extra crispy, please. With two cokes. *(hangs up)* Said they'll be here in 5 minutes, Penny. Get ready!

Penny powders her nose.

Delivery Boy rides up on roller skates.

DELIVERY BOY: Delivery!

Pablo walks out to meet him. He takes the food and walks behind the counter and begins to unwrap it.

PABLO: Chicken, chicken, coke, coke, yes good, good ...

Penny joins him at the counter. They begin to eat chicken with their hands, while Penny is transfixed by the Delivery Boy.

Delivery Boy is oblivious, doing deep bends and various exercises.

Penner has perched himself in the corner, crouching, watching Penny.

PABLO *(taking his sweeeeet time, eating chicken as he goes)*: Hey, did you ever hear the story of this girl named Penny?? Penny was a hardworking, conscientious girl, who lived on her own. Her dream in life was to go on an ocean cruise around the world.

So she scrimped, and she saved, and she saved, *(*PENNER STARTS TO CRAWL*)* and she scrimped until finally, one day, she had enough money to go on her ocean cruise.

So, she booked passage on a cruise liner—first class all the way ... The cruise started off in a grandiose scale, dancing and parties every night. *(*PENNER STROKES PENNY'S LEG*)* But Penny was a cautious girl, so she never drank, but just danced the night away. *(*PENNER TAKES HER HAND TOO*)* One night, after they had been at sea for a week, Penny was walking back to her cabin, when the heel on her left shoe broke throwing her off balance. *(PENNY STUMBLES)* If that wasn't enough, the ship chose that moment to tilt to the left. *(Penny falls down onto the toilet, legs spread)* As a result, Penny was thrown overboard. *(Penner starts eating her out, Penny still holding the chicken and staring at the Delivery Boy)* A shout was raised, and after about five minutes they found Penny. Hauling her aboard, the ship's crew realized that it was too late, poor Penny was dead. Normally, they would have done a burial at sea, but as I said before, Penny was a very conscientious girl and had written a will. In it, she specified that she wished for her body to be cremated, and kept in a jar on her parents' fireplace mantel. Her wishes were fulfilled, which just goes to show you that a Penny saved is a Penny urned!!!

A loud THUMP is heard, something fell in the bathroom during the act.

PABLO: What the hell was that?? PENNY! Where the hell are you!! PENNY
GODDAMMIT are you in there with that goddam Penner again!! PENNY!!!!
FOR CHRISTSAKES PENNY

Pablo busts open the bathroom curtain and finds them in the act.

PABLO: Get the hell outta here you dirty piece of shit!! What the hell did I say to you
before!! I'm gonna get the cops to evacuate you and your goddamn peanuts!!
Get your sweaty balls outta my shop you lush!! Penny!! You crazy ho!!

DELIVERY BOY: Uh, that'll be 15 bucks ... *(He just wants to get outta there at this
point.)*

PABLO: Ah, of course! One minute ... Penny! Goddamit Penny *(licking his fingers and
wiping them down his shirt)*

*Penny is unphased. She takes off her gloves and apron and starts to change into her
DATE NITE LOOK.*

PENNER *(back in his lair totally calm after the ruckus)*: Damn, that chicken smells
good.

TELEPHONE POLE: It sure does, mmhmm!!

PENNER: Oh Telly, why can't we ever order lunch together? I sure get hungry after all!!
that making love. You could call, couldn't you??

TELEPHONE POLE: Mmmmhmmm I suuuure can!

*The Penner gets out his guitar, and 'Call Me' by Lyndsey de Paul comes on. Duet between
him and telephone pole, butterfly on bass.*

*As the song finishes, a drunken shout comes from upstairs: banging of a beer bottle is
heard against the railing.*

'Big Black Funky Slave' by Eddie Simpson comes on.

*Drunk Man comes out. He is heartbroken over a woman. He is wearing a worker's blue
jumpsuit.*

*He swills beer and spits it on the ground yelling. He punches the wall and hits the railings
with his beer bottle.*

He gets downstairs with a yell, staggers up to the laden, spilling beer everywhere.

DRUNK *(to the Penner)*: Heyyyyyyyyyyyyyyy.

PENNER: Hi there.

DRUNK: EYYYYYY why u do that?

PENNER: I'm not doing anything.

TELEPHONE POLE: He's reaaal drunk!

PENNER: I think you should get a cup of coffee or something.

DRUNK: I DON'T WANNNNAAAAACOFFFFEE.

PENNER: Ok, it was just a suggestion.

DRUNK: AHHHHHHHH. *(tips over bottle, it is empty)* U gotta beeer??

PENNER: No man, go to the bodega, it's just down the street.

DRUNK: I DONNNWANNA GO TO NOOOOOOO BODDDEGGGAAAAAA.

PENNER: Wow, alcohol. The rose colored glasses of life. You know what, I have a
bottle of whisky here. Looks like you could use a drink.

DRUNK: YEEEEEEAAAAAAAAAAAAAAAAA gimmmmme.

PENNER *(takes a big guzzle first)*: Here you go!

Drunk swigs from the bottle, he falls over.

PENNER *(yelling into the window)*: Hey Penny!!! This man needs a foam!!

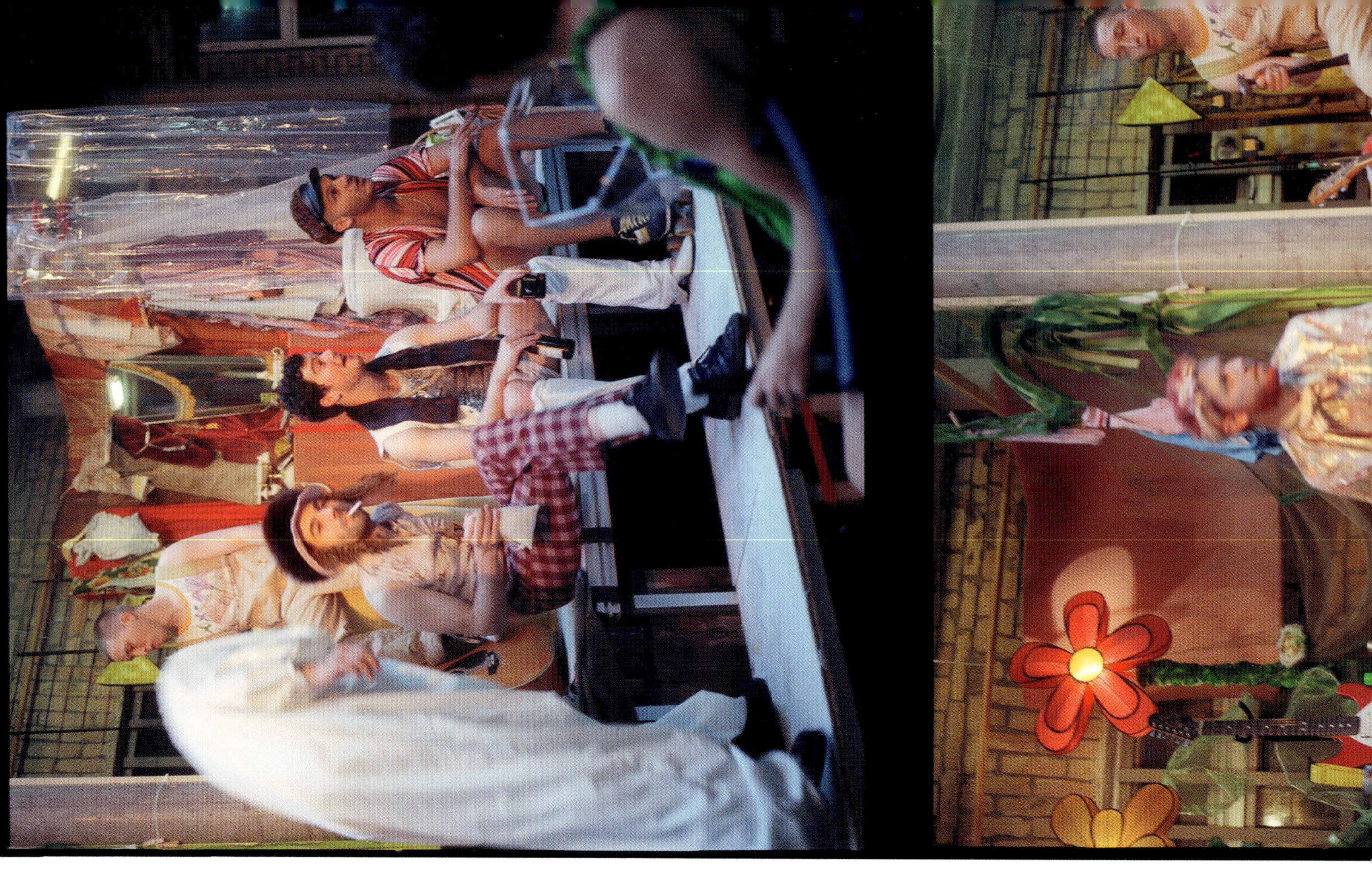

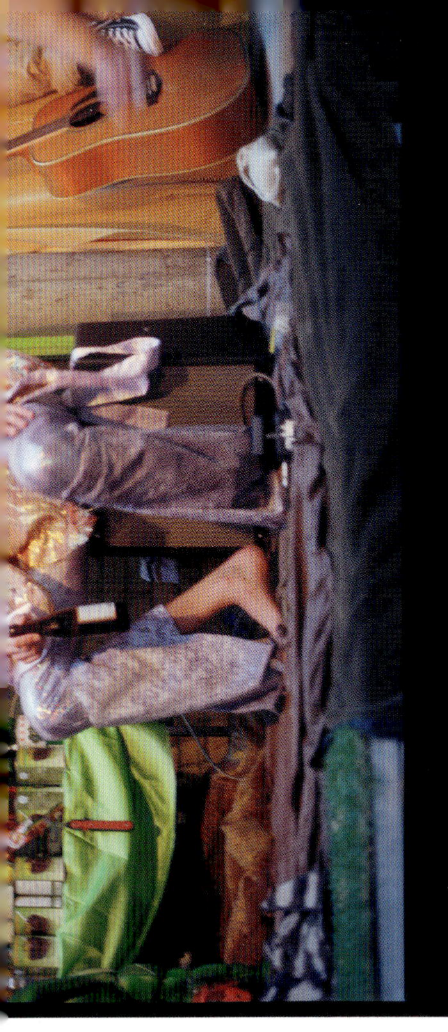
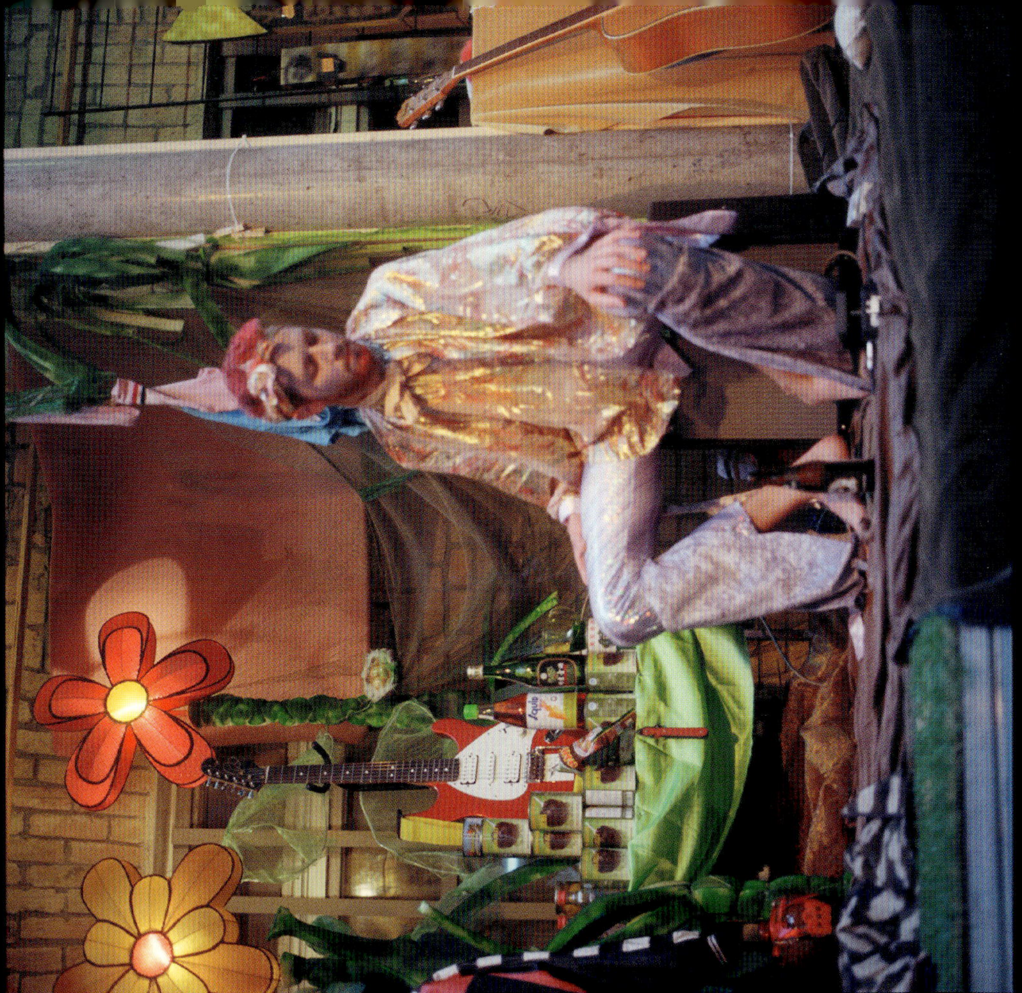

Penny runs out with a foam for him. Penny takes a wad of cash out of his pocket and shakes her head. The Drunk gets all comfy with his schaum under his head. The butterfly flies over and sits on top of him.

PENNER: Hey Penny, remember me?

Penny twirls her hair, shrugs, goes back inside.

PENNER: So what's up with you? Hung up on a lady?

DRUNK: AAAArrrrssssh.

PENNER: Let me tell you a little bit about my lady ... she's the best one of all ...
Her name is Penny ...
(in his 'poet' mood)
Succulent as she is divine,
I drink her down like a goblet of plum wine.
Like dew on the honeysuckle's vine,
Where the bee sucks,
There suck I
In a cowslip's bell
I lie.
There I couch
When owls do cry
On the bat's back
I do fly.
All summer at ACUD
Merrily, merrily
Shall I know
Which blossom
Hangs in the nude.
She's the only address I call home
Posted outside,
Like a garden gnome.
I wait there
While she sells foam.
I come to her out of the blue
To help her out
A twist and a nut,
Just a turn of the ole Phillips screw.
Love and harmony combine,
And round our souls entwine,
While thy branches mix with mine,
And our fruits together toot.
Such wilt thou be to me,
Who when at ACUD obliquely run;
Thy firmness makes my circle just,
And makes me end,
Where I just come.

DRUNK: BahhhhhhhhHHHHHHHHHHHHHHHHh Goddamn poemmmzllll

The drunk runs offstage.

The Chimney Sweeps enter with their brooms, they are all sooty faced with hats and jump-suits that are also filthy with soot. One of them has a limp. They do a little dance. Penny comes out and joins in on their dance.
The music fades, they pose, applause.
They all squeeze into the schaumstoffladen.

 PABLO: Hello fellas. What can I get for you?
 CHIMNEY SWEEP 1: Something soft, please. Our bodies are aching.
 CHIMNEY SWEEP 2 *(piping up from the back)*: Yea! I got stuck in a chimney today! They had to pour oil down so I could wiggle out!
 PABLO: Well sirs, I would say you've got the hardest jobs in the world.
 CHIMNEY SWEEP 3: Yea! You know, I haven't seen my family in ten years. They sold me to the chimney sweep master when I was only six!! Now I am just a serf.
 PABLO: Well that is just terrible to hear, just terrible!
 CHIMNEY SWEEP 2: And then, Master Chimney beat me because I couldn't clean fast enough! He hit me ten times on the head with his metal pail!
 PABLO: Well, I'll be damned.
 HEAD CHIMNEY SWEEP: It is really hard for us. Just last year I got chimney sweep cancer! It was on my scrotum and then they had to remove it! Now I will never ever have children or a wife. No happily ever after for me, nope.
 PABLO: Who needs it anyway??
 CHIMNEY SWEEP 2: Sometimes soot gets into my eyes and they are so swollen that they shut! And I can't see a single thing!
 PABLO *(getting realllllly bored)*: That's just terrible.
 CHIMNEY SWEEP 3: Yeah. I got stuck once in the flue and then my leg got alllll bent outta shape. Now I walk with a limp until the day I die!
 PABLO: Well I'll say, it's a tough life for a chimney sweep!
The Chimney Sweeps all nod their heads sadly.
 CHIMNEY SWEEP 1: You've got no idea.
 PABLO: Well take these foams!
 CHIMNEY SWEEP 1: How much are they? We don't have very much money.
 PABLO: You know what, all these will cost you is a PRETTY PENNY!
 CHIMNEY SWEEP 1: A Penny? That's a deal!
 PABLO: PENNY??
Penny goes up to each of them and gives them a kiss.
 PABLO: Poor chaps. They can't catch a break. Penny, we've really got it made!
Bubble Boy comes on from downstairs. He has a big bubble boy suit on because he cannot be touched by the outside world. He goes up to the laden and then jams himself inside.
 BUBBLE BOY: Hi.
 PABLO: Hello young man, how are you?
 BUBBLE BOY: I'm okay.
 PABLO: What can I get for you?
 BUBBLE BOY: I need something without germs.
 PABLO: What are you talking about?
 BUBBLE BOY: I have an immunodeficiency. Ever since I was a little kid I have lived inside a bubble. I have never touched even my own mother's hands. My doctor

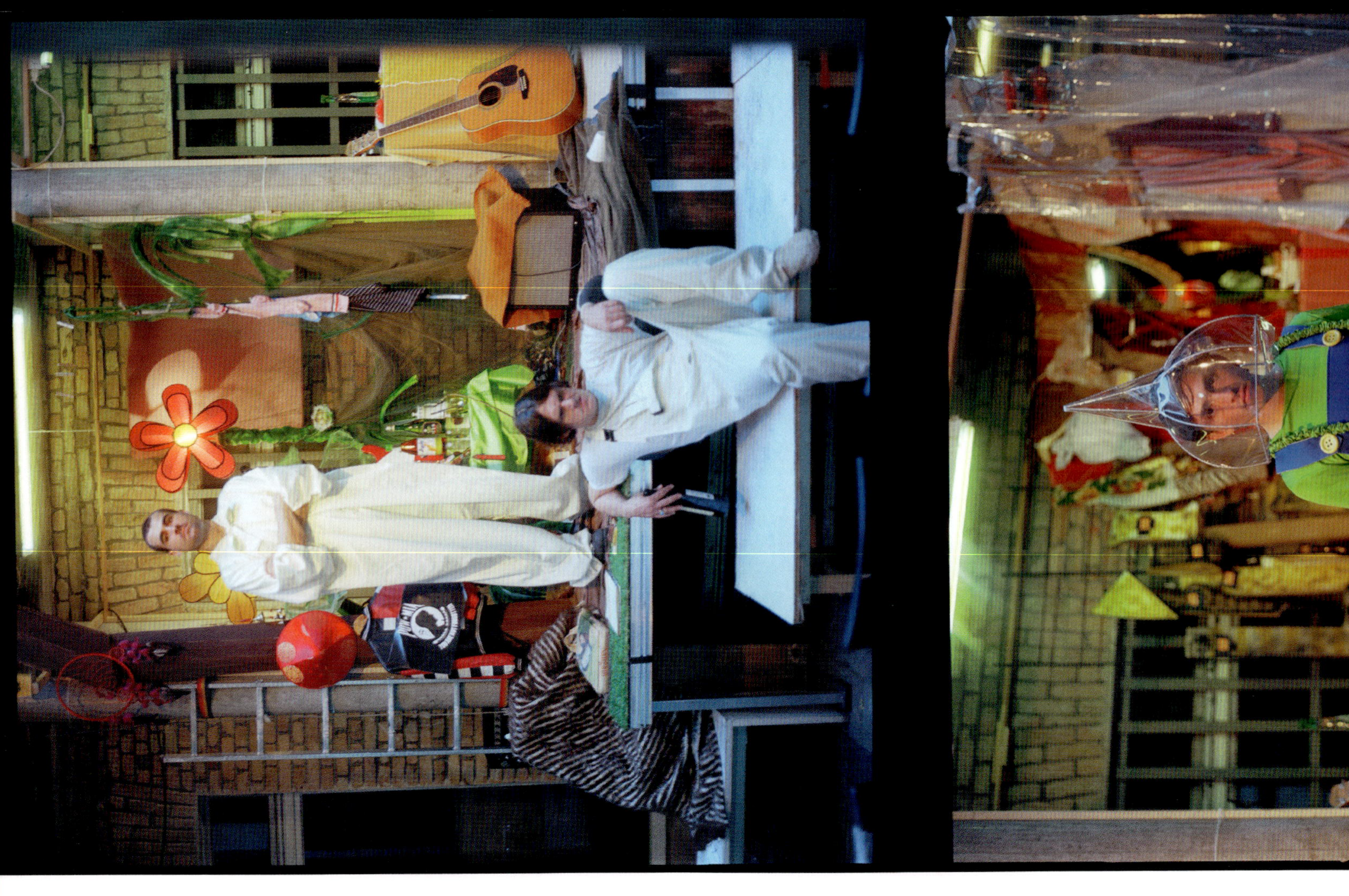

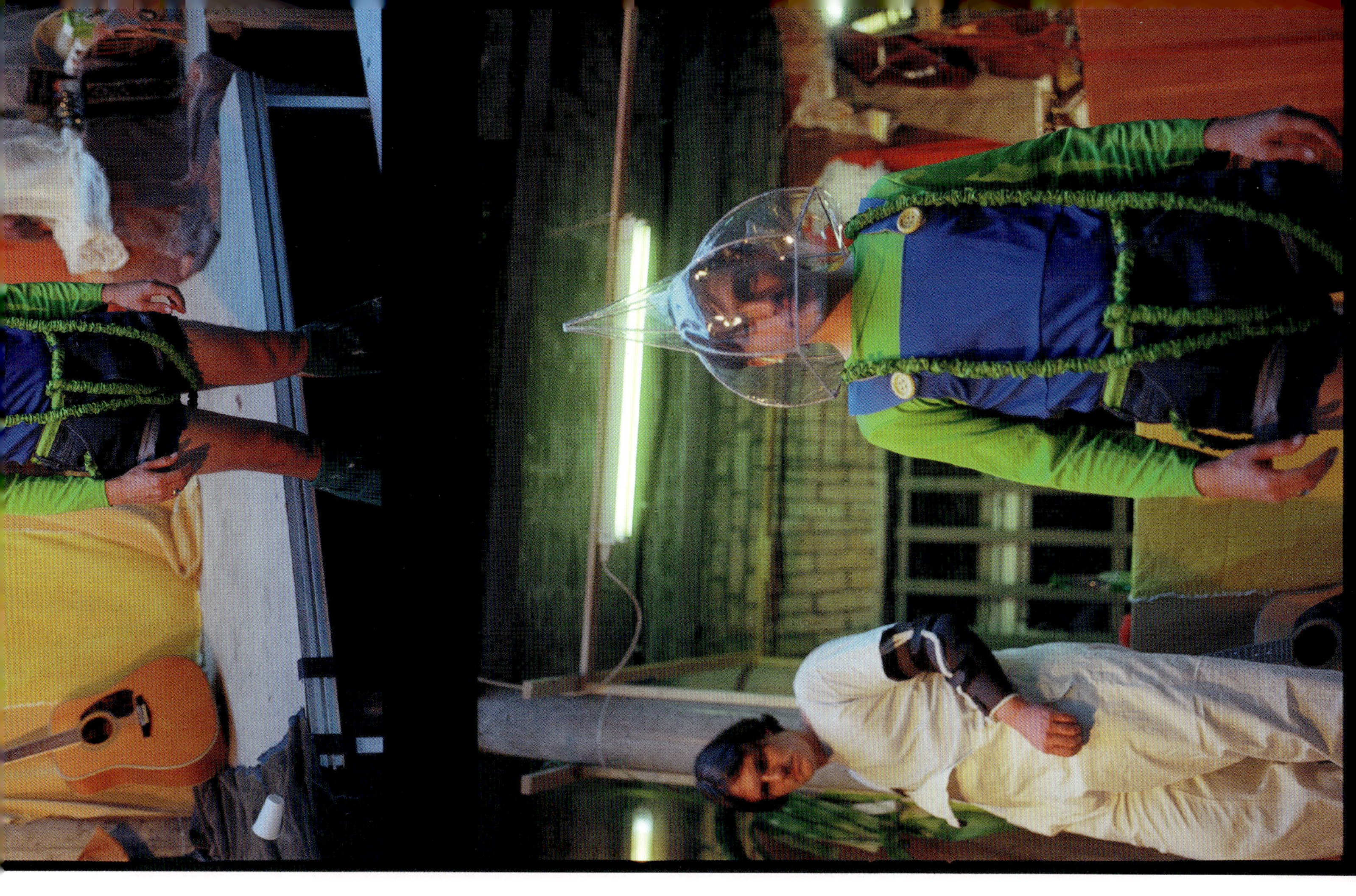

says that if I come into contact with the world I will die! I have never kissed a girl,
never felt sand sift through my fingers. I have never felt a breeze across my face!
I have never even looked into the eyes of my one friend, I only ever see him
through the foggy glass of my bubble. Eventually he stopped visiting because he
wanted to play sports with the other boys. So mostly I am just alone now.
Sometimes I talk to my grandma on the telephone.
*Penny sees Bubble Boy and her heart is wrenching. She starts to silently cry as he tells his
story. Pablo sees her crying and starts to pretend to cry too. He uses the teapot to drizzle
tears on his face.*

    BUBBLE BOY: After all my struggles, I just want a comfortable place to rest my head.
        But this suit is always getting in my way. I need something highly customized!!!!!
    PABLO: Right away, yes, yes. Penny! Please take his measurements immediately!!!
        We are gonna fix you right up!!
*Penny wipes her tears and gets a measuring tape and safety pins. She starts taking
measurements.*
A loud POPPING sound is heard.

    BUBBLE BOY: What was that??????? OH NO! MY SUIT, MY SUIT. IT'S GOTTA
        HOLE!!!! AHH.
He runs outside the laden, Penny runs after him, freaking out.

    BUBBLE BOY: Oh my god!! The air! It smells so fresh and good!!
        I am going to die!!
He runs over to the Penner, sees the flower.

    BUBBLE BOY: I have never even smelled a flower before!!!
*Takes a deep breath of the flower. Starts sneezing and coughing, grabbing his throat,
clearly dying. They try and make him as comfortable a bed as possible. They roll over the
drunk and put his foam under the Bubble Boy. Bubble Boy lays his head in Penny's lap.*

    BUBBLE BOY: GOODBYE WORLD!! *(dies)*
THE CLOCK STRIKES SIX.
Penny silently wipes her tears, rolling his corpse off her lap.
'Love for the Sake of Love' by Claudja Barry comes on.
Penny goes inside. Shuts her curtain. QUICK CHANGE into her DATE NITE LOOK.
*Penny flings open the door looking gorgeous for date nite. She runs outside, eagerly
awaiting El Coco to come pick her up. Checking her watch.*

    PENNER: Penny, where are ya goin Penny?
Penny ignores him, looking for El Coco.

    PENNER: Penny why'd you have to wear that dress, Penny, you know it's my favorite
        dress!! *(He is getting desperate, on his knees imploring her.)* PENNY, you're not
        gonna go out with that Jackass are you Penny—PENNYYY!!!! Please Penny!
She completely ignores him.
*Finally, El Coco enters and struts to the laden. She jumps into his arms. She waves
goodbye as he carries her offstage.*

    PENNER *(crawling after them)*: No, Penny, no!! Don't do this to me Penny, I love ya
        Penny, PENNNYYY!!
Penny blows air kisses to Pablo and the Penner, waving. Butty flutters after them.

THE END

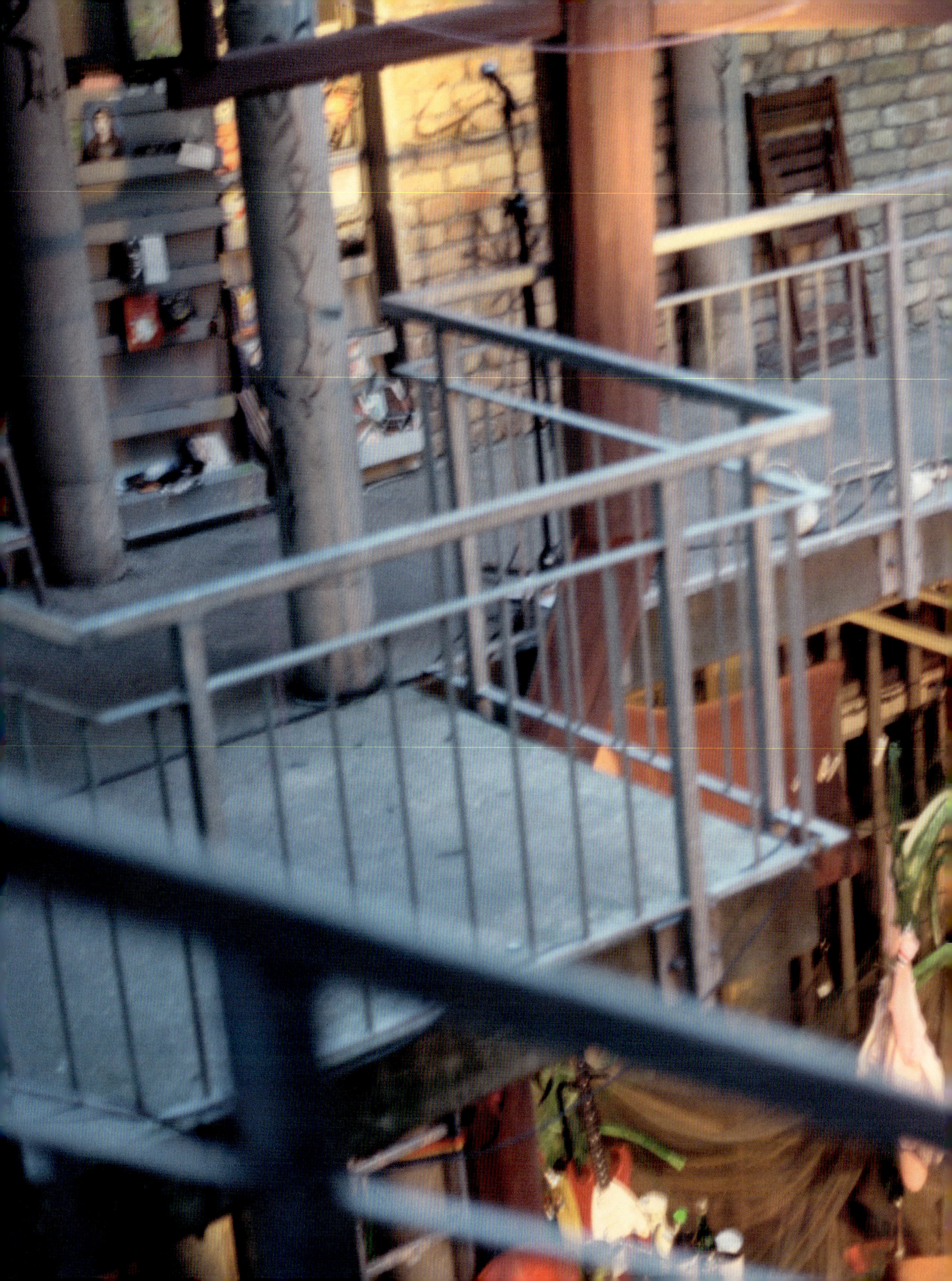

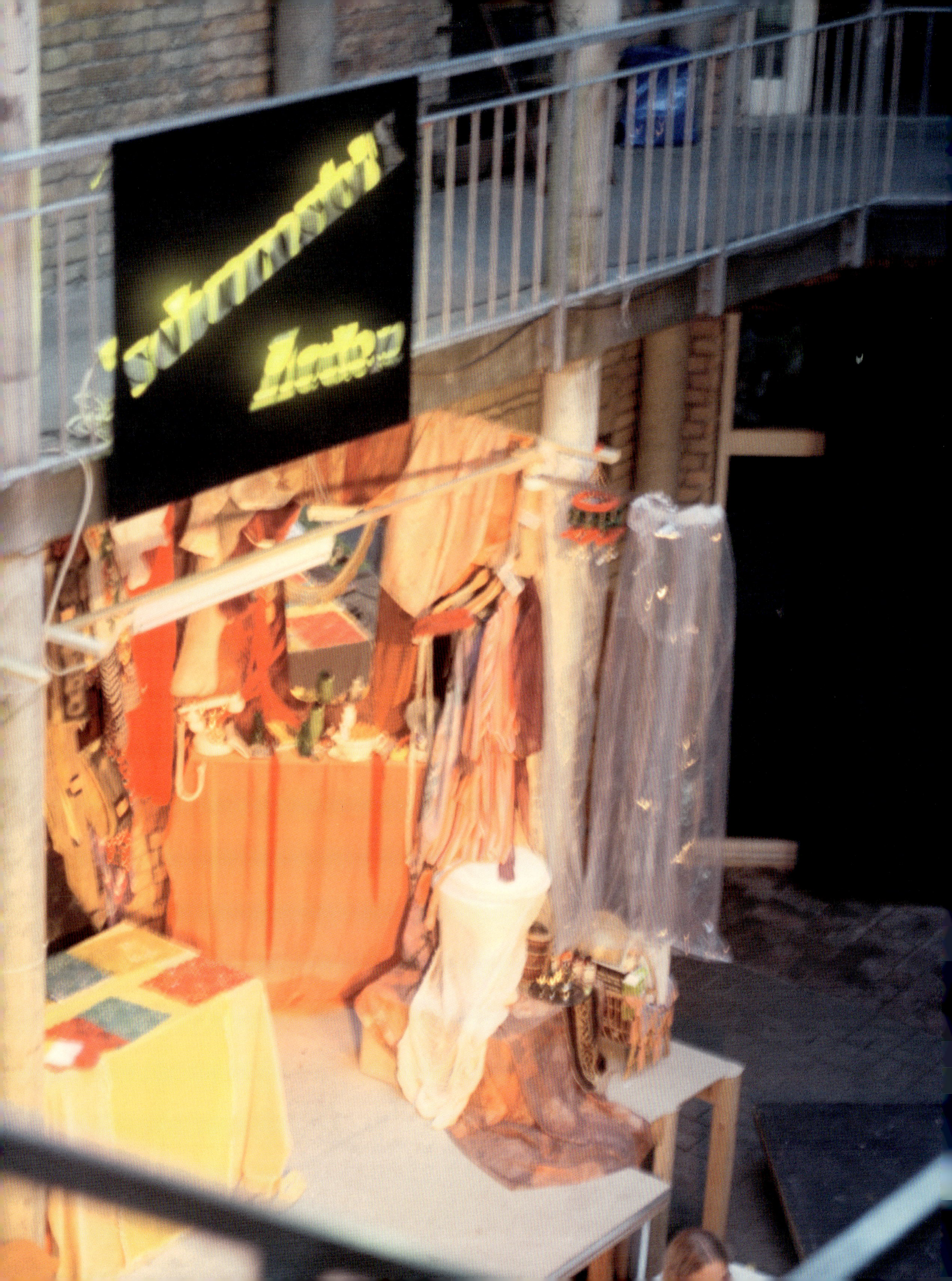

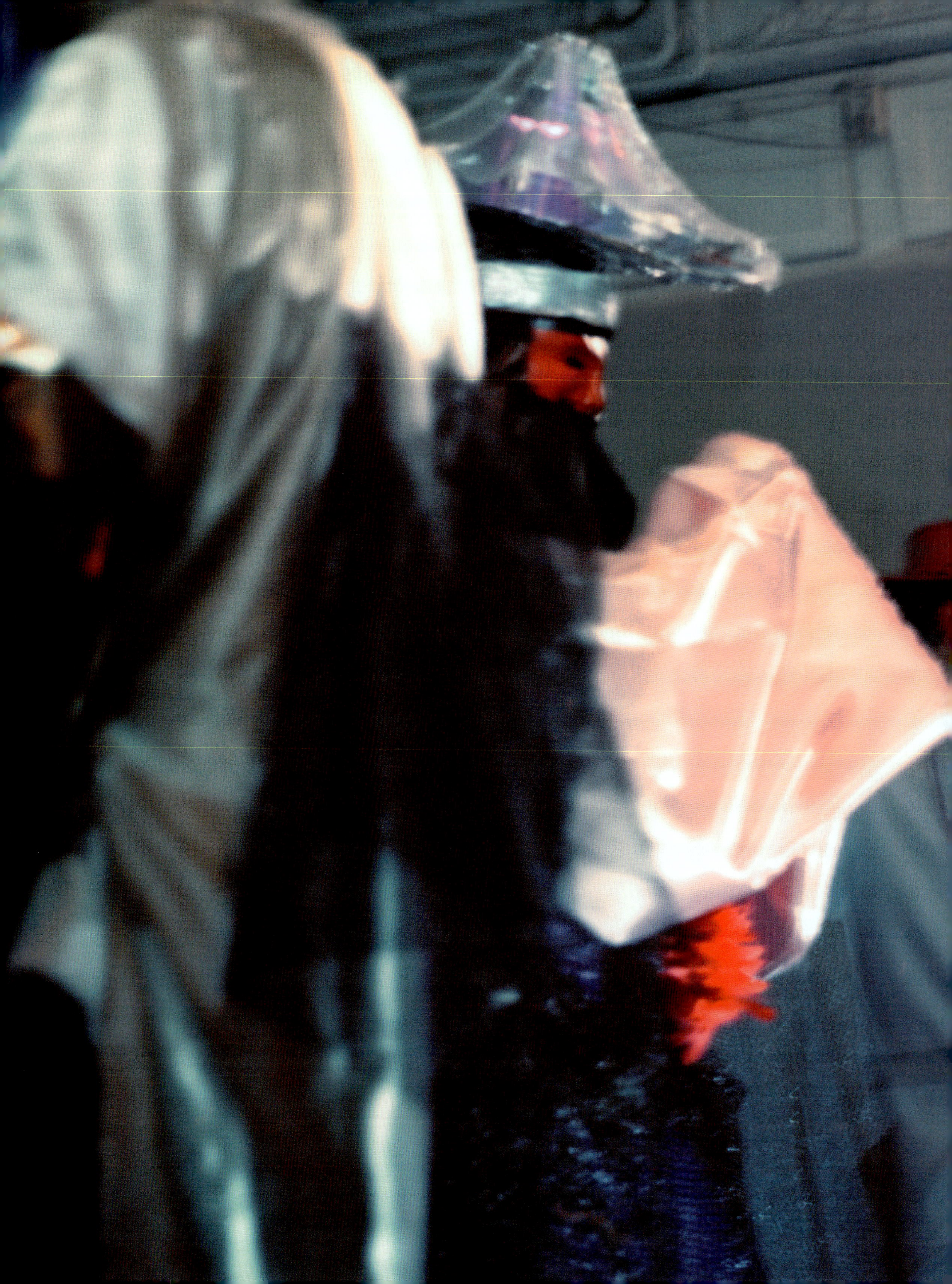

DD MOOD

Written by Georgia Gardner Gray
Originally performed at New Theater Berlin, October 30, 31 & November 1, 2014

Taschi—Natascha Goldenberg
Silvia—Sydney Beaumont
Maria—Tamen Perez
Primo—Grayson Revoir
Jil / Stenographer—Jil Lange
Bianca / Stenographer—Bianca Heuser
British Father / Monster—Maximilian Zentz Zlomovitz
British Mother / Hanz—Tobias Spichtig
Gertrude—Emma Bayley
Pip—Billy Rennekamp
Therapist—Mia von Matt
Second Old Man—Michele di Menna
Third Old Man—Felix Mura

Set by Georgia Gardner Gray
Flower arrangements by Heike-Karin Föll
Costumes by Georgia Gardner Gray

Setting: Dunkin' Donuts, Sony Center, Potsdamer Platz, Berlin. Summer.

SCENE 1
Curtain. 'One Day (Vandaag)' by Bakermat plays as Taschi opens the shop: sweeps, sets up tables and chairs, puts out donuts, etc. After she's finished she lights a cigarette and looks at a magazine, boredly. There are WASPS everywhere (large puppets about the size of a shoe being waved from off stage). It seems as if the whole place has been overtaken. Behind the counter the donuts are COVERED in wasps. The wasps are buzzing around behind the counter and annoying the customers waiting online. Loud ambient BUZZZING is heard. They are crawling all over the donuts.
Silvia & Maria enter with heavy backpacks. They are very loud and obnoxious.

    SILVIA: ¿Que pasa con estas avispas?
    MARIA: ¿Sabes adonde estamos? ¡No tengo idea de adonde estamos! ¿Como hacemos para encontrar internet? ¿Y el hostal? ¡Necesitamos averiguar como llegar!
    SILVIA: ¡Jajaja estamos perdidas!
    SILVIA: ¡Ayyy estoy taaaan agotadaa! ¡Tengo taaantaa hambree y taaanta sed! ¡Necesito azucar, YA!
    MARIA: ¡¿Que son estas avispas?! ¡¿Que pasa en este lugar?! ¡Que asco! ¡No puedo mas con este bulto, pesa demasiado! ¡Necesitamos wifi para encontrar el hostal!
    SILVIA: ¡Necesito cafe!
    MARIA: ¡Y wifi!
    TASCHI *(annoyed)*: Möchten Sie etwas bestellen?
    SILVIA: I woood liike cafe ... ¿Como se dice leche?
    MARIA: ¿Meelk?
    SILVIA: No se que quiero, ¿que quierooo? Quiero, woood liike ... ¿Frambuesa? ¿Crema?
    MARIA: NO NO ¡chocolaaateee! ¡¡¡¡¡Dulce de leche!!!!!! ¿Mango? ¡Tal vez tienen mango! ¿Coco?
    TASCHI: DONUT?! KAFFEE? WHAT YOU WANT?
    SILVIA: ¿Bathroom?
    MARIA: ¿Wifi?
    TASCHI *(pointing)*: STARBUCKS, SONY CENTER.
    MARIA: ¡Vamanos, Silvia!
Maria and Silvia gather their bags and exit.
Primo walks on stage, he is our guy. His fingers do a few taps as he takes a look at the donuts. The wasps buzz around him, he tries to swat them away.
    PRIMO: Ich hätte gern Nummer dreizehn, bitte.
    TASCHI: Nummer dreizehn, Donut mit Eiskaffee? Milch, Zucker?
    PRIMO: Ohne Milch, aber mit Zucker.
Taschi prepares the coffee. Primo continues to swat away the wasps.
    PRIMO *(referring to the wasps in bad German)*: Sie haben harte Arbeit!
    TASCH *(kind of smiles, but doesn't give a fuck)*: Welcher Donut?
    PRIMO: Boston Cream bitte. *(She rings him up.)* Danke.
Primo sits down, and his thoughts are played as voiceover, spoken as thoughts would be— slowly and with pauses. Taschi continues smoking and reading her magazine.
    PRIMO VOICEOVER: Every day started with DD. It did not matter what ... small

inconveniences might stand in my way. It was doubtful that I should be in any
particular rush. The combination of sugar, fat and caffeine has this pleasing effect
on me that I just cannot deny myself ...
(Primo stirs the sugar into his Eiskaffee and savors the first sip.)
I like a classic DD: Double Choc, Boston Creme, or maybe just Chocolate Frosted.
The fancy flavors don't really suit my purpose. DD is where I start my day.
No matter what time of day it is. Then is the time.
*Jil and Bianca enter, walk up to the counter. They are talking. He takes an interest in them.
They order quietly from Taschi.*
I doubt the DD really has the same effect on other people. They just come and go,
in and out. Get the donut, get the coffee, ja. I know what I am here for, but I wonder
what it is that brings them here ...
(Primo ponders this question, a few beats pass.)
As I have the DD, a certain ... mood comes over me. Let's call it the DD Mood.
With each sip of coffee, my mind expands. I rise to a kind of heightened state.
Thoughts come rushing. The cork is removed, and the flow begins.
(He sips, taking a look at the coffee cup.)
I don't care what's in it.
(He ravenously bites the donut, to chewing sounds)
NomNoMNoMNomNOm ahahahaha yesssssss mmmmmm
(mouth slightly full) I wouldn't ever try to stop the musings, I wouldn't fight the DD.
(chews, swallows)
Mmmmm. I take my time, I let the strange imaginings wash over me. As I drink
the DD the fantasies become more and more elaborate, the details more and
more generous. It's as if I have lost control my mind. 'DD mood' is a whole other
place entirely. And NOTHING needs to be done about it.
*Primo leans back and relaxes with the coffee. The next customers arrive, a British family:
a father, mother, and their two kids, Gertrude & Pip. Pip has a cast on his leg and is walking
on crutches.*
GERTRUDE: DADDYIIII DADDYIIII Look at all the waspsII DADDDYYYYYYYY I
CAAAAN'T GO INSIDEIIIIIII I just can'tII (starts to whimper) BUT I WANTED DD
DADDYII *(starts to cry)*
FATHER: Oh don't worry, it's fineI Daddy will go inside and get it. Don't worry sweetieI
Daddy will get it for you.
MOTHER: There is no reason to be scared Gertrude. You're a sweet little girl, but not
as sweet as Glazed Vanilla Kreme ... That's what mommy wants.
GERTRUDE: BUT I WANTED TO PICK IT FOR MYSELFIII *(crying)*
PIP: Daddy, is it a wasp or is it a bee?
FATHER: Now, now, everything is fine, Daddy will get all the different flavorsII You see,
Daddy will get an exciting box. There won't be any problem honey, no problem at
all. Now you just wait here and Daddy will get the box.
GERTRUDE: I DON'T WANT TO WAITIII I WANT TO PICK THE DONUTS DADDYIII
MUMMMMYYYYYY I WANT TO PICK THE DONUTSIII
PIP: BUT DADDDY I WANT TO PICK THE DONUTS TOOO DADDYII
(starts whimpering)
GERTRUDE: Pip is too stupid to get the DonutsI Only I know the good onesIII

PIP: DADDY I WANT A RUMPLE PUMPSKIN DADDY.
GERTRUDE: Shut up dummy! Cripples can't choose!!!
   (She shoves Pip out of the way, pushing over his crutches, and he wobbles on his cast foot.) DADDY I WANT BOO BOO BERRY!!
PIP *(scrambling back over)*: But she always gets to choose!! DADDY, I WANT THIMBLE JUICE.
FATHER: Now now, Pip! There is no reason to be upset! Daddy will get all of your favorite flavors: even chocolate with chocolate frosting if you would like.
MOTHER *(to father, pissed that he is being so accommodating)*: Nigel, just go inside. Pip, Gertrude, I've heard quite enough. Daddy will get the donuts. Now let's have a seat. But don't forget Mummy's Vanilla Kreme.

Mother waits with kids outside. They sit opposite Primo. He watches them with a strange purpose in his eyes. He is eating the donut. They don't notice him at all. Taschi is still bored. Buzzing from the wasps continues. Father walks up to the counter.

FATHER: Daddy *(stuttering)* Oh, I mean, I would like one Bavarian Creme, one Gruner Apfel ...
TASCHI: Zwölf Donuts für 6,99???
FATHER: Yes, yes.

Taschi takes a box and begins to fill it with donuts.

FATHER: Yes, let us see now. Apfel Zimt, yes that looks quite tasty, Heidelbeeren, yes, oh and let's try a Pflaumenmus, Vanilla Frosted, Kirsche Bananen, Himbeer Vanille ... Do you have a favorite?

Primo is amused by this exchange. He continues sipping coffee and eating his donut.

PRIMO VOICEOVER *(getting fully into his strange DD Mood)*: MMMMMMhmhmhmhmh hahaha. I can't even imagine ... hmhmhm actually ... Oh I cannn ... What a way to go ... no ... yessss ... mmhahahaha what a stranger ...
FATHER: Let's do one more ... Sprinkles, Boo Boo Berry, a Roasted Toasted Coconut, ah, perfect, yes. Great. Oh! And a Vanilla Kreme for the mummy.
TASCHI: Kaffee?
FATHER: I'll have a tea, thanks. Earl Grey with a splash of milk.
PRIMO VOICEOVER: Teeeaaaaa??? Hehehe.
TASCHI: NO TEE. KAFFEE MISTA.
FATHER: Ah I see. Well that will be all then. Thank you so very much.

He walks away without paying.

TASCHI: ENTSCHULDIGUNG!!!!!! BEZAHLEN BITTE!
FATHER *(jerking around in alarm)*: Oh dear, oh dear!!! Please excuse me!! I do apologize truly. My mistake. How much was it?
TASCHI: 6.99.
FATHER *(as Taschi rings him up)*: Here you are. Thank you so very much, have a lovely day.

Father takes the donuts back to the family. They rip open the package and start eating them. The kids bicker and grab for the donuts.

PIP: GIVE ME BOO BOO BERRY!! BOO BOO leg wants to eat too!!!
   (He stuffs a donut into the cast.)
GERTRUDE: EEEWWW

Mother, pissed off, shoos them all offstage. The lights go down, except for a spotlight on

Primo. Primo is fully in his DD Mood.

    PRIMO VOICEOVER: What is this? HAHA! I mean ... REAAAALLLYYY?
        ENTSCHULDIGUNG! I'm a Daddy too. Daddy LONNNNGGGGG
        LEGGGZZZZZZZZ haahahaha HHEHEHEHE.
        (He does some weird leg movement, the DD Mood is getting full blown.)
        Yyyeeeeeaaaaa ... Vooodoo Daddy, I'm a ... PAAPAAAA ... mmmm mmmm mmm
        (He starts dancing in his seat, the strange spider dance but with a beat now.)
        Mmm. Fuck it, fuck it DADDDDYYYYY. Bae bae bae DADDDDYYYYYY.

*While he is dancing a little in his seat, sipping coffee, taking bites of the donut, the Dunkin'
Donuts scene is blacked out and no longer visible. The buzzing fades and finally subsides.
Taschi holds up a twig under Primo's spotlight. Primo turns around and looks at it
surprised. He finally speaks aloud.*

    PRIMO: O! A twig.

*He watches the twig, still sipping, when suddenly there is a crack of thunder. Another voice
comes on the loudspeaker ... a stranger voice. It is singsongy and annoying. It recites a
poem while thunderstorm noises play in the background.*

    MONSTER VOICEOVER: The twig that bursts forth with life and squeams
        With the gentle tickles from mother queen
        Brings such a restful peace to this former tart
        There is nothing between us but a heart
        The sea between us now a single wave
        I'm nothing more than your docile slave.
        With this wooded branch
        I scribble my initial
        On your sweet egg
        Bringing forth our proteges.
        First one ... Then two. And I did like them.
        But what about ...

*The Monster emerges. He is a demented version of the father from the British family, with
the mother and children attached to him as appendages.*

    THE MONSTER *(tormented)*: MEEEEEEEEEEEEEEEEEEII MEEEEEEEEEEEEEEEEIII
        MEEEEEEEEEEEEEEEEEEIIII WHAT ABOUT MEEEEEEEEEIIIIII I am A MONSTERRRI
        A MONNNNSSTTERRRRRRRRRI A MONNNNSSSTTTERRRRRRRRRRR.
        WHHATTT HAVE I BEEECCOOMMMEEE??? I AMM OVVVEEERRRRRRRRRRR.
        I AM FINISHHEEDD. SOMEEEBODDYY HEEELLLLPPPP MEEEEEEE.
        (pause, this time in a more normal voice) It's time to see my therapist again!

SCENE 2

*The Monster collapses onto the Dunkin' Donuts counter. The Therapist enters and perches
regally on a stool. Her Stenographer enters. She is a Siamese twin, played by Jil & Bianca
from before. They set up their computer, and each has one hand typing. They type
incessantly. The Stenographer and the Therapist only speak to each other in German.
The Therapist sits and listens silently as the Monster speaks his monologue.*

    THE MONSTER *(in annoying singsong voice)*: Sooooooooo I didn't really do anything
        today ... I was boooooooredddd and thennnn ... I got a coooofffeeeeee ... I was at
        wooorkkk but I didn't do annnyyytthhinnnggggggg realllyyyyy ...

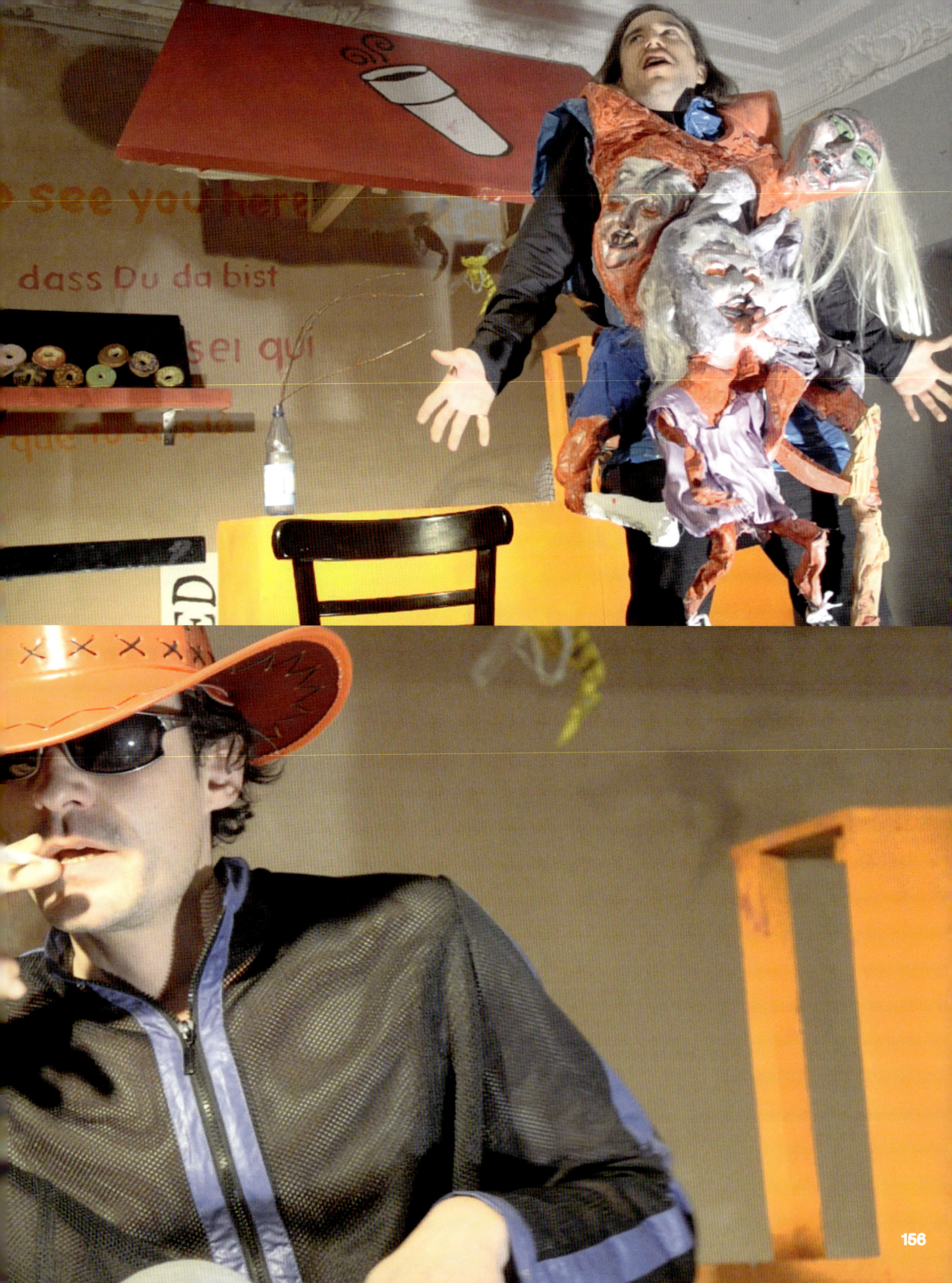
see you here
dass Du da bist
sei qui

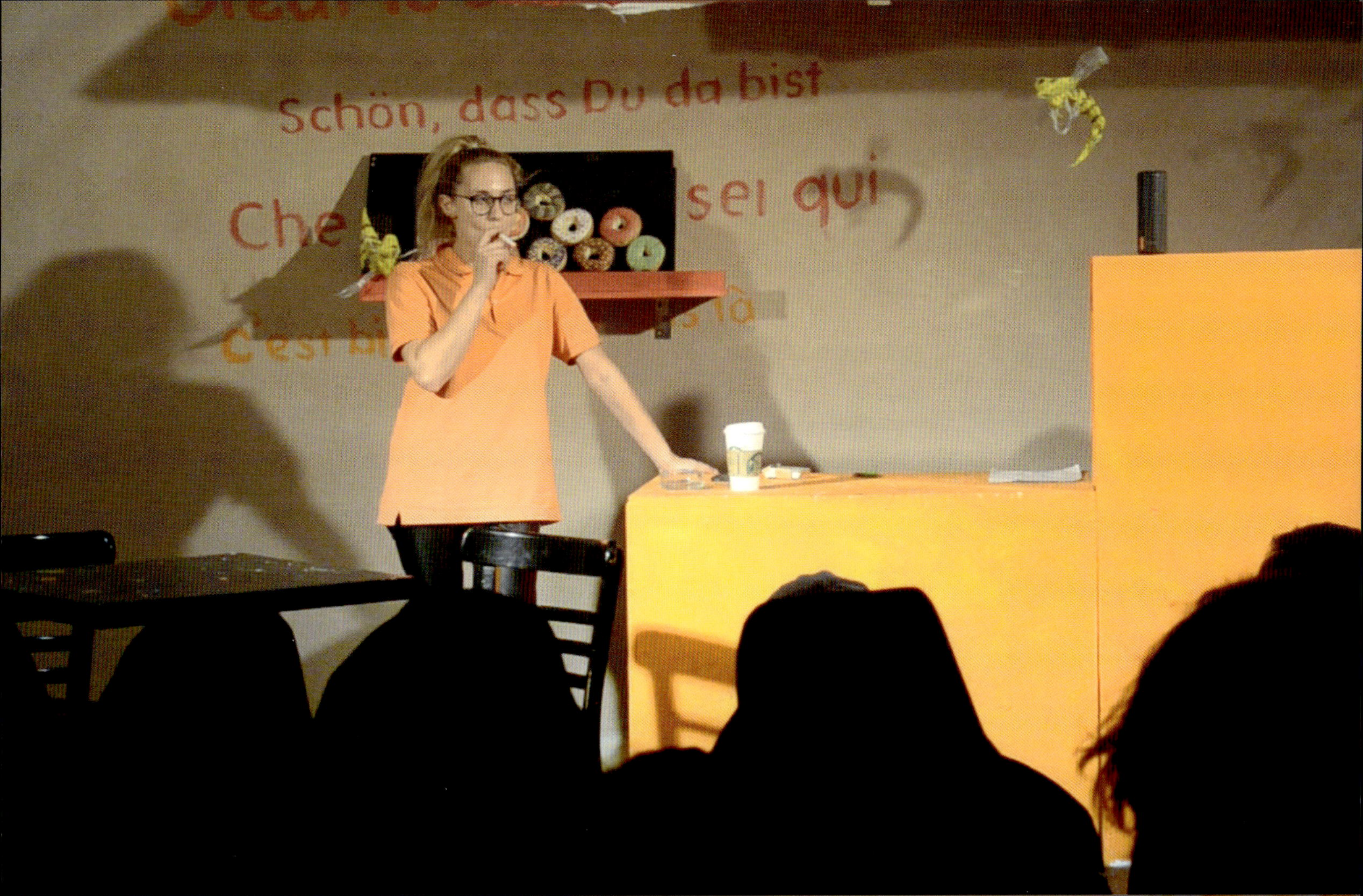

Schön, dass Du da bist
Che ... sei qui
C'est bi...

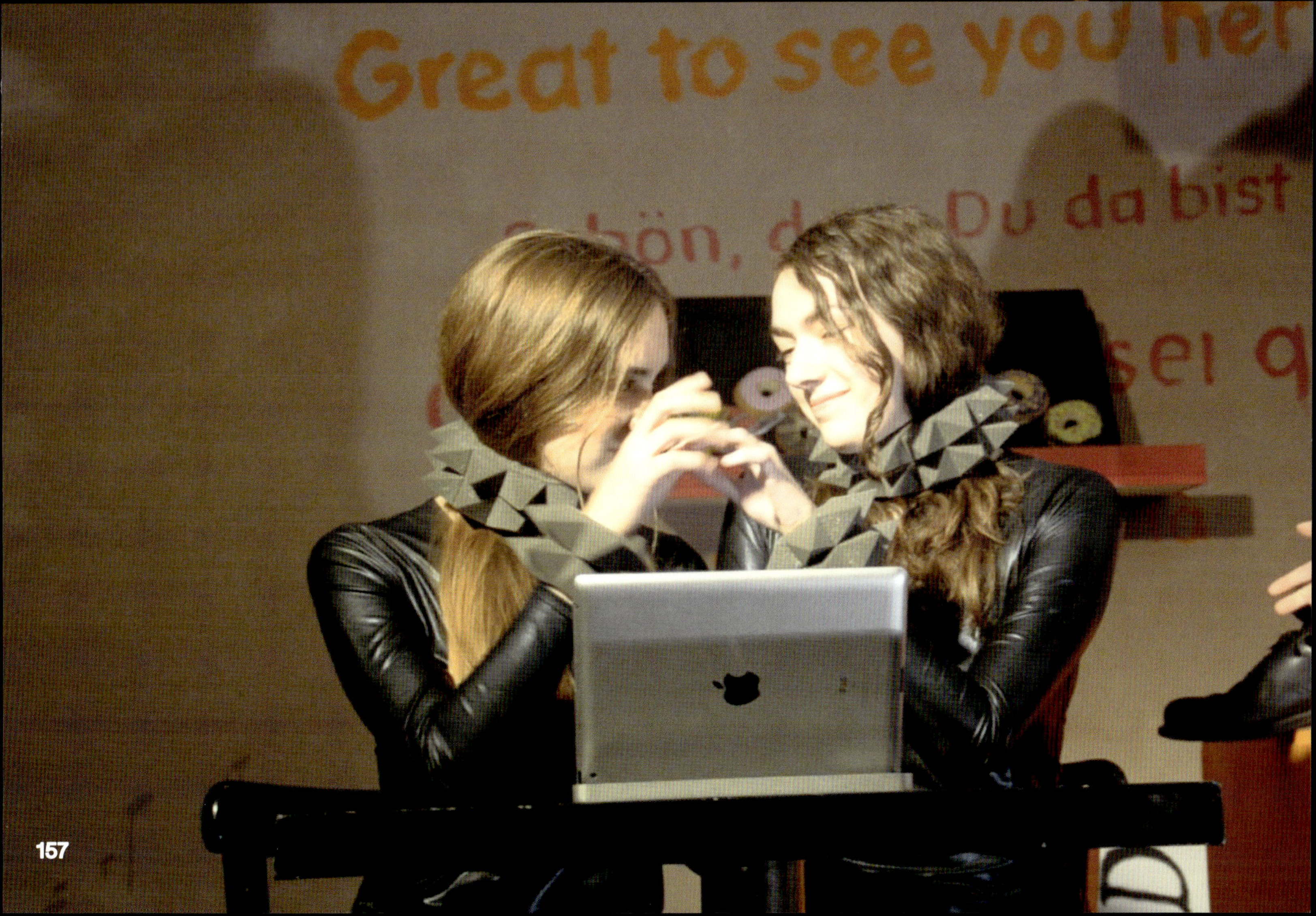

Great to see you her
Schön, d... Du da bist
sei q

He plays around with his appendages, fiddling around, slapping his wife's face, playing with the little girl's hair, flicking the little boy's face, licking fingers. Therapist continues to listen silently. Stenographer types.

> SOOOOOO thennnnnn, I wennt hooommmmeeeeeeee ... I was soooo exhausted. So thennn I watcheda movvieee. I coullldnntt deciddeee which movieee ... so I started one moovviieeeee but it wasn't goood ... Then I started another oneeee but I passsed outll EEheheheheHEHElll *(giggling nervously and stupidly)*

> THERAPIST *(harshly to Stenographer)*: Boredom. Mental dullness. Response to stimuli coming from outside or inside is greatly diminished. Apparent absence of all fantasy formations leading to a deficient cognitive state.

> STENOGRAPHER *(repeating in unison while typing feverishly)*: Langeweile. Geistige Trägheit. Reaktion auf Reize von außen oder innen stark vermindert. Scheinbare Abwesenheit aller Fantasy-Formationen, die zu einem mangelhaften kognitiven Zustand führen.

> THE MONSTER *(shifts his weight around on the chair)*: Soooooo thhheeennnnnn wifeyy was yelling at me againlll She was like: BLAH BLAH BLAHB LAHB LAHBLAH. Soooooooooo ANGRYIlllll About what??????? I DUNNO she's always going on and on and onlll She's like: I want to go outlllllllllll I'm like: I don wannnaaaaalllll I'm like: I jus wanna chilllllllll But then she's all mad and is like: I DON'T WANNA GO ALONElll U NEVER DO ANYTHINGIllll

> THERAPIST: Disinterest in social activities, co-dependency. The aversive experience of wanting, but being unable, to engage in satisfying activity.

> STENOGRAPHER *(repeating in unison)*: Desinteresse an sozialen Aktivitäten, Co-Abhängigkeit. Die aversive Erfahrung, eine befriedigende Tätigkeit ausüben zu wollen, aber nicht dazu in der Lage zu sein.

> THE MONSTER: SOOOOOOOOO thennnnn she's like: I want to makkkeeee LOOOVVVVEEEEllllll and I'm like: EWWWWWWWIlll I'm sooo sick of youullllllll JUST CHILLL OUTTT let's go to BEDI I'M TIREDIlll She's like: WHY ARE YOU TIRED???? YOU DIDN'T DO SHIT TODAYI THEN im like: ZZZZZZZZZZZZZZZZZZZZ already asleepIlll HAHA HAHA AHAHA

> THERAPIST: Failures of attention. Alienated and passive. Immersed in tedium. Defunct libidinal forces.

> STENOGAPHER *(repeating in unison)*: Störungen der Aufmerksamkeit. Entfremdet und passiv. In Langeweile eingetaucht.

The Monster seems not to notice anything that's going on, he just continues babbling while the Therapist pronounces his disorders.

> THE MONSTER: So theeeennnnn I had this CRAAZZZIIIIEEE dream. I was sur-rounded by FISH and they were nibbling at my skin. I was like STOOOPP ITT ITS TICKKLING MEEEEEEEEEII EEheheheehhe *(He squirms around on the chair just remembering it.)* Then the FISHIES took hold of ME, and brought me down the river really quickly like WOOOOOOOOOOOSSSHHHHHHHH and it was like that vacation in COLORADOOO—except canoe was MEEEEE AND THENNNNNN I woke up and I realized I was JUST SOOOOOOO SWEEATTY but I was too lazy to get upp and change the sheets agaaaaiiinnnnn even tho they always turn YEL-LOWWYY EWWWWWWWWWWWW hahahahaha.

> THERAPIST: Profound boredom drifting here and there in the abysses like a muffling

fog. Everything levelled into remarkable indifference. Life passing at an excelled
rate. No participation in the outside world.

STENOGAPHER: *(repeating in unison)*: Tiefe Langeweile, schweben hier und da in die
Abgründe wie ein dumpfer Nebel. Alles nivelliert sich in einer bemerkenswerten
Gleichgültigkeit. Das Leben zieht an ihm vorbei. Keine Teilnahme an der Außenwelt.

The Monster has apparently lost interest.

THERAPIST: I think we should go the classic route. There is not much else to be done.
No need for recovery.

STENOGRAPHER: Wie Sie möchten.

*The Stenographer starts printing out papers and papers from a printer on the counter. The
Monster farts. Upon the farting noise, the Stenographer does a choreographed crab walk
to the printer and starts picking up the pages. They hand them one by one to the Therapist.
The Therapist raises a hand to signal 'stop'. The printing stops. The Stenographer shuffles
to the back and they light a cigarette together.*

THERAPIST: Mista, it is my opinion that your course of treatment has come to an end.
It is time that I propose to you my final solution and may I advise that you take
action immediately, before your condition spreads. Please take this pamphlet and
read it carefully.

*The Monster turns around and looks at the Therapist absently. The Stenographer pulls out
the THE ASSISTED SUICIDE PAMPHLET. It is oversized, like a folding screen, and the
Stenographer sets it up in front of the monster. It says 'ASSISTED SUICIDE PAMPHLET'
and there are a few images of Primo dressed up as a doctor, or Primo with a pile of pills
and a bottle of wine. Primo with a tear streaming down his face. Primo as a cancer patient.
Descriptions are written next to them, very basic.*

THE MONSTER: UMMMMMMMmmmmmmmm whhhaaaaaaaaa??? *(pause, then
screaming)* Ohhhhhnooooooooooooooo IIIIIIIII

'Take Me to the Hospital' by The Prodigy begins to play as the Monster screams. Blackout.

SCENE 3

*The lights go up. We are back in Dunkin' Donuts. Taschi is behind the counter. Primo is
sitting where the Therapist was sitting before. He is perfectly poised calmly sipping his
coffee. He sips and we wait a beat. The audience is watching him. The buzzing of the
wasps comes on again. Three old men, slightly gangster, TK Maxx Potsdamer Platz style,
sit at the table drinking beers, playing cards and joking among themselves. One is
smoking a cigarette. Primo's voiceover returns.*

PRIMO VOICEOVER: Watching the people sometimes made me want a cigarette,
but if I were to smoke it would be almost tooo much ... the nicotine on top of
everything else, the DD Mood could be altered in an unpredictable way ... for one
there's no bathroom in DD. This is its only fault. Aha, but there's always the Art
Cinema next door. They have that huge, unguarded bathroom in the basement ...
Fuck it. I will just ask for one.
*(Primo climbs down from his little seat and slowly makes his way to the old men's
table, staring at one old man in particular.)*
This guy seems ... nice enough ... He would give me one ... hehheheh mmmmmm
look at that jacket ... actually really nice ... I should ask him where he got it from,

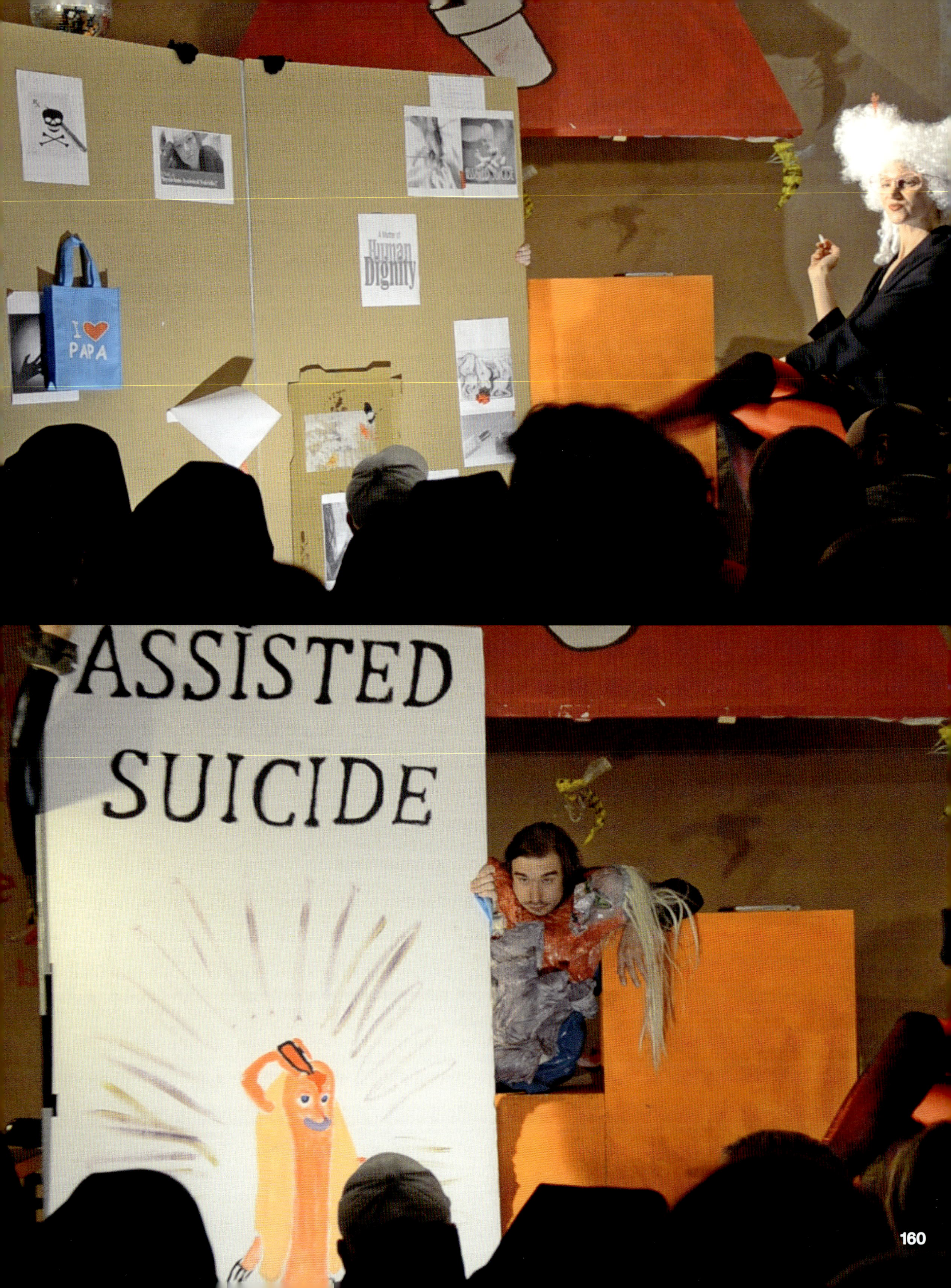
I ♥ PAPA
A Matter of Human Dignity
ASSISTED SUICIDE

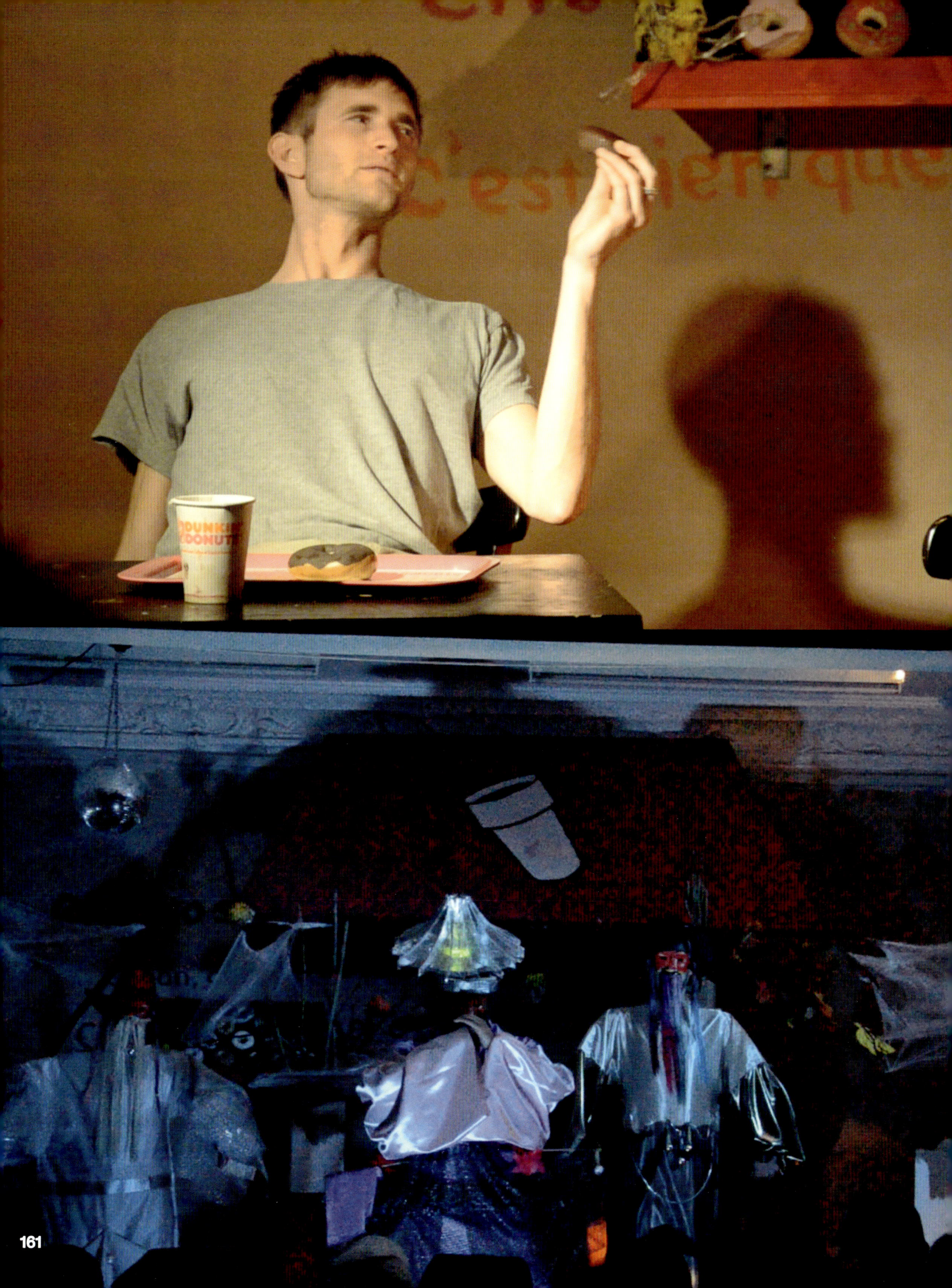
DUNKIN DONUTS
c'est bien que

or even maybe ...
(Primo is distracted by what is going on outside the window. He is starting to get weird jittery, paranoid vibes.)
Ah the bus! Whoa! Was that a mouse??? Oh no, just a birdie ... *(laughs nervously)* My god, get out of the bike lane you fat idiots! Haha whoa. Relax relax relax. It's not that serious ... They don't know ... Aww, the birdies are fat too.
(Primo remembers what he wanted to do and taps Hanz on the shoulder)
PRIMO: Entschuldigung Sie, haben Sie ein zie cigarette?
HANZ *(immediately addressing him in English)*: Ah yes, I have one for you.
PRIMO: Oh, thank you so much.
HANZ: Lighter?
PRIMO: Ah, yes. Thanks so much. *(lights his cigarette)* By the way, I really like your jacket. Where is it from?
HANZ: Oh, HAHA. You don't want to know. That's a little secret, you see.
PRIMO: Uhhh, okay. Ha ha.
HANZ: Let's just say I found it on the side of the road ... Hahaha ... Yes ... You know what, it is quite warm today. And I don't need this jacket anymore. If you really like it so much, you can have it.
PRIMO *(exaggerated politeness)*: Oh, no no no!! I couldn't take it. Really. It's too much.
HANZ: No! Take it! You should just have it! Brotherhood of the travelling whatever the fuck ... You should take it ... I have had it too long already.
PRIMO: What?? Are you serious? I mean, that's crazy.
HANZ: What the hell is crazy about that? You callin' me crazy?? Here. I said you should have it. That jacket has seen enough from me. Now wear it.
PRMO: Wow. Thank you so much!!! Hey, what's your name?
HANZ: Hanz. Mit zed.
They shake hands. Primo puts the jacket on. Hanz is shirtless. Primo hurries back to his little perch. He grabs his coffee and takes a long sip. He sighs relief. The lights go purple. A slowed down version of 'Airflow' by Aphex Twin comes on.
Primo takes a long drag of his cigarette, staring at the old men intently. The old men then shuffle offstage. Stagehands carry on Ikebana-style flower arrangements. Each old man comes back onstage, dressed head to toe like a Peking Opera dancer, with full robes, masks, hats and beards. A projection comes on of a video shot inside Sony Center. It splices together the fountain and other promotional Sony Center videos. A slowed down version of 'Airflow' by Aphex Twin comes on. Taschi and Primo leave the stage. The old men do a choreographed dance enacting an argument. Finally, each one spins offstage. Old man 1 is last. The music continues to play.
Taschi returns and sweeps up.

Curtain

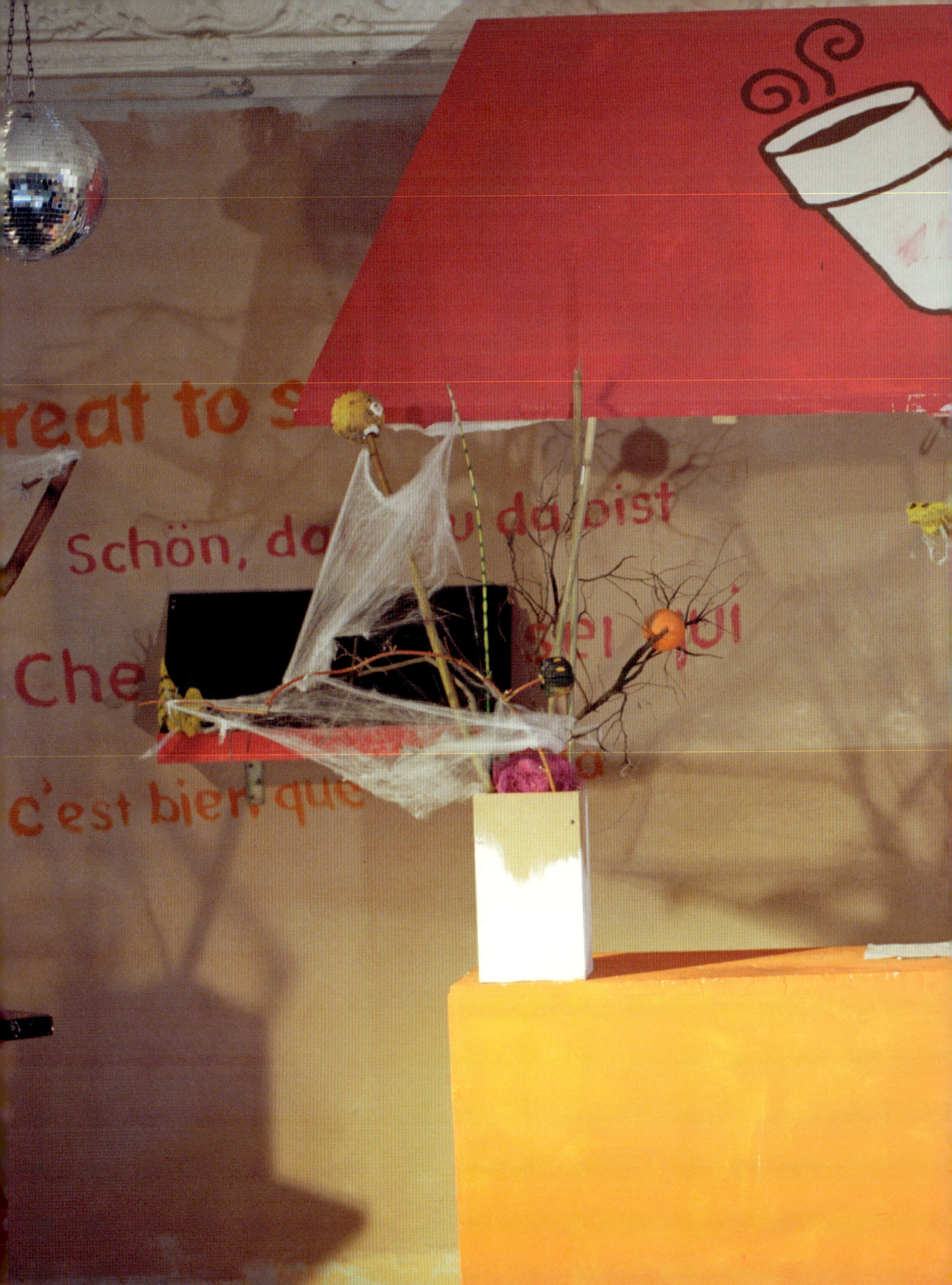
reat to s
Schön, da u da bist
Che
c'est bien que

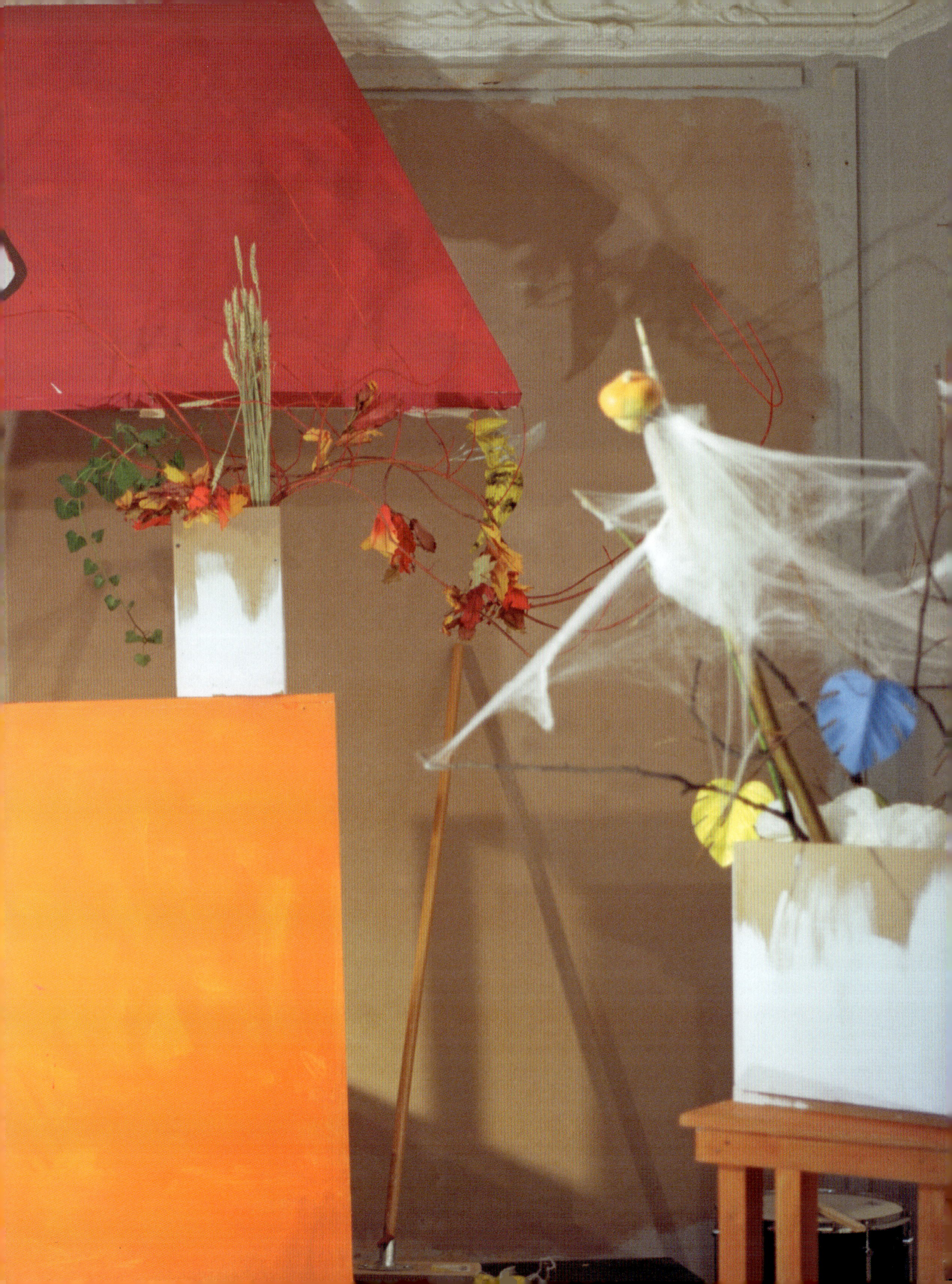

POSEN UND STIMMUNGEN
MEIKE BEHM IM GESPRÄCH MIT
GEORGIA GARDNER GRAY

MEIKE BEHM: Georgia, erzähl doch bitte kurz, wie Du zur Kunst gekommen bist und ob es für Dich einen wichtigen Moment gab, an dem Du beschlossen hast, Künstlerin zu werden und Aspekte der Welt auf künstlerische Art und Weise zu reflektieren.

GEORGIA GARDNER GRAY: An einen bestimmten Moment, an dem ich diese Entscheidung im Allgemeinen gefällt habe, erinnere ich mich nicht, aber ich erinnere mich an den Moment, als ich beschloss, mit dem Malen zu beginnen. Ich hatte das Bedürfnis, direkt, kommunikativ und explizit zu sein. Während meiner Schulzeit hatte sich ein Strohmann auf meiner Schulter aufgebaut – eine Art Schreckgespenst, das ich aufgesaugt hatte. Er sagte mir immer, Direktheit heiße Marktfähigkeit – das Einzige, was ein echter Künstler um jeden Preis vermeiden müsse. Jedes Mal, wenn meine Absicht zu laut oder meine Gefühle zu direkt zum Vorschein kamen, fühlte ich mich schuldig und unternahm etwas, um ihn zu verbergen; um eine Distanz zu schaffen, die in irgendeiner Weise politisches Engagement bedeuten sollte. Zugleich dämmerte mir, wie gestört dieses Vorgehen war. Ich hatte kein Interesse daran, Kunst für ein Nischenpublikum zu machen, dem ebenfalls dieser Dämon auf der Schulter saß. So beschloss ich, mich dieses Gefühls der Entfremdung zu entledigen.

Das ist ein interessanter Punkt – dass Du keine Kunst für ein Nischenpublikum machen wolltest. Ist das einer der Gründe, warum Du Dich für das Medium der Malerei und eine Bildsprache zwischen der abstrakten und der figurativen Malerei entschieden hast?

Ja genau. Die Malerei ist aufgrund ihrer langen Geschichte imstande, sehr eindringlich zu kommunizieren. Es gibt einen solchen Fundus an Bildern, auf den man aufbauen kann , und so viele etablierte Kodes, aus denen man schöpfen kann. Ihre Sprache ist sehr menschlich. Sie gestattet so viel Improvisation. Das liebe ich an der Malerei – ihre vielen verschiedenen Register.

Da stimme ich Dir zu. In Deinen Arbeiten beschäftigst Du Dich sehr mit dem Thema Rollenspiel. In der heutigen Gesellschaft spielen wir alle von Zeit zu Zeit eine Rolle und sind uns dessen häufig nicht bewusst. Siehst Du die heutige Gesellschaft als System von Menschen, die eine Rolle spielen?

Ich glaube, dass wir uns als Gesellschaft allgemein immer mehr unter dem Aspekt sehen, welche Rollen wir spielen: welche Gender-Rolle, welche politische Rolle, welche berufliche Rolle. Wir fühlen uns unter Druck, uns richtig darzustellen, auf der richtigen Seite der Geschichte zu stehen. Social Media geben uns das Gefühl, permanent unser Erbe zu hinterlassen. Wir bemühen uns um eine Art der Transparenz zwischen dem, was wir innerlich fühlen, und dem, wie wir wahrgenommen werden. Wir möchten nur das kommunizieren, was uns genehm ist, und das außen vor lassen, was uns nicht gefällt. Dieser Druck, klare Symbole zu schaffen, wird meiner Ansicht nach durch Social Media noch verstärkt. Das Problem besteht für mich darin, dass es keine wirklich richtige Darstellung gibt, und in der Realität macht jede gesunde Persönlichkeit ständig Kehrtwenden und wechselt ständig zwischen unendlich vielen Rollen und Stimmungen, die sich nicht so leicht definieren lassen. Mit diesen Unterscheidungen schaden wir uns meines Erachtens nur selbst, denn sie führen zu einer sehr traurigen und unmenschlichen Vergröberung.

Du bist in den USA aufgewachsen, lebst heute aber in Berlin. Siehst Du einen Unterschied, was das Spielen von Rollen in diesen beiden Ländern angeht.

Ich kann im Grunde nur für Berlin und New York sprechen, über den Rest von Amerika oder Deutschland kann ich eigentlich nichts sagen. In Berlin verstehen die Menschen die übergeordneten Verhaltensregeln in der Gesellschaft und halten sich normalerweise an sie – so als läge ihnen das im Blut. Es herrscht die stillschweigende Übereinkunft, dass das Einhalten von Regeln zu einer gewissen Art von Freiheit führt, die man genießen kann. Daher findet man in der befreiten Sex- und Clubkultur in Berlin nicht die Gewalt, die man in den USA finden würde. Trotzdem kommt es mir manchmal wie eine Kontrolle vor. Ich bin mit dieser internalisierten Infrastruktur nicht aufgewachsen. In New York kann jeder tun und lassen, was er oder sie

will. Man wächst in der Realität auf, für die man sich entscheidet: Jedes Kind kann Präsident der Vereinigten Staaten und Millionär werden. Man formt sein Weltbild um die Vorstellung, dass man eine ganz besondere Person ist – ob das nun stimmt oder nicht. Man improvisiert und vertauscht die Regeln, damit man weiter im Mittelpunkt stehen kann: Man ist die Ausnahme der Regel. In Berlin wird das nicht unbedingt geduldet, und es ist auf eine Art und Weise ernüchternd, an die ich mich wohl nie ganz gewöhnen werde. Beide Systeme sind auf unterschiedliche Weise menschlich und unmenschlich. Diese deutsche Art kommt mir zum Beispiel manchmal beklemmend und stumpfsinnig vor – aber weil die Menschen die Ruhe bewahren, funktioniert die ganze Gesellschaft viel reibungsloser und mit dem Gefühl ganzheitlicher Verantwortung. Das Problem in Berlin besteht meiner Ansicht nach darin, dass die Menschen die Regeln nicht genug hinterfragen und nicht infrage stellen, was es heißt, sie zu verstehen und sich an sie zu halten: Was geht durch diese pauschale Akzeptanz verloren? Die große pluralistische Vielfalt, die man an einem Ort wie New York erlebt, geht dabei verloren. Aber New York ist natürlich auch eine Stadt voller Illusionen: voller Egomanen, die kaum funktionieren können oder auf Kosten anderer funktionieren. Und wegen dieses New Yorker Ethos kann jemand wie Donald Trump überhaupt erst existieren.

Kommen wir auf Deine Kunst zurück. Können Deine Bilder als kritische Auseinandersetzung mit dem zeitgenössischen Phänomen des Rollenspiels in der Gesellschaft verstanden werden? Hinterfragen sie die Regeln, die für die Rückkehr zu einer pluralistischen Vielfalt nötig sind?

Ich stelle diese Beziehung immer gerne auf eine Art dar, die sie destabilisiert, die sie wieder überraschend wirken lässt. Manchmal habe ich das Gefühl, dass ich mich über das Motiv und die Personen lustig mache, die ich male, oder generell über die Tatsache, dass ich male. Ich spiele selbst verschiedene Rollen. Häufig wähle ich ein Thema, das beinahe stereotyp erscheint, und erfinde es dann neu, damit es wieder besonders scheint. Oder ich nehme etwas, das ich direkt beobachtet habe, und überhöhe es, um die Spannung zutage zu fördern. Ich bin nicht altruistisch, aber ich versuche, die Dinge zu überspitzen und auch zu unterhalten. Wenn ich den Eindruck habe, ich moralisiere, unternehme ich etwas, um auch diesen Eindruck zu verwischen. Ich suche nicht nach einem Ruheplatz außerhalb der Entschlossenheit des Werkes selbst. Da ist durchaus Humor am Werk.

Ja, diesen Humor mag ich sehr. Der scheint auch in den Titeln der Arbeiten durch. Sie sind keineswegs unwichtig, findest du nicht auch? Einige erinnern mich an die expressionistischen Werke des deutschen Malers Ernst Ludwig Kirchner, zum Beispiel *Ladies in the Toilet*. Kirchner nahm damit zum gesellschaftlichen Wandel in der Weimarer Republik Stellung. Kennst Du sein Werk? Andere Deiner Arbeiten wie *Feierabend* scheinen dagegen auf humorvolle Weise zu einer deutschen Eigenart Stellung zu nehmen. Möchtest Du damit andeuten, dass dieser geschichtliche und gesellschaftliche Wandel wichtig ist, aber auch mit Humor genommen werden sollte?

Humor kann sicherlich in den Titeln durchscheinen, und es ist häufig ein sehr trockener Humor. Was das von Dir erwähnte Beispiel *Ladies in the Toilet* angeht, so hatte ich gerade diese Ausstellung in Paris über die wenig bekannte Rolle von Fotografinnen gesehen, die sie bei der Entwicklung der frühen Fotografie gespielt haben. Da gab es Fotos, die Frauen voneinander gemacht hatten, von diesen weichen, privaten Räumen, die weder die Fotografin noch die Fotografierte je öffentlich zu machen gedachte. Die Texturen auf den Fotos waren weich und angenehm, und die Motive waren leicht erotisch, aber der Ton blieb freundlich. Mit diesem Bild wollte ich eine Szene sehr femininer, weicher Frauen in zarter Kleidung schaffen – wie sie in einem privaten und intimen Augenblick zusammen auf der Toilette stehen: ein Augenblick, der sie über einer illegalen, auf einem iPhone verteilten Substanz zusammenschweißt. *Ladies in the Toilet* fängt vielleicht einen Hauch der Dekadenz ein, die diese sich erweiternden Erzählungen mitunter haben. Üben sie eine größere Anziehungskraft aus oder sind sie einfach breiter und flacher? Ich neige mitunter zur nihilistischen Seite, und daraus resultiert vermutlich der Humor. So gesehen könnte man sagen, dass es etwas von der Weimarer Ära hat – eine Gesellschaft oder Ästhetik, die sich ihrer progressiven Ausrichtung so sicher ist, ist mir immer suspekt.

MEIKE BEHM: Georgia, please tell us briefly how you came to art and whether there was an important moment when you decided to become an artist and to reflect on the world in an artistic way.

GEORGIA GARDNER GRAY: I cannot remember a moment that I made this decision generally, but I do remember when I decided to begin painting. I felt a desire to be direct, communicative and explicit. I had a a straw man that was built up during my schooling—this looming specter that I had absorbed. It was always sitting on my shoulder, telling me that being direct meant being marketable, which was the one thing a real artist must avoid at all costs. So every time my intention came out too loud or my feeling came out too direct, I would feel guilty and make some move to cloak it; to create a distance that would somehow signify political engagement. It dawned on me how dysfunctional this process was. It didn't interest me to make art for a niche audience that also had this demon sitting on their shoulder. I decided that I wanted to get rid of this alienated feeling.

That's an interesting point—not wanting to make art for a niche audience. Is this one of the reasons you choose the medium of painting and a formal language between abstract and figurative painting?

Yes, exactly, painting has an ability to communicate strongly because of its long history. There is so much visual language to build upon and so many established codes to draw from. Its language is very human. It allows for so much improvisation. I love this about painting: its many different registers.

Yes, I agree. In your work, you deal a lot with the subject of role play. In today's society everyone plays roles from time to time and we're often not aware of it. Do you see today's society as a system of role-playing individuals?

I think that in general as a society we come to see ourselves more and more in terms of what role we play: what

gender role, what political role, what professional role. We feel pressure to represent ourselves accurately, to be on the right side of history. Social media gives us the feeling that we are constantly leaving our legacy. We strive to create some kind of transparency between what we feel inside and how we are perceived. We want to only communicate what we desire to be seen and eliminate what does not please us. I think this pressure to symbolize clearly is magnified by social media. The problem I see with this is that there is no real accurate representation, and in reality any healthy personality is constantly flipping and switching between an infinite number of roles and moods that are not so easily defined. I think that creating these distinctions really plays to our own detriment and causes a very sad and inhuman oversimplification.

You grew up in the USA but today you live in Berlin. Do you see a difference in role-playing in these two places?

Well, I can only be specific about Berlin and New York, the rest of America or Germany I can't really account for. In Berlin people understand the overarching rules of behavior within the society and generally abide by them. It's as if they have it in their blood. They have a tacit understanding that following rules leads to a certain type of freedom that they can enjoy. This is why you find the liberated sex and club culture in Berlin without the violence you would find in the US. Still though, for me it can feel like control: I did not grow up with this internalized infrastructure. In New York, it is a free for all. You grow up in whatever reality you choose: every kid can be the President of the United States and a millionaire. You shape your world around finding yourself exceedingly special, regardless of whether or not it's true. You improvise and permutate the rules so that you can continue to find yourself at the center: the exception to the rule. This is not really tolerated in Berlin, and it is very sobering in a way I don't think I will ever totally get used to. Both systems are human and inhuman in different ways: for example I find the German version to be oppressive and mind-numbing at times—but then because people keep it cool, the whole society functions much more smoothly and with a sense of holistic responsibility. The problem I find in Berlin is that people do not question the rules enough, and what it means to

understand and abide by them: what is lost by this blanket acceptance. What is lost is the great pluralistic diversity that you experience in a place like New York. But then New York is a deluded city: full of ego maniacs who can barely function, or who function at the expense of others. This ethic of New York is what allows someone like Donald Trump to exist.

To get back to your art, can the paintings be read as a critical approach to this contemporary phenomenon of role-playing within society? Do they question the rules required for a return to a pluralistic diversity?

I always like to present these relations in a way that destabilizes them, in a way that makes them seem surprising again. I feel like sometimes I am making fun of what and who I am painting, or of even making a painting at all. I am taking on different roles myself. A lot of the time I will take a subject matter that almost feels stereotypical and then reimagine it so that it feels particular again. Or I will take something that I directly observed and make it heightened to draw out the tension. I am not altruistic, but I am trying to push and also to entertain. If I ever feel like I am being moralistic, I will do something to destabilize that too. I don't search for any resting place outside of the resolution of the work itself. There is a humor there.

Yes, I like this humor a lot. It can also be felt in the titles of the works; they are important, aren't they? Some remind me of the Expressionistic works of German painter Ernst Ludwig Kirchner, for instance *Ladies in the Toilet*. He was commenting on changes in society during the Weimar Republic. Are you familiar with this work? But other ones, such as *Feierabend* seem to offer humorous commentary on something particularly German. Are you trying to suggest that these changes in the times and in society are important, but have to be regarded with humor?

Humor can definitely come through in the titles, and often in a deadpan way. For example, in the painting you mention *Ladies in the Toilet*, I had just seen this exhibition in Paris about the unsung role that female photographers played in the development of early photography. It featured photographs of women taken of each other of these soft, private spaces that neither the photographer nor the subject had any notion of making public. The textures were soft and pleasing in the photographs, and the subjects were slightly erotic, while the tone stayed friendly. So in this painting, I wanted to make a scene of very feminine, soft women in their delicate clothes—together in a private and intimate moment in a toilet: a bonding moment over an illicit substance doled out on an iPhone. The *Ladies in the Toilet* may catch the whiff of a decadence that these expanding narratives can at times accommodate. Do they provide more traction or are they just broader and flatter? I can tend to the nihilistic side, and I think that is where the humor stems from. In this sense, you could say there is something similar to the Weimar era about it—I am always suspicious of a society or an aesthetics that is so secure in its progressive tack.

GEORGIA GARDNER GRAY

*1988, New York, lebt und arbeitet in Berlin / lives and works in Berlin

AUSBILDUNG / EDUCATION
2006–2011
BFA, Cooper Union for the Advancement of Science and Art, New York

AUSZEICHNUNGEN / AWARDS
2018
Lingener Kunstpreis / Lingen Art Award

EINZELAUSSTELLUNGEN / SOLO EXHIBITIONS
2019
Präsentation / presentation kuratiert von / curated by Patrick Armstrong, The Downer, Berlin
„Pigeon Feather Stick", Drehbuch und Regie / play written and directed, als Teil von / as part of „Disappearing Berlin", Schinkel Pavilion, Berlin
„Buddha Bless This Show", Croy Nielsen, Wien / Vienna
2018
„Works 2015–2018", Kunsthalle Lingen, Lingen (Ems)
„Controller", Art Basel Statements, Basel (mit / with Croy Nielsen)
„Concorde: Saturn Returns", Grüner Salon, Volksbühne, Berlin
2017
„Concorde", UKS / Kunstnernes Hus, Oslo
„Precious Provincials", Kunstverein Hamburg, Hamburg
2016
Paris Internationale, Paris (mit / with Croy Nielsen)
„Georgia Gardner Gray", Acud macht Neu, Berlin

AUSGEWÄHLTE GRUPPENAUSSTELLUNGEN / SELECTED GROUP EXHIBITIONS
2018
„All'estero & Dr. K.'s Badereise nach Riva: Version B", kuratiert von / curated by Saim Demircan, Croy Nielsen, Wien / Vienna
„HERE HERE – DAS ICH UND ALLES ANDERE", kuratiert von / curated by Tenzing Barshee, Braunsfelder Family Collection, Köln / Cologne
„The Hard Facts of Tragedy in April", Lomex Gallery, New York
2017
CONDO New York, Bodega, New York
„Monday is a day between Tuesday and Sunday", Tanya Leighton, Berlin
2015
„New Theater: Selected Plays", Whitney Museum of American Art, New York
„The People's Biennial", kuratiert von / curated by Bradley Kronz, New York
2014
„The Pipe at the Gates of Dawn", kuratiert von / curated by Grayson Revoir, Jan Kaps, Köln
„DD Mood", Drehbuch und Regie / play written and directed, New Theater, Berlin
„Gun Making Seminar", Performance im Freien in Zusammenarbeit mit / outdoor sculpture performance in cooperation with Meisterschule, Gillmeier Rech, Berlin

PUBLIKATIONEN / PUBLICATIONS
2018
Works 2014–2019, herausgegeben von / published by Meike Behm und dem Freundeskreis des Lingener Kunstpreises / and Friends of the Lingen Art Award, Mousse Publishing, Mailand / Milan
2016
Georgia Gardner Gray, herausgegeben von / published by Elodie Evers, Berlin und / and ACUD, Berlin

AUSGEWÄHLTE PRESSE / SELECTED PRESS
2019
Feldhaus, Timo, „Portrait Georgia Gardner Gray", *Monopol Magazin*, März / March
Bradley, Kimberly, „Georgia Gardner Gray", *Frieze*, April
2018
Sharp, Chris, „The New Symbolism", *Garage Magazine*, März / March
2017
Meier, Anika, „Georgia Gardner Gray", *Monopol*, Juni / June

S. / p. 89
Bahnhof Zoo, 2017
Öl und Lack auf Leinwand / Oil and
varnish on canvas
190 × 160 cm
Courtesy: Anthony Adler

S. / p. 91
Aldi Paintings, 2017
Öl und Lack auf Holz / Oil and acrylic on
Board
Maße variabel / Dimensions variable

S. / p. 94
Groupies in a Green World, 2017
Öl und Lack auf Leinwand / Oil and
varnish on canvas
95 × 85 cm
Courtesy: Privatsammlung,
Deutschland / Private collection,
Germany

S. / p. 97
Horse Medicine, 2017
Öl und Lack auf Leinwand / Oil and
varnish on canvas
120 × 120 cm
Courtesy: Privatsammlung, Norwegen /
Private collection, Norway

S. / p. 98
Die Richter, 2016
Öl und Lack auf Leinwand / Oil and
varnish on canvas
67 × 50 cm
Courtesy: Privatsammlung / Private
collection, Berlin

S. / p. 103
Good Girl, 2017
Öl und Lack auf Leinwand / Oil and
varnish on canvas
90 × 65 cm
Courtesy: Privatsammlung /
Private collection

S. / p. 105
Caffeine, 2017
Öl und Lack auf Leinwand / Oil and
varnish on canvas
90 × 65 cm
Courtesy: Sammlung Luigi Giordano /
Luigi Giordano Collection

S. / p. 106
Clingy Punk, 2017
Öl und Lack auf Leinwand / Oil and
varnish on canvas
99 × 70 cm
Courtesy: Georgia Gardner Gray

S. / p. 111
In my Altbau, 2017
Öl und Lack auf Leinwand / Oil and
varnish on canvas
240 × 115 cm
Courtesy: Privatsammlung, Norwegen /
Private collection, Norway

S. / p. 112
1500, 2016
Öl und Lack auf Stoff / Oil and
varnish on fabric
40 × 37 cm
Courtesy: Privatsammlung /
Private collection

S. / p. 113
Turbulence, 2017
Öl und Lack auf Leinwand / Oil and
varnish on canvas
68 × 66 cm
Courtesy: Key Sammlung / Key Collection

S. / p. 114–115
The Paris RER Regional Train, 2017
Öl und Lack auf Leinwand / Oil and
varnish on canvas
160 × 160 cm
Courtesy: Sammlung De Iorio /
De Iorio Collection

S. / p. 119
Portrait of the Artist's Mother, 2016
Bleistift auf Papier / Pencil on paper
41 × 53 cm
Courtesy: Privatsammlung, Norwegen /
Private collection, Norway

S. / p. 120
Private Meeting, 2017
Öl und Lack auf Leinwand / Oil and
varnish on canvas
44 × 63 cm
Courtesy: BDU Sammlung /
BDU Collection

S. / p. 123
Crumpling Your Stupid Idea, 2017
Öl und Lack auf Leinwand / Oil and
varnish on canvas
90 × 65 cm
Courtesy: Privatsammlung /
Private collection, Berlin

S. / p. 124
*Backstage, Still Alone, Swinging from a
Hippie Tree*, 2017
Öl und Lack auf Leinwand / Oil and
varnish on canvas
240 × 115 cm
Courtesy: Privatsammlung,
Deutschland / Private collection,
Germany

S. / p. 127
XYZ, Fast Asleep, 2017
Öl und Lack auf Leinwand / Oil and
varnish on canvas
120 × 90 cm
Courtesy: Privatsammlung /
Private collection

S. / p. 129
Payment in Butter, 2017
Öl und Lack auf Leinwand / Oil and
varnish on canvas
120 × 160 cm
Courtesy: Alexander Adler

IMPRESSUM / COLOPHON

Dieser Katalog erscheint anlässlich der Ausstellung / This catalogue is published on the occasion of the exhibition
Georgia Gardner Gray „Arbeiten 2015 bis 2018. Lingener Kunstpreis 2018"
Kunsthalle Lingen
15.09.–11.11.2018

Die Ausstellung und der Katalog wurden ermöglicht durch den Freundeskreis des Lingener Kunstpreises. / The exhibition and the catalogue were made possible by the Friends of the Lingen Art Award.
Annette u. Robert Koop
Margriet u. Richard Lange
Elke Raberg u. Jochen Kopp
Marleen u. Dr. Radulf Oberthür
Bärbel u. Helge Kropik
Marita Kamp u. Heino Deeken
Silvia Buddelmann u. Heiner Schepers
Christa Nitze-Ertz u. Dr. Klaus Ertz
Ulrike u. Harald Müller
Karin u. Gerhard Ripken
Maria u. Peter Leuschner
Annette u. Dr. Johannes Höing
Drs. Doris u. Heribert Lange
Waldtraut Jelkmann
Drs. Brigitta u. Georg Lindgen
Sigrid u. Dipl. Ing. Wilhelm Hohoff
Annakatrin u. Gerd Schulz
Gisela Klukkert
Martina u. Dr. Horst Niemann
Renate u. Dr. Wolfhard Schmidt
Anne u. Dr. Walter Höltermann
Antje u. Dr. Michael Adams
Peter Lütje u. Meike Behm
Andrea u. Winfried Reiprich
Ulrike Kopp
Dr. Annemarie u. Dr. Gunther Bensch
Michaela u. Dr. Martin Kruse
Christel Grunewaldt-Rohde
Anke u. Bernhard Merswolke
Gerlinde u. Heinz Diekamp
Petra Niwiera
Katrin Lindenlauf-Gnaß u. Christian Gnaß
Nasrin u. Michael Oldiges
Maria Newmerschyzky
Eva-Maria u. Wolfgang Paus
Ursula u. August Feldmann
Dr. Marie-Elisabeth Averkamp
Elke Schiedeck u. Heinz Schulte
Brigitte u. Jochen Brackmann
Gundula Zieschang
Gerda Klukkert u. Alfons Kordsmeier
Andrea u. Christoph Stöckler
Margret Kleinert u. Georg Aehling
Marion Hofschröer
Ulrich Dörrie
Anja Bünker
Petra Revermann u. Bernd Müller
Harald Pschorn
Schirmherr / Patron: Hermann Bröring

Die Summe für den Lingener Kunstpreis stellten in diesem Jahr Maria und Peter Leuschner zur Verfügung. Dafür dankt ihnen die Kunsthalle Lingen außerordentlich. / The sum for the Lingen Art Award was donated by Maria and Peter Leuschner. Kunsthalle Lingen is extremely grateful for their support.

Weiterer Dank gilt dem Land Niedersachsen, dem Landkreis Emsland, der Stadt Lingen (Ems), der Kulturstiftung Heinrich Kampmann und RWE. / Kunsthalle Lingen is grateful to Land Niedersachsen, Landkreis Emsland, Stadt Lingen (Ems), Kulturstiftung Heinrich Kampmann and RWE.

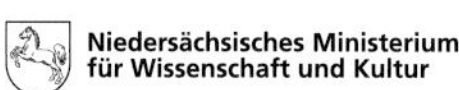
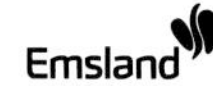
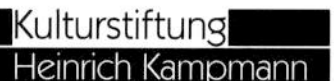
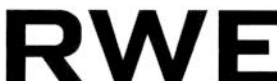

Kunstverein Lingen Kunsthalle
Kaiserstraße 10a
49809 Lingen (Ems)
Tel. +49 (0)591 5 99 95
info@kunsthallelingen.de
www.kunsthallelingen.de

Vorstand / Board Members:
Georg Aehling, Annette Höing, Heinz Diekamp, Monika Schwegmann, Dieter Gäckler

AUSSTELLUNG / EXHIBITION
Direktorin und Kuratorin / Director and Curator: Meike Behm
Assistentin der Direktion / Assistant to the Director: Maria-Anna Berlage
ART SHOP, Projekt kküche, Philosophie in der Kunsthalle / Project kküche, Philosophy at Kunsthalle: Peter Lütje
Leiter Kunstvermittlung / Head of Art Mediation: Ulrich Dörrie
Kunstvermittlung / Art Mediation: Claudia Arns, Silvia Bessler, Lea Masselink
Praktikantin / Intern: Selma Körber
Aufbau / Installation: Noor Dolati, Michael Schneider

Aufsicht / Guards: Maxi Harmel, Frederike Herbers, Jasmin Last, Michael Möller, Lina Völkers, Christina Schaaf

KATALOG / CATALOGUE
Herausgeber / Editor: Meike Behm, Freundeskreis des Lingener Kunstpreises / Friends of the Lingen Art Award
Lektorat / Editing: Meike Behm (deu), Naomi Buck (eng)
Korrekturlesen / Proofreading: Meike Behm (deu), Georgia Gardner Gray (eng), Claudia Kotte
Übersetzungen / Translations: Claudia Kotte
Druck / Printing: Druckhaus Köthen
Fotonachweis / Photo Credits: Fred Dott, Hamburg; Calla Henkel & Max Pitegoff; kunst-dokumentation, Wien / Vienna; Roman Mensing, Münster / Munster; Joachim Schulz, Berlin
Gestaltung / Design: Dan Solbach

© 2018 Kunsthalle Lingen, Georgia Gardner Gray, Autorinnen und Autoren, Fotografen / authors, photographers

Erschienen und vertrieben bei / Published and distributed by
Mousse Publishing
Contrappunto s.r.l.
Corso di Porta Romana 63
20122, Milan–Italy

Erhältlich durch / Available through:
Mousse Publishing, Milan
moussepublishing.com
DAP | Distributed Art Publishers, New York
artbook.com
Vice Versa Distribution, Berlin
viceversaartbooks.com
Les presses du réel, Dijon
lespressesdureel.com
Antenne Books, London
antennebooks.com

ISBN 978-88-6749-382-1
Printed in Germany

Dank / Acknowledgements
Oliver Croy, Henrikke Nielsen, Dan Solbach, Calla Henkel & Max Pitegoff, Eva Birkenstock, Sigrid Hohoff, Richard Lange, Maria und Peter Leuschner, Marita Kamp, Kristina Szepanski, Monika Schwegmann, Stadt Lingen (Ems)